Courtroom
DRAMA

120 of the World's
Most Notable Trials

CONTRIBUTORS

John S. Bowman

Rodney Carlisle

Stephen G. Christianson

Kathryn Cullen-DuPont

Teddi DiCanio

Colin Evans

Michael Golay

Bernard Ryan Jr.

Tom Smith

Eva Weber

Janet Bond Wood

NEW ENGLAND PUBLISHING ASSOCIATES

Edited and prepared for publication by
New England Publishing Associates, Inc.

GENERAL EDITORS
Elizabeth Frost-Knappmann,
Edward W.Knappmann, and
Lisa Paddock

EDITORIAL ADMINISTRATION
Ron Formica and Christopher Ceplenski

PICTURE EDITOR
Victoria Harlow

Courtroom
DRAMA

120 of the World's Most Notable Trials

Elizabeth Frost-Knappman,
Edward W. Knappman,
and Lisa Paddock, Editors

Victoria Harlow, Picture Editor

VOLUME 1

THE CONSTITUTION

FAMILY LAW AND
REPRODUCTIVE RIGHTS

FREEDOM OF SPEECH

HUMAN RIGHTS

NEGLIGENCE

U·X·L ®

AN IMPRINT OF GALE

Detroit   New York   Toronto   London

Courtroom Drama:
120 of the World's Most Notable Trials

Staff

Jane Hoehner, *U•X•L Senior Editor*
Carol DeKane Nagel, *U•X•L Managing Editor*
Thomas L. Romig, *U•X•L Publisher*

Mary Beth Trimper, *Production Director*
Evi Seoud, *Assistant Production Manager*
Shanna Heilveil, *Production Associate*

Cynthia Baldwin, *Product Design Manager*
Barbara J. Yarrow, *Graphic Services Supervisor*
Tracey Rowens, *Senior Art Director*

Margaret Chamberlain, *Permissions Specialist (Pictures)*

Library of Congress Cataloging-in-Publication Data

Courtroom drama : 120 of the world's most notable trials / Elizabeth Frost-Knappman, Edward W. Knappmann, and Lisa Paddock, editors.

p. cm.

Includes bibliographical references and index.

Summary: Covers 120 notable trials that occurred around the world, from the Salem witchcraft cases to O. J. Simpson.

ISBN 0-7876-1735-0 (set). — ISBN 0-7876-1736-9 (v. 1) — ISBN 0-7876-1737-7 (v. 2) — ISBN 0-7876-1738-5 (v. 3)

1. Trials—Juvenile literature. [1. Trials.]   I. Frost-Knappmann, Elizabeth.   II. Knappmann, Edward W.   III. Paddock, Lisa.

K540.C68 1998

347'.07—dc21

97-23014
CIP
AC

This book is printed on acid-free paper that meets the minimum requirements of American National Standard for Information Sciences—Permanence Paper for Printed Library Materials, ANSI Z39.48-1984.

This publication is a creative work fully protected by all applicable copyright laws, as well as by misappropriation, trade secret, unfair competition, and other applicable laws. The authors and editors of this work have added value to the underlying factual material herein through one or more of the following: unique and original selection, coordination, expression, arrangement, and classification of the information. All rights to this publication will be vigorously defended.

Contents

Contents

Contents

VOLUME 2:

ASSASSINATIONS

Contents

MURDER

Contents

VOLUME 3:

MILITARY TRIALS AND COURTS MARTIAL

RELIGION AND HERESY

Contents

Contents

Trials Alphabetically

A

B

I

J

K

L

M

S

T

U

**Trials
Alphabetically**

Trials Chronologically

**Trials
Chronologically**

**Trials
Chronologically**

Reader's Guide

Courtroom Drama: 120 of the World's Most Notable Trials presents twenty-five centuries of intriguing and influential trials that helped shape the course of world history. Falling into thirteen categories, the cases cover assassinations, murders, war crimes, court martials, religious crimes, espionage, treason, negligence, political corruption, freedom of speech, family law, and constitutional cases.

The earliest featured courtroom drama dates from 399 B.C. For refusing to worship the gods of the city of Athens, the philosopher Socrates was sentenced to death. The Timothy McVeigh trial, which deals with the worst act of terrorism in American history—the bombing of the Oklahoma City Federal Building in 1995—is among the more recent trials. Others are the *Jones v. Clinton and Ferguson* lawsuit brought by Paula Jones against President Bill Clinton for sexual harassment that allegedly occurred when he was governor of Arkansas. *Vacco v. Quill* and *Washington v. Glucksberg* together make up the Right to Die test cases heard by the Supreme Court in 1997.

Most of the cases in this book resulted in true trials, meaning that a court—usually a judge or a panel of judges—followed established rules and procedures and impartially examined disputes between parties over fact or law. Others are jury trials in which lawyers presented evidence to a jury that delivered a verdict.

Others are not real trials at all. The Salem witchcraft persecutions, for example, were not true trials since no attorney was present to represent the accused. Still, they were among the greatest social upheavals in colonial New England. Communist dictator Joseph Stalin's "show trials" made a mockery of justice since their verdicts were foregone conclusions.

The trials are arranged chronologically by category. There is an alphabetical listing as well. For easy reference, a Words to Know section at the beginning of each volume defines key terms. More than 120 sidebars provide related information while 172 photos enliven the text. A cumulative index concludes each volume.

Special Thanks

Our special thanks go to the following people for their help in preparing this book:

Colin Evans, for writing the essays on *Jones v. Clinton and Ferguson,* the Markus Wolf trials, the Right to Die case, the Steven Biko Inquest, the Roh Tae-woo and Chun Doo-hwan trials, and the Timothy McVeigh trial; Victoria Harlow, for obtaining all of the illustrations; Ron Formica, for trustworthy and meticulous editorial assistance; Tom Romig, for developing this three-volume set and asking us to prepare it; Jane Hoehner, for her high spirits, flexibility, and editorial advice; Rachael Kranz, for the lively sidebars; Carl Rollyson, for suggestions and support; Christopher Ceplenski, for general assistance and help in preparing the index; Amanda Frost-Knappman, for her independence, which allowed her parents to complete this project; John S. Bowman, for the Martin Guerre Trials and Reichstag Fire Trial essays; Rodney Carlisle, for the Peter Wright (Spycatcher) Trials and Boston Massacre Trials essays; Stephen G. Christianson, for the William "Big Bill" Haywood Trial, *Marbury v. Madison, Cherokee Nation v. Georgia,* Dred Scott Decision, *Reynolds v. U.S., Plessy v. Ferguson, Brown v. Board of Education, U.S. v. Nixon, Bakke v. University of California . . . Appeal, New York Times Company v. Sullivan, U.S. v. Cinque, U.S. v. Berrigan,* Harry Thaw Trials, Leo Frank Trial, Haymarket Trial, The Triangle Shirtwaist Fire Trial, Samuel Chase Impeachment, President Andrew Johnson Impeachment Trial, Aaron Burr Trial, John Brown Trial, and Tokyo Rose Trial essays; Kathryn Cullen-DuPont, for the *Packard v. Packard, Buck v. Bell, Roe v. Wade,* Anne Hutchinson's Trials, Mary Dyer Trials, *U.S. v. Susan B. Anthony,* The Trials of Alice Paul and Other National Woman's Party Members, *In the Matter of Karen Ann Quinlan,* and Hester Vaughan Trial essays; Teddi DiCanio, for the Alien and Sedition Acts, The "Great Negro Plot" Trial, Major John Andre Trial, and Salem Witchcraft Trials essays; Colin Evans, for the Sirhan Bishara Sirhan Trial, Edith Cavell Trial, *O'Shea v. Parnell and O'Shea, In the Matter of Baby M,* Chicago Seven Trial, Oscar Wilde Trials, Clarence Earl Gideon Trials, Ernesto Miranda Trial, Los Angeles Police Department Officers' Trials, *Bounty* Mutineers Court-Martial, William Calley Court-Martial, Samuel Sheppard Trials,

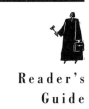

Angela Davis Trial, Guildford Four Trial, *Titanic* Inquiry, *Silkwood v. Kerr-McGee,* Oliver North Trial, Manuel Noriega Trial, Thomas More Trial, Mary Queen of Scots Trial, Walter Raleigh Trials, Gunpowder Plot Trial, Charles I Trial, Roger Casement Trial, and John Demjanjuk Trial essays; Michael Golay, for the Charlotte Corday Trial, Red Brigades Trial, Joan of Arc Trial, Giordano Bruno Trials, Galileo Galilei Trial, Louis XVI and Marie Antoinette Trials, Alfred Dreyfus Trials, The Moscow Purge Trials, József Cardinal Mindszenty Trial, The Nuremberg Trial, and Klaus Barbie Trial essays; Edward W. Knappman, for the John Peter Zenger Trial and John Thomas Scopes Trial (The "Monkey" Trial) essays; Bernard Ryan Jr., for the Alger Hiss Trials, Trial of Julius and Ethel Rosenberg and Morton Sobell, *Schenck v. U.S. Appeal, Ulysses* Trial, Hollywood Ten Trials, The Scottsboro Trials, Sacco-Vanzetti Trial, Bruno Richard Hauptmann Trial, Baader-Meinhof Trial, O. J. Simpson Trial, The Teapot Dome Trials, Socrates Trial, Martin Luther Trial, Vidkun Quisling Trial, Henri Philippe Pétain and Pierre Laval Trials, Ezra Pound Trial, Jiang Qing and the Gang of Four Trial, Tiananmen Square Dissidents Trial, Tokyo War Crimes Trial, and Adolf Eichmann Trial essays; Tom Smith, for the Alexander II's Assassins Trial, Rosa Luxemburg's Assassins Trial, Indira Gandhi's Assassins Trial, Argentina's "Dirty War" Trial, Jean-Bédel Bokassa Trial, Isabel Perón Trial, Milovan Djilas Trial, Cuban Revolutionary Tribunals, Václav Havel Trials, and Anatoly Shcharansky and Alexandr Ginzburg Trials essays; Eva Weber, for the Archduke Franz Ferdinand's Assassins Trial, Anti-Hitler Conspirators Trial, Assassins of Gandhi Trial, Jomo Kenyatta Trial, The Sharpeville Six Trial, and Nelson Mandela Trial essays; and Janet Bond Wood, for the Leon Trotsky's Assassin Trial and Jesus of Nazareth Trial essays.

Comments and Suggestions

We welcome your comments on this work as well as your suggestions for trials to be featured in future editions of *Courtroom Drama: 120 of the World's Most Notable Trials.* Write: Editors, *Courtroom Drama,* U•X•L, 835 Penobscot Bldg., Detroit, Michigan 48226-4094; Call toll-free: 1-800-877-4253; or fax: (313)877-6348.

Words to Know

Note: References to other defined terms are set in **bold**

A

Abortion: a medical term meaning the termination of a fetus or pregnancy

Accessory after the fact: one who obstructs justice by giving comfort or assistance to the felon (*see* **felony**), knowing that the felon has committed a crime or is sought by authorities in connection with a serious crime

Accessory before the fact: one who aids in the commission of a felony by ordering or encouraging it, but who is not present when the crime is committed

Accomplice: a person who helps another to commit or attempt to commit a crime

Acquit: to find a criminal defendant not guilty

Affirmative action: preferences given to one group over another to ease conditions resulting from past discrimination

Alibi: a Latin term meaning "elsewhere"; a criminal defense which shows that the defendant was unable to commit an act because he or she was at some other place

Alimony: an agreement or court order for support payments to either husband or wife after their marriage has ended

Amicus curiae: a Latin term meaning "friend of the court;" a person or organization not party to the lawsuit who provides the court with information

Words to Know

Annulment: to make void; to wipe out the effect of an action or agreement, such as an annulment of a marriage so that it never existed legally

Anti-Semitism: discrimination against or dislike of Jewish persons

Apartheid: a governmental policy of strict racial discrimination and **segregation**

Appeal: a legal request for a new trial or reversal of conviction

Appellant: a party which appeals a decision or a case to a higher court

Appellate jurisdiction: the power of a higher court or other tribunal to review the judicial actions of a lower court

Appellee: the party opposing the party which appeals a decision or case to a higher court; the opponent of the appellant

Arraignment: the procedure by which a criminal defendant is brought before the trial court and informed of the charges against him or her and the pleas (guilty, not guilty, or **no contest**) he or she may enter in response

Asylum: any place that provides protection or safety

Authoritarian: not questioning authority

B

Bench warrant: an order from the court giving the police or other legal authority the power to arrest an individual

Bigamy: having more than one legal spouse

Brief: a written argument a lawyer uses in representing a client

C

Cartel: an association between countries or other financial interests to fix prices of a resource or product to create a **monopoly**

Change of venue: the removal of a lawsuit from a county or district to another for trial, often permitted in criminal cases where the court finds that the defendant would not receive a fair trial in the first location because of adverse publicity

Circumstantial evidence: indirect evidence which can lead a jury or judge to conclude the existence of a fact by inference

Civil disobedience: breaking a law in order to draw attention to its unfairness

Civil liberties: rights reserved for individuals that are protections from the government

Civil rights: rights that civilized communities give to people by enacting positive laws

Claimant: the party, customarily the **plaintiff,** asserting a right, usually to money or property

Class action: a lawsuit a person brings on behalf of all members in a group sharing a common interest

Clemency: the act, usually by a chief executive such as a president or governor, of forgiving a criminal for his or her actions, as when **pardon** is granted

Co-conspirator: one who engages in a **conspiracy** with others; the acts and declarations of any one conspirator are admissible as evidence against all his or her co-conspirators

Cold war: the period of tense relations, from 1945–1990, between the former Soviet Union (and its Eastern allies) and the United States (and its Western European allies)

Common law: principles and rules established by past judicial decisions

Communism: an economic system in which all property and means of production are owned by the community or society as a whole, and all members of the community or society share in the products of their work

Communist Party: the political party that believes, supports, and advances the principles of **Communism**

Community property: everything acquired by a wife or husband after marriage, except for gifts and inheritances

Commutation: change or substitution, such as when one criminal punishment is substituted for another, more severe one

Compensatory damages: monetary damages the law awards to compensate an injured party solely for the injury sustained because of the action of another

Conspiracy: the agreement of two or more people to jointly commit an unlawful act

Contempt of court: an act that obstructs or attempts to obstruct the administration of justice, such as when someone fails to follow a specific court order

Coroner: a public official who investigates the causes of death

Coroner's inquest: an examination by the coroner, often with the aid of a jury, into the causes of a death occurring under suspicious circumstances

Corpus delicti: proof that a crime has been committed, which ordinarily includes evidence of the criminal act and evidence of who is responsible for its commission

Coup: the sudden, forcible, sometimes violent overthrow of a government

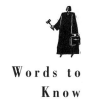

Court of chancery: courts that follow rules of **equity,** or general rules of fairness, rather than strictly formulated **common law;** distinctions between courts of equity and courts of law have essentially disappeared at both the state and federal levels

Cross-examination: questioning a witness, by a party or a lawyer other than the one who is called the witness, about testimony the witness gave on **direct examination**

D

Declarative judgment of relief: a binding decision of the rights and status of parties that does not require any further action or relief

Defamation: speech (**slander**) or writings (**libel**) that damages the reputation of another

Deliberations: any method used to weigh and examine the reasons for and against a verdict, usually by a jury

Deposed: one who is removed from a high office of government

Direct evidence: testimony at trial by a witness who actually heard the words or saw the actions in question

Direct examination: initial questioning of a witness by the lawyer who called him or her

Dissent: a legal opinion of one or more judges in a case who disagree with the legal opinion of the majority of judges; to disagree with

Dissenter: one who voices disagreement with the opinion of the majority

Dissident: one who expresses disagreement with the policies of a government or other ruling authority

Diversity jurisdiction: one basis for granting federal courts the power to hear and determine cases, applicable to cases arising between citizens of different states or between a citizen of the United States and a citizen of a foreign country

DNA: deoxyribonucleic acid; a molecule that appears in all living cells, and is the "building block" of life

Double jeopardy: in criminal law, the Constitutional prohibition against putting a person on trial more than once for the same offense

Due process: relevant only to actions of state or federal governments and their officials; it guarantees procedural fairness when the state deprives an individual of property or liberty

E

Emancipated: freedom from control by another

Equity: legal principle of general fairness and justice

Ex parte: a Latin term meaning "without a party"; a judicial proceeding brought for the benefit of one party without the participation of the opposing party

Excommunicated: one who is expelled from membership in a church by church authority

Executive priviledge: the right of the executive branch to keep matters confidential

Exile: being ordered to leave one's country and being prohibited to return

Expert witness: a witness, such as a psychiatrist or ballistics expert, with special knowledge concerning the subject he or she will testify about

Extenuating circumstances: factors which would reduce a defendant's criminal punishment

Extortion: a criminal offense, usually punished as a felony, consisting of obtaining property from another through use or threat of force, or through illegitimate use of official power

Extradition: the surrender by one state or country of an individual accused or convicted of an offense outside its borders and within those of another state or country

F

Fascism: a system of government (first established by Benito Mussolini in Italy in 1922) usually characterized by one ruling political party led by a strong leader that forcibly holds down any opposition, controls its people very closely, and advocates war

Fascists: individuals who believe, support, and advance the priciples of **fascism**

Felony: high crimes, such as burglary, rape, or homicide, which unlike **misdemeanors,** are often punishable by lengthy jail terms or death

G

Gag order: a court order restricting attorneys and witnesses from talking about or releasing information about a case; also, an order to restrain an unruly defendant who is disrupting his or her trial

Genocide: the intentional and systematic destruction, in whole or in part, of a racial, ethnic, or religious group

Grand jury: traditionally consisting of twenty-three individuals empaneled to determine whether the facts and accusations presented by prosecutors in a criminal proceeding require an **indictment** and trial of the accused

Guardian ad litem: a person appointed by the court to represent the interests of a child or one not possessing legal capacity in legal proceedings

Guerilla: a member of a small military force who make surprise attacks against an enemy army

H

Habeas corpus: a Latin term meaning "you have the body"; a procedure for a judicial ruling on the legality of an individual's custody. It is used in a criminal case to challenge a convict's confinement, and in a civil case to challenge child custody, deportation, and commitment to a mental institution (see **Writ of *habeas corpus***)

Hearsay: a statement, other than one made by a witness at a hearing or trial, offered to prove the truth of a matter asserted at the hearing or trial

House arrest: confinement under guard to quarters other than a prison

Hypocrisy: pretending to be what one is not

I

Immunity: exemption from a duty or penalty; witnesses are often granted immunity from prosecution in order to compel them to respond to questions they might otherwise refuse to answer based on the Fifth Amendment's privilege against self-incrimination

Impeach: to charge a public official with a wrongdoing while in office

Impeachment: criminal proceedings against a public official, such as a president or a supreme court justice, accused of wrongdoing while in office

In re: a Latin term meaning "in the matter of"; used to signify a legal proceeding where there are no adversaries, but merely a matter, such as an estate, requiring judicial action

Indicted: when someone is charged with a crime by a **grand jury**

Indictment: a formal written accusation drawn up by a public prosecuting attorney and issued by a grand jury against a party charged with a crime

Injunction: a judicial remedy requiring a party to cease or refrain from some specified action

Interspousal immunity: a state common law rule, now largely abolished, prohibiting tort actions, or lawsuits concerning certain civil wrongs, between husbands and wives

J

Judicial notice: recognition by a court during trial of certain facts that are so universally acknowledged or easily verifiable (for example, historical facts, geographical features) that they do not require the production of evidence as proof of their existence

Jurisdiction: a court's authority to hear a case

L

Libel: a method of **defamation** expressed by false and malicious publication in print for the purpose of damaging the reputation of another

M

Manslaughter: unlawful killing of another without malice or an intent to cause death. It calls for less severe penalties than murder. Most jurisdictions distinguish between voluntary, or intentional, manslaughter and involuntary manslaughter, such as a death resulting from an automobile accident

Martial law: the law enforced by military forces in substitution for the ordinary government and adminstration of justice when a state of war, rebellion, invasion, or other serious disturbance exists

Martyr: a person who chooses to suffer or die rather than give up his or her faith or principles

Marxism: economic and political philosophy founded by Karl Marx, also known as Socialism

Misdemeanor: any criminal offense less serious than a felony. It is generally punished by a fine or jail (not a penitentiary) and for a shorter period than would be imposed for a felony

Mistrial: a trial terminated and declared void before a verdict is reached because of serious error in procedure or other major problem

Monopoly: an organization, such as a corporation or **cartel,** that has exclusive control of a service or product in a given market

Mutiny: an act of defiance or resistance to a lawful authority, usually by a member or members of one of the armed forces against a higher ranking officer or officers

N

Nationalized: the transfer of ownership or control of land, resources, and industries from private interests to the government

No contest: a type of plea available in a criminal case that does not require a defendant to admit responsibility to the charge, however, the consequences are the same as a guilty plea

O

Opportunism: acting in a way to further one's own interest without any regard to the consequences

P

Pacifist: one who opposes war or the use of force to settle disputes

Pardon: an act, usually of a chief executive such as a president or governor, that relieves a convict from the punishment imposed for his or her crime

Parole: a conditional release of a prisoner after he or she has served part of a sentence

Patriotism: love and loyal support for one's own country

Perjury: the criminal offense of making false statements or lying while under oath

Pernicious: having the power of killing, destroying, or injuring

Plaintiff: the party who initiates a lawsuit, seeking a remedy for an injury to his or her rights

Police power of the state: the power of state and local governments to impose upon private rights restrictions that are necessary to the general public welfare

Precedent: a court decision which serves as a rule for future cases involving similar circumstances

Pro bono: a Latin term meaning "for the good of the people"; when an attorney takes a case without charging a fee

Pro se: a Latin term meaning "for oneself"; representing oneself without an attorney

Prosecution: the act of conducting a lawsuit or criminal case

Prosecutor: a person who handles the **prosecution** of persons accused of crime

Punitive damages: compensation above actual losses awarded to a successful plaintiff who was injured under circumstances involving malicious and willful misconduct on the part of the defendant

R

Reasonable doubt: the degree of certainty required for a juror to find a criminal defendant guilty. Proof of guilt must be so clear that an ordinary person would have no reasonable doubt as to the guilt of the defendant

Redress: to correct or compensate for a fault or injustice

Regime: a political system in power

Repression: strict control of another

Reprieve: a temporary relief or postponement of a criminal punishment or sentence

Republicanism: belief in a republican form of government in which all power rests with the citizens who are entitled to vote, as in the United States

Resistance fighters: members of an organization that secretly work against a government or army in power

S

Sedition: a form of treason consisting of acts intending to overthrow or disrupt the government

Segregation: practice of separating groups of people in housing, public accomadations, and schools based on race, nationality, or religion

Show trial: a trial whose outcome has been decided before it starts

Slander: false and malicious words spoken with the intent to damage another's reputation

Stalemate: any situation making further action impossible; a deadlock

Subpoena: a Latin term meaning "under penalty"; a written order issued by a court authority requiring the appearance of a witness at a judicial proceeding

T

Temporary insanity: a criminal defense which asserts that, because the accused was legally insane at the time the crime was committed, he or she did not have the necessary mental state to commit it, and is therefore not legally responsible

Totalitarian: a government in which one political party or group has complete control and refuses to recognize any other political party or group

Tribunal: an officer or body having authority to judge a case

U

Unanimous: complete agreement

**Words to
Know**

V

Voir dire: a Latin term meaning "to speak the truth"; the examination of possible jurors by lawyers to determine their qualifications to serve

W

Writ of *habeas corpus:* a procedure used in criminal law to bring a petitioning prisoner before the court to determine the legality of his or her confinement (*see **Habeas corpus***)

Writ of *mandamus:* an order issued by a court, requiring the performance of some act or duty, or restoring rights and privileges that have been illegally denied

Picture Credits

The photographs and illustrations appearing in *Courtroom Drama: 120 of the World's Most Notable Trials* were received from the following sources:

On the cover, clockwise from upper left: Crowds at the Bruno Richard Hauptmann Trial (**National Archives and Records Administration**); Salem Witchcraft Trials (**The Library of Congress**); John Demjanjuk (**AP/Wide World Photos**). On the back cover: Scottsboro Trial defendant Haywood Patterson (**National Archives and Records Administration**).

United States Supreme Court. Reproduced by permission: 4, 31, 37, 120, 212; **The Library of Congress:** 6, 11, 12, 16, 17, 25, 106, 107, 108, 113, 124, 138, 158, 173, 174, 178, 184, 191, 192, 198, 252, 253, 256, 303, 336, 342, 382, 387, 425, 518, 524, 531, 532, 580, 604, 642, 643, 649, 650, 651, 669, 695, 700, 701, 707, 749; **Utah State Historical Society. Reproduced by permission:** 24; **Reproduced by permission of Elizabeth Frost-Knappman:** 41; **Official White House photo:** 44; **Photograph by Bettye Lane. Reproduced by permission:** 48, 98; **AP/Wide World Photos. Reproduced by permission:** 55, 142, 149, 211, 222, 228, 235, 236, 337, 369, 374, 412, 440, 448, 468, 498, 500, 504, 543, 760, 783, 789, 794, 833; **Illinois State Historical Society. Reproduced by permission:** 72, 406, 407; **Virginia State Library & Archives. Reproduced by permission:** 85; **Mrs. A. T. Newberry. Reproduced by permission:** 86; **Reproduced by permission of Sarah Weddington:** 90; **National Archives and Records Administration:** 114, 197, 298, 324, 328,

Courtroom DRAMA

120 of the World's Most Notable Trials

THE
CONSTITUTION

Marbury v. Madison: 1803

Plaintiffs: William Marbury, William Harper, Robert R. Hooe, and Dennis Ramsay

Defendant: James Madison

Plaintiffs' Claims: That Madison had illegally refused to deliver judicial commissions to their rightful recipients

Chief Defense Lawyer: U.S. Attorney General Levi Lincoln

Chief Lawyer for Plaintiffs: Charles Lee

Justices: Samuel Chase, William Cushing, John Marshall, Alfred Moore, William Paterson, and Bushrod Washington

Place: Washington, D.C.

Dates of Hearing: February 10–11, 1803

Verdict: Plaintiffs could not force Madison to deliver the commissions, because the Judiciary Act of 1789 was unconstitutional

SIGNIFICANCE: *Marbury v. Madison* may be the most important case in American history. It gave the courts power to decide whether acts of Congress or the president are constitutional. This is called the principle of judicial review.

In the late eighteenth and early nineteenth centuries, there were two main political parties in America, the Federalists and the Democratic Republicans. After the presidential election of 1800, there was a tie vote in the Electoral College—the group whose job it is to elect the president officially. When there is a tie, the House of Representatives decides the win-

ner. On February 17, 1801, it took a bitter battle and thirty-six ballots to elect Democratic-Republican Thomas Jefferson president.

Last Minute Appointments

The outgoing president was Federalist John Adams. His secretary of state was the famous lawyer John Marshall. Before he left office, Adams nominated Marshall as chief justice of the Supreme Court. In January 1801, Marshall's nomination was confirmed. He was sworn in as chief justice on February 4. However, he also continued to serve as secretary of state until March 3, when Adams's term as president ended. Mean-

Chief Justice John Marshall in an engraving by Alonzo Chappell.

while, Adams and his party appointed as many new Federalist judges as possible before Jefferson came to power.

On February 27, 1801, Congress gave Adams the power to appoint new justices of the peace in the District of Columbia. This was part of their effort to keep their control over the judiciary. On March 2, one day before his term ended, Adams appointed forty-two new justices of the peace. Congress approved them the next day. As secretary of state, Marshall signed and sealed the judicial commissions. However, they were not delivered by the end of the day on March 3. When Jefferson's term began March 4, he ordered his new secretary of state, James Madison, not to deliver the commissions. Jefferson declared that since the appointing documents had not been delivered, the appointments were not valid.

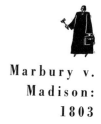

THE POWER OF JUDICIAL REVIEW

The *Marbury v. Madison* case established that the judicial branch has the power to review all laws. It can then throw out those that are unconstitutional. That is, if a law contradicts the U.S. Constitution, then that law is not valid. Supreme Court decisions to find laws unconstitutional have led to many social changes. In 1954, in *Brown v. Board of Education,* the Supreme Court found that laws which segregated (separated) education on the basis of race violated the Fourteenth Amendment. The Fourteenth Amendment says that all citizens, regardless of race, are entitled to equal protection under the law. In 1973, in *Roe v. Wade,* the Supreme Court found that laws banning many types of abortion (termination of a pregnancy) were illegal on the grounds that the Ninth Amendment guarantees the right to privacy. As a result of these decisions, school segregation was ended and abortion became legal.

Marbury Goes to Court

After he had demonstrated his power, Jefferson allowed most of Adams's appointees to take office. However, he did not allow William Marbury to do so, so Marbury filed a petition with the Supreme Court. On December 16, 1801, he asked the court to order Madison to deliver his commission. Three other unconfirmed appointees added their names to Marbury's petition. They were William Harper, Robert R. Hooe, and Dennis Ramsey. By this time Marshall had been chief justice for more than nine months. Under the Judiciary Act of 1789, the Supreme Court had the power to issue the order Marbury requested. It was called a "writ of mandamus."

On December 18, 1801, Marshall called a hearing on Marbury's petition. The hearing began on February 10, 1803. Charles Lee, a Federalist and former attorney general, was the lawyer for Marbury and the others. Jefferson's attorney general, Levi Lincoln, represented Secretary of State Madison.

Lee said that Madison, as secretary of state, was an official of the executive branch of the government. He was bound to obey the president.

However, Madison was also a public servant. As such he had to perform his duty and deliver Marbury's commission. Therefore, the court must exercise its power under the Judiciary Act to issue a writ of mandamus against Madison. Attorney General Lincoln said only that the issue of the commissions was purely political. As such, the judiciary had no control over them.

Marshall Proclaims the Doctrine of Judicial Review

On February 24, 1803, Chief Justice Marshall issued the court's opinion. He proceeded in three steps. First, he reviewed the facts of the case. He

Secretary of State James Madison, defendant in Marbury v. Madison, which established the principle of judicial review.

stated that Marbury had the right to receive his commission. Not to do so, he declared, would violate Marbury's right to receive it.

Second, Marshall analyzed Marbury's legal remedies. He concluded that the Judiciary Act clearly entitled Marbury to the writ of mandamus he requested.

The third and final issue Marshall addressed was whether the writ could be issued by the Supreme Court. The Judiciary Act would allow the court to issue it. However, Marshall was concerned about the extent of the court's constitutional authority. The relevant passage appears in Article II, Section 2, Paragraph 2 of the Constitution, which reads:

> In all cases affecting ambassadors, other public
> ministers and consuls, and those in which a State

shall be a Party, the Supreme Court shall have original jurisdiction. In all other cases . . . the Supreme
Court shall have appellate jurisdiction. . . .

If the court did not have original jurisdiction, it did not have the power to hear the evidence and decide Marbury's case. Therefore, Marbury would have to go to a lower court—a federal district court—first. If the district court rejected his petition, then could he appeal to the Supreme Court.

Marshall addressed the critical question: Could the Supreme Court use the power that the Judiciary Act granted it to issue Marbury's writ? The Constitution seemed to say it could not.

Marshall declared that the court would not issue the writ. No act of Congress—in this case, the Judiciary Act—could make an act forbidden by the Constitution lawful. Therefore, because the Judiciary Act violated the Constitution, it could not be enforced. Marbury and the others could not get their writ of mandamus directly from the Supreme Court.

In announcing this decision, however, Marshall established the doctrine of judicial review. This doctrine holds that federal courts—and above all, the U.S. Supreme Court—have the power to declare laws invalid if they violate the Constitution.

Marshall's decision meant that the court would not give his fellow Federalist Marbury a writ of mandamus. Still, Marshall's decision was brilliant. In refusing to confront Jefferson, Marshall still forged a new and powerful tool for the judiciary, judicial review.

The case left several issues unresolved. One was whether Marshall should have removed himself from deciding the case because he had served as Adams's secretary of state. Still, *Marbury v. Madison* permanently established the doctrine of judicial review. It changed forever the role of the courts. This power to overturn unconstitutional laws is the basis for the courts' power today.

Suggestions for Further Reading

Baker, Leonard. *John Marshall: A Life in Law.* New York: Macmillan, 1974.

Berger, Raoul. *Congress v. the Supreme Court.* Cambridge: Harvard University Press, 1969.

Beveridge, Albert J. *The Life of John Marshall.* Atlanta: Cherokee, 1990.

Bickel, Alexander M. *The Least Dangerous Branch: The Supreme*

**THE
CONSTITUTION**

Court at the Bar of Politics. New Haven: Yale University Press, 1986.

Cusack, Michael. "America's Greatest Justice?" *Scholastic Update* (January 1990): 11.

Ellis, Richard E. *The Jeffersonian Crisis: Courts and Politics in the Young Republic.* New York: Oxford University Press, 1971.

Levy, Leonard Williams. *Judicial Review and the Supreme Court.* New York: Harper & Row, 1967.

McHugh, Clare. "The Story of the Constitution: Conflict and Promise." *Scholastic Update* (September 1987): 8–11.

Warren, Charles. *The Supreme Court in United States History.* Littleton: F. B. Rothman, 1987.

Cherokee Nation v. Georgia: 1831

Plaintiffs: Cherokee Indian Nation

Defendant: State of Georgia

Plaintiff Claim: That under the Supreme Court's power to resolve disputes between states and foreign nations, the court could forbid Georgia from unlawfully attempting to move the Cherokee from their lands

Chief Defense Lawyer: None

Chief Lawyer for Plaintiffs: William Wirt

Justices: Henry Baldwin, Gabriel Duvalt, William Johnson, John Marshall, John McLean, Joseph Story, and Smith Thompson

Place: Washington, D.C.

Date of Decision: March 5, 1831

Decision: The court ruled that Indian nations were not foreign nations, but dependent, domestic nations, and therefore could not sue

SIGNIFICANCE: The Cherokee based their case on a clause in the Constitution that allowed foreign nations to seek redress (compensation) in the Supreme Court for damages caused by U.S. citizens. But the court ruled that Indian nations were not foreign, but domestic. By refusing to help the Cherokee, the U.S. Supreme Court left the Indians at the mercy of land-hungry settlers. In the end, the Cherokee were forced to leave their lands in Georgia and travel along the "Trail of Tears" to Indian Territory (present-day Oklahoma).

**THE
CONSTITUTION**

ON THE "TRAIL OF TEARS"

The "Trail of Tears" was the end of a seven-year process of forcing Indian nations out of the American Southeast. Between 1831 and 1833, some 15,000 Mississippi Choctaw were forced into the new Indian Territory west of Arkansas (present-day Oklahoma). Pneumonia in winter and cholera in summer killed hundreds of Choctaw. They were soon joined by the Chickasaw and Creek indians. After a bitter war in Florida, the Seminole were also forced into Indian Territory. Finally, in October 1838, some 15,000 to 17,000 Cherokee were forced out of Georgia. The U.S. government imprisoned any Cherokee who refused to abandon their lands, and burned their homes and crops. The Cherokee remember the trek as "The Trail Where They Cried," while U.S. historians refer to it as "The Trail of Tears." Some 4,000 Cherokee men, women, and children lost their lives along the way. One soldier wrote: "I fought through the Civil War and have seen men shot to pieces and slaughtered by thousands, but the Cherokee removal was the cruelest work I ever knew."

The Cherokee Indians originally inhabited much of the land along the southeastern coast of the Atlantic Ocean. In the seventeenth and eighteenth centuries, European settlers pushed the Cherokee from many of their lands. Unlike most Indians, however, the Cherokee were able to resist somewhat by adopting the white man's ways. After the American Revolution, the Cherokee copied white farming methods and other aspects of the white economy. The Cherokee sent some of their children to white schools and permitted mixed marriages. They also signed treaties with the federal government that seemed to protect what remained of Cherokee lands.

Gold in Cherokee Territory

The number of Cherokee living in Georgia was especially large, having succeeded by adapting to white men's ways. Cherokee plantations even had Negro slaves working on them. Then in 1828, prospectors discovered gold in Cherokee territory. Georgia wanted to give the land to whites, and laws were put in place to force the Cherokee to leave. However, the Cherokee fought back, hiring white lawyers to represent them.

The chief lawyer for the Cherokee was William Wirt. He took their case directly to the Supreme Court, asking for an order to prevent Georgia from removing the Indians. Article III, Section 2, of the U.S. Constitution gives the Supreme Court original jurisdiction in cases where a state is one of the parties. The Cherokee did not have to go through the Georgia state courts first. They could not use the lower federal courts. Unfortunately, Article III, Section 2, generally limits the court's jurisdiction to cases involving American citizens, and Indians were not yet recognized as citizens. The only basis Wirt could use to argue for jurisdiction was the court's power to hear disputes "between a State, or the Citizens thereof, and foreign States, Citizens or Subjects."

Associate Justice Joseph Story did not vote with the majority in the 1831 Cherokee Nation v. Georgia *decision, which led to the "Trail of Tears."*

Wirt had to convince the court that the Cherokee were a foreign nation. On March 5, 1831, he pleaded their case before Supreme Court Justices Henry Baldwin, Gabriel Duvalt, William Johnson, John Marshall, John McLean, Joseph Story, and Smith Thompson. Georgia refused to send a lawyer to defend itself. The refusal was based on Georgia's strong support of the right of states to control their own affairs, called "states' rights."

The Cherokee
Phoenix *was first
published on
February 21, 1828,
by Elias Boudinot, a
Cherokee educated
by Christian
missionaries.
Symbolizing the
tribe's progress, the
newspaper used the
English as well as
the Cherokee
alphabet. This issue
is dated April 10,
1828, from New
Echota, Georgia.*

Supreme Court Hears Arguments for the Cherokee Nation

Wirt reminded the court that the Cherokee had clear rights to the lands in Georgia:

> The boundaries were fixed by treaty, and what was within them was acknowledged to be the land of the Cherokee. This was the scope of all the treaties.

Next, Wirt begged the court to prevent what was about to happen to the Cherokee:

> The legislation of Georgia proposes to annihilate them, as its very end and aim. . . . If those laws be fully executed, there will be no Cherokee boundary, no Cherokee nation, no Cherokee lands, no Cherokee treaties. . . . They will all be swept out of existence together, leaving nothing but the monuments in our history of the enormous injustice that has been practiced towards a friendly nation.

That same day, the Supreme Court turned down Wirt's claim. The Cherokee and other Indian tribes were only "domestic dependent nations," not foreign nations. The court, therefore, had no authority to help them.

A year later, the court did hear another case concerning the Cherokee. But the court only agreed to decide *Worcester v. Georgia* (1832) because it concerned white missionaries who had been jailed in the course of their work with the Cherokee.

Without the support of the Supreme Court, the Cherokee could not resist efforts to drive them off their lands. In 1838, over 7,000 soldiers forced the Cherokee to leave for Indian Territory. Over 4,000 Cherokee died during the long journey west along what became known as the "Trail of Tears."

Suggestions for Further Reading

Guttmann, Allen. *States' Rights and Indian Removal: The Cherokee Nation v. the State of Georgia.* Boston: D.C. Heath, 1965.

Lumpkin, Wilson. *The Removal of the Cherokee Indians from Georgia.* New York: Arno Press, 1969.

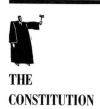

**THE
CONSTITUTION**

Peck, Ira. "Worcester v. Georgia: The Campaign to Move the Cherokee Nation." *Senior Scholastic* (November 1982): 17–20.

Warren, Mary Bondurant. *Whites Among the Cherokees.* Danielsville: Heritage Papers, 1987.

Wilkins, Thurman. *Cherokee Tragedy.* Norman: University of Oklahoma Press, 1986.

Dred Scott Decision: 1856

Appellant: Dred Scott

Defendant: John F. A. Sanford

Plaintiff Claim: That Scott, who was a slave, had become a free man when his owner had taken him to a state designated as "free" under the 1820 Missouri Compromise

Chief Defense Lawyers: Hugh A. Garland, H. S. Geyer, George W. Goode, Reverdy Johnson, and Lyman D. Norris

Chief Lawyers for Appellant: Samuel M. Bay, Montgomery Blair, George Ticknor Curtis, Alexander M. Field, Roswell M. Field, and David N. Hall

Justices: John A. Campbell, John Catron, Benjamin Curtis, Peter Daniel, Robert Cooper Grier, John McLean, Samuel Nelson, Roger B. Taney, and James M. Wayne

Place: Washington, D.C.

Date of Decision: 1856 December Term

Decision: That Dred Scott was still a slave, regardless of where his owner took him

SIGNIFICANCE: The Dred Scott decision ended the Missouri Compromise, which outlawed slavery within the Louisiana Purchase territory north of about 36 degrees latitude (this included the states of Illinois, Indiana, Ohio, Pennsylvania, New York, Vermont, Main, New Hampshire, Massachusetts, Rhode Island, Connecticut, New Jersey, and Michigan territory). It added to the rivalry between North and South and paved the way for the Civil War.

Dred Scott was born in Virginia sometime during the late 1790s. The exact date and place are not known. Because Scott was black and born into slavery, no one would have taken much interest in such details. Most would have noted his birth merely as the arrival of another piece of property.

Dred Scott's Journey

Scott's owner was Peter Blow, who owned a fairly successful plantation. In 1819, Blow moved with his family and several slaves—including Scott—to Alabama to start a new plantation. Blow tired of farming, and in 1830 moved to St. Louis, Missouri. St. Louis was a frontier town that was enjoying a population and business boom, and Blow opened a hotel there. But he and his wife became ill; both were dead by 1832.

The U.S. Supreme Court held that that Dred Scott was his owner's property and that the only "rights" to be considered were those of the owner.

Scott's travels westward mirrored the expansion of the United States during this time period. American colonists had pushed west from the original thirteen states on the Atlantic seaboard to the Mississippi River and beyond. This expansion gave rise to serious political problems. Southern states wanted to bring slavery and the plantation way of life into the new territories. Northerners wanted to keep the territories free. Each side was afraid that as the territories became states, the other side would take the upper hand in Congress as new senators and representatives were added.

In 1820, the North and South struck a bargain called the Missouri Compromise. Missouri was admitted to the Union as a free state. This status kept the political balance in Congress. Further, the Missouri Compromise outlawed slavery north of Missouri's northern border, which is about 36 degrees latitude. Any territory south of this line could adopt slavery.

After the Blows' deaths, their estate sold Scott to a doctor named John Emerson. Emerson took Scott with him to Illinois and to those parts of the Wisconsin and Iowa Territories that would become Minnesota. Both Illinois and Minnesota were within the free territory of the Missouri Compromise. Emerson returned to St. Louis and died December 29, 1843. He left everything, including Dred Scott, to his wife. He appointed his wife's brother, John F. A. Sanford, as the administrator of his estate.

Scott Sues for Freedom

Tired of a lifetime of slavery, Scott tried to buy his freedom from the widow Emerson. He was unsuccessful. But Scott had received more education than most slaves, and he realized that his travels in free territory

An illustration of the Fugitive Slave Law, 1851.

gave him some claim to his own freedom. On April 6, 1846, he sued for his freedom in the Missouri Circuit Court for the City of St. Louis. Because Sanford was the executor for John Emerson's estate, which legally owned Scott, the case bears his name. Unfortunately, his name was misspelled in the court records, and the case has come to be known as *Scott v. Sandford.*

The legal grounds for Scott's suit were assault and false imprisonment. A slave could be punished and kept as property, but a free person could not. But the real issue was whether Scott was a slave or a free man. On June 30, 1847, the case came to trial before Judge Alexander Hamilton. Scott's lawyer committed a technical error in presenting evidence, and that same day the jury reached a verdict in favor of Sanford. Judge Hamilton granted Scott a new trial, however, and this trial opened on January 12, 1850.

At the second trial, the jurors found that Scott was a free man. They based their decision on some earlier cases which held that although Missouri was a slave state, if a slave had resided in free state or territory, he was freed. Scott's freedom was short-lived, however.

Sanford appealed to the Missouri Supreme Court. After more than two years, this court handed down its decision on March 22, 1852. This decision reversed the earlier verdict. Scott was, the court declared, still a slave. The judge's decision was phrased in terms of states' rights and the legality of slavery in Missouri. Its real basis, however, was the rise to power of pro-slavery Democrats in the court itself. Judge William Scott justified the court's decision by stating that blacks were destined to be slaves.

Scott Tries Federal Courts

Following the Missouri Supreme Court's decision, the case was sent back to Judge Hamilton in St. Louis. Judge Hamilton was supposed to issue the final order dismissing the case and returning Scott to slavery. Hamilton delayed doing so, however, thus giving Scott time to hire a new lawyer and get his case into the federal courts. His new lawyer was Roswell M. Field. Field realized that Sanford had moved to New York City and was therefore no longer a citizen of Missouri. But legal rules give federal courts jurisdiction over trials between citizens of different states. Therefore, Field began a new trial on November 2, 1853, in federal court under what is called "diversity jurisdiction." Diversity jurisdiction made it possible for Scott, as a citizen of Missouri, to sue Sanford, as a citizen of New York, in federal court. The issue of Scott's freedom was now before Judge Robert

CONDEMNED TO SLAVERY

After Dred Scott finally lost his case, he and his wife were made the property of Taylor Blow. Scott later worked—as a slave—for Mr. and Mrs. Theron Barnum, serving as a porter in their St. Louis hotel. The long struggle to win his freedom had worn him out, and on September 17, 1858—one year after losing his case—he died of tuberculosis. However, after the Civil War ended slavery, Scott's descendants went on to build new lives. Dred Scott Madison became a police officer. In a later generation, John A. Madison became a lawyer who practiced in the very court where Dred Scott had been denied the right to sue.

W. Wells of the U.S. Court for the District of Missouri, located in St. Louis.

During the circuit court's spring 1854 term, Wells held that Scott was a Missouri "citizen" for purposes of diversity jurisdiction (despite Scott's status as a slave). The case then went to trial on May 15, 1854. In this third trial concerning Scott's freedom, the jury ruled in Sanford's favor: Scott was still a slave. Field promptly appealed to the U.S. Supreme Court. He convinced the distinguished lawyer Montgomery Blair to represent Scott before the Supreme Court in Washington, D.C., although Scott had no money to pay him.

Southerners who favored slavery realized the significance of the case. They helped Sanford hire a well-regarded lawyer, Henry S. Geyer. Like Blair, Geyer came originally from Missouri and had made a name for himself as a Washington lawyer.

Victory for Slavery, Defeat for Scott

The Scott case was filed with the Supreme Court on December 30, 1854. It was set to be heard during the court's February 1856 term before Justices John A. Campbell, John Catron, Benjamin R. Curtis, Peter Daniel, Robert Cooper Grier, John McLean, Samuel Nelson, Roger Brooke Taney, and James M. Wayne.

THE CONSTITUTION

The political makeup of the court would play a major role in the outcome of the case. Southern and pro-slavery justices had a clear majority. Campbell was from Alabama; Catron was from Tennessee; Curtis was from Massachusetts, but he was sympathetic to the South; Daniel was from Virginia; Grier was from Pennsylvania, but he was a conservative who favored states' rights; Nelson was from New York, but like Grier, he was a defender of states' rights; Taney, the chief justice, was from Maryland and acted as the leader of the court's Southern majority; Wayne was from Georgia. McLean, from Ohio, was the only judge who was openly anti-slavery. The justices were also conscious of the fact that 1856 was an election year. The Scott decision could have serious political consequences.

During the February 1856 term, the justices listened to the parties' arguments for three days. Scott's attorneys presented the "free soil" case, the one favored by Northerners. This position held that once a slave stepped into a free state or territory, he or she was emancipated (set free). Otherwise, the Free Soilers argued, the power to prohibit slavery was meaningless. Sanford's attorneys presented the states' rights argument, which favored slavery. Scott had been a slave in Missouri, and he had returned to Missouri, where he had applied to Missouri courts under Missouri law. Therefore, they reasoned, Missouri was entitled to declare Scott a slave.

Not surprisingly, most of the justices were in favor of rejecting Scott's plea for freedom. However, they could not agree on the legal grounds for reaching this decision. Some justices wanted to rule that a slave could not sue in federal court. Others wanted to discuss Congress's power to prohibit slavery in the territories and the constitutionality of the Missouri Compromise. The justices decided to postpone their decision until after the presidential election. They ordered the lawyers to reargue the case during the court's December 1856 term.

In November 1856, Democrat James Buchanan was elected president. Buchanan, unconcerned with the slavery issue, would do nothing during the next four years to prevent the country from splitting apart and moving toward civil war.

After the second round of arguments in December, Chief Justice Taney finally announced the court's decision. Taney and six other justices voted that Scott was still a slave. Taney refused to recognize that blacks had any rights as citizens under the Constitution. He went on to say that Scott was a slave wherever he went. Therefore, Scott's owner could reclaim him as property any time, because the Constitution forbids Congress from depriving Americans of their life, liberty, or property without due process of law. And Scott, said Justice Taney, was property.

Using the same arguments, Taney went on to declare the Missouri Compromise unconstitutional:

> An Act of Congress which deprives a citizen of the United States of his property, merely because he came himself or brought his property into a particular Territory of the United States, and who had committed no offense against the laws, could hardly be dignified with the name of due process of law.

Scott was a slave once again, and the South had won an important victory. The Missouri Compromise had held the nation together for nearly forty years, and now it was swept away. The North would eventually succeed in abolishing slavery, but only after many bloody Civil War battles.

Dred Scott Decision: 1856

Suggestions for Further Reading

Ehrlich, Walter. *They Have No Rights: Dred Scott's Struggle for Freedom.* Westport, CT: Greenwood Press, 1979.

Fehrbacher, Don Edward. *Slavery, Law, and Politics: The Dred Scott Case in Historical Perspective.* New York: Oxford University Press, 1981.

Kutler, Stanley I. *The Dred Scott Decision: Law or Politics?* Boston: Houghton Mifflin, 1967.

McGinty, Brian. "Dred Scott's Fight for Freedom Brought Him a Heap O' Trouble." *American History Illustrated* (May 1981): 34–39.

Sudo, Phil. "Five Little People Who Changed U.S. History." *Scholastic Update* (January 26, 1990): 8–10.

Reynolds v. U.S.:
1879

Defendant: George Reynolds

Crime Charged: Bigamy (a legal term for marrying a second spouse while the first is still living)

Chief Defense Lawyers: George W. Biddle and Ben Sheeks

Chief Prosecutor: William Carey

Judge: Alexander White

Place: Salt Lake City, Utah

Date of Trial: October 30–December 10, 1875

Verdict: Guilty

Sentence: Two years imprisonment and a $500 fine

SIGNIFICANCE: The Mormons, a religious group that settled in Utah, permitted its men to have many wives, a practice known as polygamy. In *Reynolds v. U.S.,* the Supreme Court found that laws banning polygamy were constitutional. They did not violate the Mormons' right to free exercise of their religion. This remains the most important legal case to address the issue of polygamy.

After a long trek westward, in the middle of the nineteenth century the Mormons finally settled in the land that would become the state of Utah.

The Mormons are followers of a religious prophet named Joseph Smith, and their religion is called the Church of Jesus Christ of Latter Day Saints. They hold a variety of beliefs, the most controversial of which was that a man could have more than one wife.

Most of the United States had known about the Mormon practice of polygamy since 1852. Most Americans were traditional Christians who believed in monogamy—having only one spouse. Until the Mormons arrived, however, there were no federal laws against bigamy or polygamy. The government left the Mormons alone for many years, but in 1862, President Abraham Lincoln signed the Morrill Anti-Bigamy Act into law. The Morrill Act outlawed polygamy throughout the United States in general and in Utah in particular. The government did not do much to enforce the law, however, because it was absorbed with the Civil War.

Reynolds v. U.S.: 1879

Congress Strengthens Anti-Bigamy Law

After the Civil War was over, Congress again took up the issue of Mormon polygamy. The Morrill Act was strengthened with the Poland Law in 1874. The Poland Law increased the powers of the federal courts in the territory of Utah. Because federal judges were not appointed by local politicians, they were more likely to be non-Mormons who would be more aggressive in enforcing the anti-polygamy law.

Mormon leader Brigham Young's advisor, George Q. Cannon, was also a territorial delegate to Congress. Together, the two men decided to challenge the federal government in court. They were confident that if the government tried any Mormons for bigamy, the United States Supreme Court would throw out the convictions. Their belief was based on the First Amendment right to free exercise of religion. Young and Cannon arranged to bring a "test" case to court. They chose Young's personal secretary, a devout Mormon and practicing polygamist named George Reynolds, to act as the defendant.

Young and Cannon were successful. The government indicted Reynolds for bigamy in October 1874. When the first trial failed because of problems with jury selection, Reynolds was retried in October 1875. Federal prosecutors charged that Reynolds was then married to both Mary Ann Tuddenham and Amelia Jane Schofield. They had little trouble proving that Reynolds lived with both women, even though they had some trouble serving Schofield with a subpoena (a document ordering a person

to appear in court under penalty for failure to do so). The following dialogue is taken from the prosecution's questioning of Arthur Pratt, a deputy marshal sent to serve the subpoena:

Question: State to the court what efforts you have made to serve it.

Answer: I went to the residence of Mr. Reynolds, and a lady was there, his first wife, and she told me that this woman was not there; that that was the only home that she had, but that she hadn't been there for two or three weeks. I went again this morning, and she was not there.

Question: Do you know anything about her home, where she resides?

Answer: I know where I found her before.

Question: Where?

Answer: At the same place.

Following the presentation of more clear evidence that Reynolds had two wives, Judge White gave instructions to the jury. These instructions completely undermined Reynolds's defense that the First Amendment protected his practice of the polygamy permitted by his Mormon faith:

*George Reynolds
surrounded by his
twelve sons.*

Mormon leader
Brigham Young
(center) and his
cabinet.

**THE
CONSTITUTION**

[If you find that Reynolds] deliberately married a second time, having a first wife living, the want of consciousness of evil intent, the want of understanding on his part that he was committing crime, did not excuse him, but the law . . . in such cases, implies criminal intent.

The jury found Reynolds guilty on December 10, 1875. On July 6, 1876, the territorial supreme court affirmed his sentence. Reynolds then appealed to the U.S. Supreme Court. On November 14 and 15, 1878, his lawyers argued before the highest court in the land that Reynolds's conviction must be overturned on First Amendment grounds.

The Supreme Court Destroys Mormon Hopes

On January 6, 1879, the Supreme Court upheld the trial court's decision. The Supreme Court said that the First Amendment did not protect polygamy, basing its decision on historic American cultural values. Reynolds's sentence of two years in prison and a $500 fine stood.

The court's decision rocked the Mormons, who initially vowed to defy the court. Later, however, they seemed to accept their fate. In 1890, Mormon leader Wilford Woodruff issued a document called the Manifesto, which ended "any marriages forbidden by the law of the land." After 1890, most Mormons abandoned polygamy.

The *Reynolds* case is still the leading Supreme Court case on the issue of polygamy. In 1984, a U.S. district court considered the case of Utah policeman Royston Potter, who was fired from his job because of bigamy. District Court Judge Sherman Christensen rejected Potter's First Amendment defense, and the U.S. Tenth Circuit Court of Appeals upheld this ruling. In October 1985, the U.S. Supreme Court refused to hear Potter's appeal. By refusing to hear cases like Potter's the court in effect reinforces *Reynolds* as the law of the land.

Many legal scholars have criticized the court for not altering or overturning its opinion in *Reynolds*. It has been more than a century since this decision was handed down. During that time, the court has greatly expanded First Amendment protection of free exercise of religion. In the 1960s and early 1970s, the court increased constitutional protection for the civil rights of women, minorities, and other classes of persons whose equality under the law had not been a part of the old common law on

FIGHTS OVER POLYGAMY

The Mormon practice of polygamy had been controversial for almost as long as the religion existed in the United States. In 1857, 2,500 Army troops were sent into Utah to install a governor to replace Mormon leader Brigham Young. Mormons responded angrily. The result was the "Utah War," in which Mormons killed 120 people passing through Utah on their way to California. For years, Utah had been refused statehood because of its sanctioning of polygamy. The controversy spread to the Mormon community itself. In 1873, Ann Eliza Webb Young made history by moving out of the home owned by her husband, Brigham Young, and demanding a divorce. She became a nationwide crusader against polygamy. Throughout the 1880s and 1890s, the battle continued. Over 1,000 Mormons were fined or imprisoned for polygamy. Not until Mormons themselves outlawed this practice was Utah's application for statehood accepted, on January 4, 1896.

which *Reynolds* was based. To date, however, the Supreme Court has not reconsidered its decision in this case.

Suggestions for Further Reading

Cannon, George Quayle. *A Review of the Decision of the Supreme Court of the United States, in the Case of Geo. Reynolds vs. the United States.* Salt Lake City: Deseret News Printing, 1879.

Casey, Kathryn. "An American Harem." *Ladies Home Journal* (February 1990): 116–121.

Embry, Jessie L. *Mormon Polygamous Families: Life in the Principle.* Salt Lake City: University of Utah Press, 1987.

Firmage, Edwin Brown. *Zion in the Courts: A Legal History of the Church of Jesus Christ of Latter-day Saints, 1830–1900.* Urbana: University of Illinois Press, 1988.

**THE
CONSTITUTION**

Foster, Lawrence. *Religion and Sexuality: The Shakers, the Mormons, and the Oneida Community.* Urbana: University of Illinois Press, 1984.

Wagoner, Richard S. *Mormon Polygamy: A History.* Salt Lake City: Signature Books, 1989.

Plessy v. Ferguson: 1896

Appellant: Homer A. Plessy

Respondent: J. H. Ferguson

Appellant Claim: That Louisiana's law requiring blacks to ride in separate railroad cars violated Plessy's right to equal protection under the law

Chief Defense Lawyer: M. J. Cunningham

Chief Lawyers for Appellant: F. D. McKenney and S. F. Phillips

Justices: David J. Brewer, Henry B. Brown, Stephen J. Field, Melville W. Fuller, Horace Gray, John Marshall Harlan, Rufus W. Peckham, George Shiras, and Edward D. White

Place: Washington, D.C.

Date of Decision: May 18, 1896

Decision: That laws providing for "separate but equal" treatment of blacks and whites were constitutional

SIGNIFICANCE: After the Supreme Court's decision in *Plessy v. Ferguson,* "separate but equal" became the law of the land. However, legal segregation (separation) would not be completely overruled for more than sixty years.

After the Civil War, many states in the South and elsewhere in the country enacted laws that discriminated against African Americans. These laws ranged from restrictions on voting, such as reading tests and poll taxes,

DISSENTING OPINION

Justice John Marshall Harlan offered the only dissenting (differing) opinion to *Plessy v. Ferguson.* He argued that the decision was contrary to the spirit of the Constitution, and that it would prove dangerous to African Americans: "Our Constitution is color-blind, and neither knows nor tolerates classes among citizens. . . . In my opinion, the judgment this day rendered will, in time, prove to be quite as pernicious [destructive] as the decision made by this tribunal in the Dred Scott case. . . . The present decision. . . will not only stimulate aggressions. . . upon the admitted rights of colored citizens, but will encourage the belief that it is possible, by means of state enactments, to defeat the beneficent purposes which the people of the United States had in view when they adopted the recent amendments of the Constitution."

to requirements that blacks and whites attend separate schools and use separate public facilities, such as washrooms.

Plessy Tests State Segregation Law

On June 7, 1892, Homer A. Plessy bought a train ticket to travel from New Orleans to Covington, Louisiana. Plessy's ancestry was one-eighth black and seven-eighths white. Under Louisiana law, he was considered black and therefore required to ride in the "blacks only" railroad car. Plessy sat in the "whites only" car. He was promptly arrested and thrown into the New Orleans jail.

John A. Ferguson presided over Plessy's trial in federal district court. Plessy faced trial for the crime of riding in a "whites only" car and was found guilty. The Louisiana Supreme Court upheld his conviction. Plessy then appealed to the U.S. Supreme Court for an order forbidding Louisiana—in the person of Judge Ferguson—from carrying out his conviction.

Plessy Goes to the Supreme Court

On April 13, 1896, Plessy's lawyers argued before the Supreme Court in Washington, D.C. They said that Louisiana had violated Plessy's Fourteenth Amendment right to equal protection under the law. Attorney General Cunningham argued that the law merely made a distinction between blacks and whites. It did not, he said, necessarily treat blacks as inferiors. In theory, at least, the Louisiana law provided for "separate but equal" railroad accommodations.

The only justice who disagreed with the Supreme Court's decision in Plessy v. Ferguson *was John Marshall Harlan.*

On May 18, 1896, the court issued its decision upholding the Louisiana law:

A [law] which implies merely a legal distinction between the white and colored races—a distinction which is founded in the color of the two races, and which must always exist so long as white men are distinguished from the other race by color—has no tendency to destroy the legal equality of the two races.

The court also upheld Plessy's sentence, a $25 fine or two days in jail. And the court endorsed the "separate but equal" doctrine. In doing so, the court ignored the fact that blacks had almost no power to make sure their separate facilities were "equal" to those used by whites. In the

**THE
CONSTITUTION**

years to come, black railroad cars, schools, and other facilities were rarely as good as those of whites.

It was not until the 1950s and 1960s that the Supreme Court began to reverse *Plessy.* In the landmark 1954 decision *Brown v. Board of Education,* the court held that separate black and white schools are unconstitutional. Later cases abolished the separate but equal doctrine in other areas concerning civil rights.

Suggestions for Further Reading

Jackson, Donald W. *Even the Children of Strangers: Equality Under the U.S. Constitution.* Lawrence: University Press of Kansas, 1992.

Kull, Andrew. *The Color-Blind Constitution.* Cambridge, MA: Harvard University Press, 1992.

Brown v. Board of Education: 1954

Appellants: Several parents of African American children of elementary school age in Topeka, Kansas

Defendant: Board of Education of Topeka, Kansas

Appellant Claim: That the segregation (separation) of white and African American children in the public schools of Topeka solely on the basis of race denied the African American children equal protection under the law guaranteed by the Fourteenth Amendment

Chief Defense Lawyers: Harold R. Fatzer and Paul E. Wilson

Chief Lawyers for Appellants: Robert L. Carter, Thurgood Marshall, Spottswood W. Robinson, and Charles S. Scott

Justices: Hugo L. Black, Harold H. Burton, Thomas C. Clark, William O. Douglas, Felix Frankfurter, Robert H. Jackson, Sherman Minton, Stanley F. Reed, and Earl Warren

Place: Washington, D.C.

Date of Decision: May 17, 1954

Decision: Segregated schools violate the equal protection clause of the Fourteenth Amendment

SIGNIFICANCE: *Brown v. Board of Education* held that racially segregated schools are unconstitutional. It overturned the "separate but equal" doctrine that had been the law of the land since *Plessy v. Ferguson* (1896).

**THE
CONSTITUTION**

Sometimes events of great importance happen to seemingly unimportant people. This happened to Oliver Brown. His desire for his children to attend the public school closest to home resulted in a transformation of race relations in the United States.

All-White School Turns Away Linda Brown

Oliver Brown was born in 1919 and lived in Topeka, Kansas, where he worked as a welder for a railroad. Brown and his family lived literally on the wrong side of the tracks. Their house was close to Brown's place of work, and their neighborhood was next to a major railroad switchyard. The Brown family could hear trains coming and going day and night. Because the Topeka public school system was racially segregated, the Brown children had to walk through the switchyard to get to the black school a mile away. There was another school only seven blocks away, but it was only for white students.

In September 1950, Brown's daughter, Linda, was about to enter third grade. Brown took her to the whites-only school and tried to enroll her. He had not been politically active in the past. His only major activity outside of work was serving as an assistant pastor in the local church. Now, he was simply tired of seeing his daughter being forced to walk through a switchyard to get to school. The principal of the all-white school refused to enroll Linda, though. Brown then sought help from McKinley Burnett, head of the local branch of the National Association for the Advancement of Colored People (NAACP).

NAACP Takes On Topeka Board of Education

The NAACP had been looking for a chance to challenge segregation. Segregation, in the public schools and elsewhere, was a fact of life in Topeka, as in so many other places. Few were willing to contest it. Now that he had Brown, Burnett decided it was time to take legal action. Several other African American parents in Topeka joined in the lawsuit.

On March 22, 1951, Brown's NAACP lawyers filed a lawsuit in the U.S. District Court for the District of Kansas. They requested an order forbidding Topeka from continuing to segregate its public schools. The court heard the case June 25–26, 1951. Brown and the other African American parents testified that their children were denied admission to white schools. One parent, Silas Fleming, explained why he and the other parents wanted to get their children into all-white schools:

It wasn't to cast any insinuations that our teachers are not capable of teaching our children because they are supreme, extremely intelligent and are capable of teaching my kids or white kids or black kids. But my point was that not only I and my children are craving light; the entire colored race is craving light, and the only way to reach the light is to start our children together in their infancy and they come up together.

Next, the court listened to expert witnesses who testified that segregated schools were unequal because they sent a message to black children that they were inferior. This shame could never be removed from a segregated school system. Dr. Hugh W. Speer, chairman of the University of Kansas City's department of elementary education, testified:

[I]f the colored children are denied the experience in school of associating with white children, who represent 90 percent of our national society in which these colored children must live, then the colored child's curriculum is being greatly curtailed [lessened]. The Topeka curriculum or any school curriculum cannot be equal under segregation.

The Board of Education's lawyers responded that most of Kansas City's bathrooms and other public facilities were segregated, too. Segregated schools were preparing African American children for the realities of life as black adults. Segregation touched every part of life in Topeka and many other places. It was beyond the court's power, said the lawyers, to rule on anything in this one suit but the legality of public school segregation.

Next, the board argued that segregated schools did not necessarily cause any harm. After all, Frederick Douglas, Booker T. Washington, and George Washington Carver—all famous African Americans—had achieved greatness despite obstacles far worse than segregated educational facilities. The falsity of this argument was obvious, however. While some extraordinary people could rise above any difficulty, for the majority of African Americans segregation resulted in fewer opportunities. Dr. Horace B. English, a psychology professor at Ohio State University, testified:

There is a tendency for us to live up to, or perhaps I should say down to, social expectations and to

EARL WARREN SPEAKS OUT

The unanimous Supreme Court decision in *Brown* was written by Chief Justice Earl Warren on May 17, 1954. Warren wrote: "To separate [children] from others of similar age and qualifications solely because of their race generates a feeling of inferiority as to their status in the community that may affect their hearts and minds in a way unlikely ever to be undone. . . . We conclude that in the field of public education the doctrine of 'separate but equal' has no place. Separate educational facilities are inherently unequal.

learn what people say we can learn, and legal segregation definitely depresses the Negro's expectancy and is therefore prejudicial to his learning.

On August 3, 1951, the court handed down its decision. The three-judge panel that had heard the case noted that the most important case on the subject was *Plessy v. Ferguson. Plessy* made the doctrine of "separate but equal" law, and had not been overturned or even seriously questioned by the Supreme Court. Therefore, regardless of the experts' testimony that separate but equal schools are necessarily impossible, the court was obliged to deny Brown's request for an order. The court made it, clear, however, that it was not entirely happy with this decision.

Fight Goes to the Supreme Court

On October 1, 1951, the plaintiffs filed a petition for appeal. Because of certain legal rules, they were able to go directly to the U.S. Supreme Court rather than going through a federal court of appeals. On June 9, 1952, the Supreme Court put the case on its schedule, adding to it other similar cases from around the country. The court set December 9, 1952, as the date for hearing the arguments in the cases.

Harold R. Fatzer and Paul E. Wilson represented the board of education. Brown and the other plaintiffs were represented by a number of lawyers sponsored by the NAACP. The chief lawyers for the appellant

Supreme Court Chief Justice Earl Warren played a key role in the unanimous outcome of Brown v. Board of Education.

parents were Robert L. Carter, Thurgood Marshall, Spottswood W. Robinson, and Charles S. Scott. The Supreme Court justices hearing the case were Hugo L. Black, Harold H. Burton, Thomas C. Clark, William O. Douglas, Felix Frankfurter, Robert H. Jackson, Sherman Minton, Stanley F. Reed, and Earl Warren.

The December 9 hearing ended in a stalemate (deadlock). The Supreme Court ordered another hearing, to take place December 8, 1953. The court instructed the parties to focus their new arguments on specific issues—those concerning the acceptance by the states of the Fourteenth Amendment in 1868. Since the appellants' lawsuit rested on the Equal Protection Clause of this amendment, the court wanted to know more about the Amendment's adoption. Although the NAACP, Brown, and the other appellants were disappointed that their case would be on hold for another year, the court had indicated that it was willing to consider overturning *Plessy v. Ferguson.*

Court Throws Out Plessy, Declares Segregation Illegal

After hearing new arguments, the court announced its decision on May 17, 1954. Instead of focusing on the Fourteenth Amendment, the opinion of the court supported the appellants' argument that segregation was by

THE CONSTITUTION

its very nature unfair. No matter how much effort the school system took to make sure that black and white schools had equal facilities, staff, books, buses, and so forth, segregated schools could never be equal. The court was ready to declare that all segregation in public schools was unconstitutional: "We conclude that in the field of public education the doctrine of 'separate but equal' has no place."

After nearly sixty years of legal discrimination, the court threw out *Plessy v. Ferguson.* It would taken another twenty years for the court's decision to be fully realized, though. In 1955, the court said that all American school systems must desegregate "with all deliberate speed." Still most schools in the South did nothing until, one by one, they were hauled into court. The process dragged on throughout the 1950s, 1960s, and even into the 1970s. Meanwhile, the country was seized by a civil rights movement. The court acted to strike down all other forms of legal segregation in American society, integrating bus stations and public libraries, restaurants, and hotels.

The process was painful and often violent. At times, the federal government had to send in army reserve units to control mass demonstrations. By the late 1970s, however, desegregation was a fact of life. *Brown v. Board of Education* made it possible to end segregated school systems. However, it also served as a guide and inspiration for further civil right decisions by the Supreme Court.

Suggestions for Further Reading

Bennett, Lerone Jr. "The Day Race Relations Changed Forever: U.S. Supreme Court Desegregation Decision of May 17, 1954 Was Hailed by Many as the 'Second Emancipation Proclamation.'" *Ebony* (May 1985): 108–112.

Kluger, Richard. *Simple Justice: The History of Brown v. Board of Education and Black America's Struggle for Equality.* New York: Alfred A. Knopf, 1976.

Orlich, Donald C. "Brown v. Board of Education: Time for a Reassessment." *Phi Delta Kappan* (April 1991): 631–632.

Sudo, Phil. "Five Little People Who Changed U.S. History." *Scholastic Update* (January 1990): 8–10.

White, Jack E. "The Heirs of Oliver Brown." *Time* (July 6, 1987): 88–89.

U.S. v. Nixon: 1974

Plaintiff: United States

Defendant: President Richard M. Nixon

Plaintiff Claims: That the president had to obey a subpoena (a document ordering a person to appear in court under penalty for failure to do so) ordering him to turn over tape recordings and documents relating to his conversations with aides and advisers concerning the Watergate break-in

Chief Defense Lawyer: James D. St. Clair

Chief Lawyers for Plaintiff: Leon Jaworski and Philip A. Lacovara

Justices: Harry A. Blackmun, William J. Brennan, Warren E. Burger, William O. Douglas, Thurgood Marshall, Lewis F. Powell Jr., Potter Stewart, and Byron R. White (William H. Rehnquist withdrew from the case)

Place: Washington, D.C.

Date of Decision: July 24, 1974

Decision: President Nixon was ordered to turn over the tapes and other documents to the prosecutors

SIGNIFICANCE: After *Nixon v. U.S.,* a president could not use executive privilege—the right to refuse to disclose confidential communications—to avoid turning over evidence to a court.

THE CONSTITUTION

On June 17, 1972, police arrested five men attempting to break into the offices of the Democratic National Committee in the Watergate Hotel in Washington, D.C. They soon found that this was no ordinary burglary. One of the burglars, James W. McCord Jr. was the security co-ordinator for The Committee to Re-Elect the President (CREEP). Also involved was E. Howard Hunt, a White House consultant. Could President Richard M. Nixon or the White House itself be involved?

At first the government investigation into the break-in went slowly. Individuals connected with the Nixon administration stalled. By the spring of 1974, however, the investigation had gathered steam. It was becoming obvious to Congress and the public that senior officials in the administration—and probably Nixon himself—were involved in covering up the burglary.

Watergate Indictments

On March 1, 1974, a federal grand jury indicted Attorney General John N. Mitchell for conspiracy to obstruct justice in a case titled *U.S. v. Mitchell.* Six other people were indicted as co-conspirators. All were senior Nixon administration officials employed in the White House or by the CREEP. They were: Charles W. Colson, John D. Erlichman, H. R. Haldeman, Robert C. Mardian, Kenneth W. Parkinson, and Gordon Strachan. Nixon was an unindicted coconspirator.

Special Prosecutor Leon Jaworski had led the investigation. On April 18, 1974, he asked Judge John Sirica of the U.S. District Court for the District of Columbia to issue a subpoena (suh-PEE-nah). Sirica did so, ordering Nixon to produce "certain tapes, memoranda, papers, transcripts, or other writings." Jaworski was able to identify the details of these discussions because he already had White House daily logs and appointment records. The material was to be turned over by May 2, 1974. It was to be used at trial on September 9, 1974.

Nixon Fights Subpoena

On April 30, 1974, Nixon turned over edited versions of forty-three conversations. These included portions of twenty conversations named in the subpoena. On May 1, however, Nixon's lawyer, James D. St. Clair, asked Sirica to withdraw the subpoena. Nixon hoped that the transcripts, which had been publicly released, would satisfy both the court and the public. He did not want to turn over the tapes themselves. Sirica denied this re-

Chief lawyer for the United States Leon Jaworski.

quest on May 20, 1974. He ordered the president or any of his employees who had the documents to turn them over to the court by May 31, 1974.

On May 24, a week before Sirica's deadline, St. Clair filed an appeal in the U.S. Court of Appeals for the District of Columbia Circuit. Both sides realized, however, that the issue of whether the court could force the president to obey subpoenas and other forms of judicial orders would finally have to be decided by the U.S. Supreme Court. Also, both sides were aware of the political stakes involved and were eager to avoid a lengthy trial. Therefore, on May 24, 1974, Jaworski took the unusual step of asking the Supreme Court to consider the case without waiting for the court of appeals to make a decision. If the Supreme Court agreed, the decision about the subpoena would be final. On June 6, 1974, St. Clair requested the same thing.

On June 15, 1974, the Supreme Court granted these requests and decided to take the case from the court of appeals. On July 8, 1974, the case came before Supreme Court Justices Harry A. Blackmun, William J. Brennan, Warren E. Burger, William O. Douglas, Thurgood Marshall, Lewis F. Powell, Potter Stewart, and Byron R. White. Justice William H. Rehnquist, whom Nixon had appointed, did not participate in the case.

When Jaworski and Lacovara went into the Supreme Court building on July 8, there were hundreds of cheering spectators on the steps. The justices themselves were also caught up in the case. They asked many questions of both sides during oral argument. Justice Lewis Powell questioned Nixon's claim that he had to keep the tapes secret to protect the

THE WATERGATE BREAK-IN

The Watergate story began June 17, 1972. Five men were arrested at the Watergate Hotel in Washington, D.C., after a break-in at the offices of the Democratic National Committee. The burglary was committed the summer before Nixon's second presidential election. All five men were carrying cash and documents linking them to Nixon's re-election committee. They wanted to plant listening devices and steal documents with information on the Democrats' campaign plans. Former White House aides G. Gordon Liddy and E. Howard Hunt were also arrested. Nixon was re-elected by a landslide. But in February 1973, a Senate committee began investigating the break-in and what seemed to be a cover-up. In March, one of the burglars, former CIA agent James W. McCord, named others involved in the break-in. One person he named was former Attorney General John Mitchell. Soon, many on Nixon's staff resigned. Acting Federal Bureau of Investigation (FBI) director L. Patrick Gray, Nixon's chief of staff H. R. Haldeman, Nixon's domestic affairs assistant John Erlichman, and presidential counsel John Dean III were among those who resigned. On July 16, 1973, White House aide Alexander Butterfield revealed that Nixon had recorded all conversations in his office. The Senate committee asked for the tapes to investigate Nixon himself.

public interest: "Mr. St. Clair, what public interest is there in preserving secrecy with respect to a criminal conspiracy?"

St. Clair responded, "The answer, sir, is that a criminal conspiracy is criminal only after it's proven to be criminal."

The government's attorneys were questioned thoroughly as well. The justices were especially concerned about the consequences of a grand jury naming a president as a co-conspirator before the prosecution had even requested an indictment. In response to Powell's questions on this point, Lacovara stated:

> Grand juries usually are not malicious. Even prosecutors cannot be assumed to be malicious. . . . I

submit to you, sir, that just as in this case a Grand Jury would not lightly accuse the President of a crime, so, too, the fear that, perhaps without basis, some Grand Jury somewhere might maliciously accuse a President of a crime is not necessarily a reason for saying that a Grand Jury has no power to do that.

The Supreme Court issued its decision on July 24, 1974, less than three weeks later. During those weeks, the justices struggled to write an opinion on which they could all agree. Although Supreme Court justices are free to dissent (disagree), they wanted to issue an unanimous decision. Important issues concerning the relationship between the executive and judicial branches of government were at stake. Multiple opinions would weaken the impact of the court's decision. Although Burger, the chief justice, was in charge of writing the opinion, all eight justices wrote or contributed to portions of it.

Nixon Ordered to Release Tapes

The main issue before the court was whether the president, because of "executive privilege," could refuse to obey judicial orders. First, the court restated the principle of its landmark 1803 *Marbury v. Madison* decision, that "it is. . . the duty of the judicial department to say what the law is."

[T]he judicial power of the United States vested in the federal courts by Article III, section 1, of the Constitution can no more be shared with the Executive Branch than the Chief Executive, for example, can share with the Judiciary the veto power, or the Congress share with the Judiciary the power to override a Presidential veto. Any other conclusions would be contrary to the basic concept of separation of powers and the checks and balances that flow from the scheme of a tripartite government. We therefore reaffirm that it is . . . the duty of this Court to say what the law is with respect to the claim of privilege presented in this case.

Next, the court addressed Nixon's two main arguments in favor of executive privilege. First, St. Clair argued that in order for the presidency to function, conversations and other communications between high officials and their advisors had to remain private. If every statement could be made public, advisors would be reluctant to speak freely, and the decision-making process would suffer. Second, St. Clair argued that the doctrine of separation of powers itself gave the president immunity from judicial orders.

The court rejected both arguments. While confidentiality was important, it could be maintained by allowing a judge to review evidence alone in chambers. The court stressed that they could

Richard Nixon leaves the White House soon after resigning the presidency.

not agree to Nixon's broad claim of executive privilege. To do so would endanger the judicial system's duty to assure that justice was done in criminal trials. Nixon had not given any specific reason why the courts should not have the tapes in the *U.S. v. Mitchell* case. Now, the court ordered the president to turn them over to Judge Sirica to inspect in his chambers.

Nixon Resigns

Ordering a president to do something is one thing. Enforcing that order is another. The judicial branch is as powerful as the other two branches of the government. However, it lacks both the military power of the executive branch and the taxing power of the legislative branch. In the end, enforcement of court orders depends on public respect for the democratic system. During oral argument, St. Clair had hinted that Nixon "had his own obligations under the Constitution." It was unclear whether Nixon would obey the court's order.

Nixon was in San Clemente, California, when he heard about the Supreme Court's unanimous decision. Within a day, he issued a public statement saying that he would comply with the court's order:

> While I am, of course, disappointed in the result, I respect and accept the court's decision, and I have instructed Mr. St. Clair to take whatever measures are necessary to comply with that decision in all respects.

Nixon turned over sixty-four tapes to Sirica. Some of these tapes contained highly incriminating conversations that occurred between Nixon and his aides shortly after the Watergate break-in. Congress was ready to impeach the president, and Nixon realized that his time was up. On August 8, 1974, he announced his resignation. Vice President Gerald Ford became president at noon on August 9, the day Nixon's resignation became effective. Ford later granted Nixon a pardon, and Nixon never stood trial. Still, *U.S. v. Nixon* set an important precedent (example). As a result of this case, it is clear that if executive privilege does exist, it does not permit the president to withhold evidence needed by the courts. Finally, the case ended the political career of Richard Nixon, who had been one of America's most popular and successful presidents.

Suggestions for Further Reading

Ball, Howard. *"We Have a Duty": The Supreme Court and the Watergate Tapes Litigation.* New York: Greenwood Press, 1990.

Berger, Raoul. *Executive Privilege: A Constitutional Myth.* Cambridge, MA: Harvard University Press, 1974.

Carlson, Margaret. "Notes from Underground: A Fresh Batch of White House Tapes Reminds a Forgiving and Forgetful America Why Richard Nixon Resigned in Disgrace." *Time* (June 17, 1991): 27–28.

Dudley, Mark E. *United States v. Nixon (1974): Presidential Powers.* New York: Twenty-First Century Books, 1994.

Friedman, Leon. *United States v. Nixon: The President Before the Supreme Court.* New York: Chelsea House Publishers, 1974.

THE CONSTITUTION

Jaworski, Leon. *The Right and the Power: The Prosecution of Watergate.* New York: Reader's Digest Press, 1976.

Stans, Maurice. H. *The Terrors of Justice: The Untold Side of Watergate.* Washington D.C.: Regnery Books, 1984.

Woodward, Bob. *The Brethren: Inside the Supreme Court.* New York: Simon & Schuster, 1979.

Bakke v. University of California. . . Appeal: 1978

Appellee: Allan Bakke

Appellant: The Medical School of the University of California

Appellee Claim: That the California Supreme Court was wrong in ruling that the school's special admissions program for minorities violated Bakke's civil rights as a white male when he was denied admission

Chief Lawyer for Appellee: Reynold H. Colvin

Chief Lawyers for Appellant: Archibald Cox, Paul J. Mishkin, Jack B. Owens, and Donald L. Reidhaar

Justices: Harry A. Blackmun, William J. Brennan Jr., Warren E. Burger, Thurgood Marshall, Lewis F. Powell Jr., William H. Rehnquist, John Paul Stevens, Potter Stewart, and Byron R. White

Place: Washington, D.C.

Date of Decision: June 28, 1978

Decision: That the school's special-admissions program was unconstitutional

SIGNIFICANCE: For the first time, the Supreme Court said there could be such a thing as reverse discrimination.

The University of California is one of the largest higher educational institutions in America. In 1968, the school opened a medical school at its Davis campus. Fifty students made up the entering class. Three years later, the class had doubled in size to 100. Then in 1968, the school set up a special admissions program to increase minority enrollment.

This program operated separately from the regular admissions program. Sixteen percent of the places in each entering class would go to minority students. The school handled minority applications separately and interviewed candidates separately. The grade point averages and standardized test scores required of special admissions applicants were significantly lower than those for regular admissions students.

*Protesters let their
feelings be known
about the U.S.
Supreme Court
decision in* Bakke v.
University of
California.

Bakke Rejected

In 1973, Allan Bakke applied to the Medical School. He achieved a combined score of 468 out of a possible 500 from his interviewers. Still the school rejected him. There were 2,464 applications for the 100 places in the 1973 entering class. By the time Bakke's application came up for consideration, the school was only taking applicants with scores of 470 or

better. However, four special admissions places went unfilled. Bakke wrote an angry letter to Dr. George H. Lowrey, associate dean and chair of the admissions committee, complaining about the unfairness of the special admissions process. He felt the school rejected him because he was white.

Bakke applied again in 1974. That year there were even more applicants for the 100 places in the entering class. The school received 3,737 applications. Lowrey was one of Bakke's interviewers and gave him a low score, which contributed to a second rejection. Furious, Bakke sued the University of California in the Superior Court of California.

Bakke claimed that the Medical School's special admissions program excluded him because of his race. Therefore, the school had violated his rights under the Equal Protection Clause of the Fourteenth Amendment of the U.S. Constitution. It had also denied his rights under the California state constitution and civil rights laws. The trial court agreed. However, it still refused to order the Medical School to admit him. Bakke then appealed to the California Supreme Court. It upheld the trial court's decision. It also ordered the school to admit Bakke.

Bakke v. University of California. . . Appeal: 1978

Reverse Discrimination Charged

The school appealed to the U.S. Supreme Court. The parties argued their cases before the court on October 12, 1977. Bakke's attorney, Reynold Colvin, was making his first appearance before the Supreme Court, and he faced several lawyers with much more experience. For example, Cox was a former Harvard Law School professor who had served as a special prosecutor during the Watergate investigation of President Richard Nixon.

Colvin soon found himself arguing about the special admissions policy with Thurgood Marshall, the only African American justice on the Court:

> Marshall: You are arguing about keeping somebody out and the other side is arguing about getting somebody in.
>
> Colvin: That's right.
>
> Marshall: So it depends on which way you look at it doesn't it?
>
> Colvin: If I may finish . . .
>
> Marshall: You are talking about your client's rights.

THE CONSTITUTION

Don't these underprivileged people have some right?

Colvin: They certainly have the right to . . .

Marshall: To eat cake.

On June 28, 1978, Justice Lewis F. Powell announced the decision. Five judges had voted to uphold the California Supreme Court's decision. The court ruled that the Medical School's policy was reverse discrimination and illegal. The court ordered the school to admit Bakke. The court also upheld the California court's decision that the school's special admissions policy end. However, schools could continue to give priority to minorities. They simply could not exclude whites from a specific percentage of the entering class. The court pointed to Harvard University's program as a model for an acceptable admissions policy. It gave consideration to race without violating the civil rights of whites:

> The experience of other university admissions programs, which take race into account in achieving the educational diversity valued by the First Amendment, demonstrates that the assignment of a fixed number of places to a minority group is not a necessary means toward that end. . . . When the [Harvard] Committee on Admissions reviews the large middle group of applicants who are admissible and deemed capable of doing good work in their courses, the race of an applicant may tip the balance in his favor just as geographic origin or a life spent on a farm may tip the balance in other candidates' cases. A farm boy from Idaho can bring something to Harvard College that a Bostonian cannot offer. Similarly, a black student can usually bring something that a white person cannot offer. In Harvard college admissions the Committee has not set target quotas for the number of blacks, or of musicians, football players, physicists or Californians to be admitted in a given year.

Bakke had won his case and would be admitted as a student. This was the first time that the Supreme Court applied civil rights protection to whites seeking admission to a university.

THE SEARCH FOR MINORITY DOCTORS

During the Bakke case, commentators who supported the Davis Medical School's position made another argument. They pointed out that many African American, Latino, and Native American communities faced a shortage of doctors. These supporters argued that educating more African American, Latino, and Native American doctors would make it more likely that at some of these new physicians would go back and practice medicine in these communities.

Suggestions for Further Reading

"Five Cases That Changed American Society." *Scholastic Update* (November 30, 1984): 19–20.

"Minorities Down at Davis Univ. Since Bakke Case." *Jet* (June 7, 1982): 8.

Mooney, Christopher F. *Inequality and the American Conscience: Justice Through the Judicial System.* New York: Paulist Press, 1982.

O'Neill, Timothy J. *Bakke & the Politics of Equality: Friends and Foes in the Classroom of Litigation.* Middletown, CT: Wesleyan University Press, 1985.

Schwartz, Bernard. *Behind Bakke: Affirmative Action and the Supreme Court.* New York: New York University Press, 1988.

Jones v. Clinton and Ferguson: 1994–1997

Plaintiff: Paula Corbin Jones

Defendants: William Jefferson Clinton and Danny Ferguson

Claim: Damages for deprivation of federally protected rights, intentional infliction of emotional distress, defamation

Chief Plaintiff Lawyers: Gilbert K. Davis and Joseph Cammarata

Chief Defense Lawyers: Robert S. Bennett, Walter Dellinger, Alan Kriegel, Carl S. Rauh, Amy R. Sabrin, and Stephen P. Vaughn

Justices: U.S. Supreme Court

Date of Decision: June 3, 1997

Place: Washington, D.C.

Verdict: That Jones's case against Clinton could go forward

SIGNIFICANCE: Should the President of the United States have special protection under the law? Or should he or she be accountable to the same law as any other member of society? This was the question facing the Supreme Court in one of its most difficult cases.

On May 8, 1991, Paula Corbin Jones was a twenty-four-year-old clerk with the Arkansas Industrial Development Commission (AIDC). Her duties that day took her to the Excelsior Hotel in Little Rock, the state's capital. There Governor Bill Clinton was going to give a speech for the AIDC. During Clinton's press conference, Jones later reported, she noticed the governor staring at her. Afterward, she said, a state trooper from the governor's security detail, Danny Ferguson, asked her to follow him to one of the hotel's rooms. He said Clinton wanted to meet her. Jones says she discussed the request with her coworker Pamela Blackard. Then, after being reassured by Ferguson, who allegedly told her, "It's okay, we do this all the time for the governor," Jones agreed to visit the governor. She later said she hoped the meeting might lead to a better job.

After her meeting with Clinton, Jones's gave this account of what happened between her and the governor: When she arrived at the room Clinton was alone. He invited her in, closed the door, and struck up a friendly conversation. He mentioned that her boss, Dave Harrington, was his "good friend." Then, according to Jones, the mood in the room changed. Without warning Clinton suddenly yanked her close and, ignoring her protests, began fondling her. Jones resisted and reminded him he was a married man.

This had no effect whatsoever on the governor, Jones claimed. He asked if she was married. When she replied that she had a regular boyfriend, he allegedly exposed himself and sexually propositioned her.

Jones said she refused him and attempted to leave the room. Clinton said, "Well, I don't want to make you do anything you don't want to do." He told her, "If you get in trouble for leaving work, have Dave [Harrington] call me immediately, and I'll take care of it." But then, she said, his tone hardened. "You are smart," he said, "Let's keep this between ourselves." Acording to Jones, she then left the room in great distress.

Did It Happen?

Two people who saw Jones soon after this meeting had widely differing recollections of how she had reacted to it. Ferguson, who said Jones was in the room for "some twenty to thirty minutes," asserted that "she did not appear to be upset in any way."

However, Pamela Blackard's version had Jones returning to the registration desk after just ten minutes. "I could see her shaking," said Blackard, "I could see. . . something was wrong." She said that after some time, and with considerable difficulty, Jones told her what had happened.

Yet, according to Ferguson, a week or so later he saw Jones and she asked him to give her phone number to Clinton. Jones recalled this meeting differently, claiming Ferguson said, "Bill wants your phone number. Hilary [Clinton's wife] is out of town often and Bill would like to see you." Jones says she refused.

SEXUAL HARASSMENT: A WIDESPREAD PROBLEM

Paula Jones accused President Bill Clinton of a crime known as sexual harassment. Sexual harrassment occurs when a person suffers unwanted sexual advances as a condition of keeping his or her job. According to Title VII of the 1964 Civil Rights Act, all employees have the right to be free of sexual harassment, which it defines as:

> Unwelcome sexual advances, requests for sexual favors, and other verbal and physical conduct of a sexual nature. . . when submission to such conduct is made a term or condition of an individual's employment, submission to or rejection of such conduct is used as the basis for promotional decision, or such conduct unreasonably interferes with work performance, or creates an intimidating, hostile, or offensive working environment.

Employers must also provide their employees with a workplace in which no one—such as a fellow employee, a customer, or a client—is harassing them.

Shortly thereafter, Jones claimed, she felt her bosses at work were acting in a hostile manner toward her. Finally, in February 1993—by which time Clinton had become president of the United States—Paula Jones left the AIDC. She later moved to California.

In January 1994, Jones saw a magazine article in which Arkansas state troopers claimed they had found women for then-Governor Clinton to date, among them someone called "Paula." Later, the officers took back this statement. However, on May 6, 1994, Jones' lawyers, Gilbert K. Davis and Joseph Cammarata, filed a lawsuit with the United States Court for the Eastern District of Arkansas, claiming President Clinton had acted improperly toward her when he was governor of that state and demanding $700,000 in damages. Also named in the brief was Danny Ferguson.

THE CONSTITUTION

On October 1, 1994, President Clinton responded in a press release:

> I have no recollection of meeting Paula Jones on May 8, 1991, in a room at the Excelsior Hotel. However, I do not challenge her claim that we met there and I may very well have met her in the past. She did not engage in any improper or sexual conduct. I regret any untrue assertions which have been made about her conduct which may have adversely challenged her character and good name. I have no further comment on my previous statements about my own conduct.

Jones's response was, "I am grateful that the president has acknowledged the possibility that he and I may have met at the Excelsior Hotel on May 8, 1991, and has acknowledged my good name and disagrees with assertions to the contrary. However, I stand by my prior statement of the events."

Clinton's Defense

After much delay, a court ruled in January 1996 that the case could move forward. This cleared the way for a trial. However, on May 28, 1996, the president's lawyers, headed by Robert Bennett, appealed to the Supreme Court. They requested that the court postpone the trial. Otherwise, the president would be diverted from his official duties. They pointed to the only previous case, *Nixon v. Fitzgerald* (1982), in which a president of the United States had been sued. On that occasion the court ruled that the president's fame made him a target of lawsuits. Therefore, it would be against the national interest to allow the suit to continue. However, that lawsuit was about Nixon's acts while he was president. Paula Jones's lawsuit concerned actions allegedly committed when Clinton was governor.

On June 25, 1996, the Supreme Court announced it would put off considering Clinton's appeal, a decision that was favorable to Bennett and Clinton. Jones's reaction was, "If the man's innocent, why did he take it all the way to the Supreme Court? He's using his power once again. He's very good at abusing power."

On January 13, 1997, Clinton's lawyers again went to the Supreme Court. They argued that the president's ability to do his job was more important than a citizen's desire for justice.

This was a point emphasized by Bennett. "We'll give Ms. Jones her day in court, but let's not do it now." Bennett claimed that what was new in this lawsuit was "subjecting [the] president to the power of any state or federal court."

Justice Antonin Scalia responded, "We see presidents riding on horseback, chopping firewood, playing golf. The notion that he doesn't have a minute to spare is not credible."

On Tuesday, June 3, the Supreme Court ruled by a nine-to-zero vote that Jones's suit could go forward while the president was still in office. The justices rejected Bennett's argument that presidents are protected under the Constitution from lawsuits involving what they allegedly do in their private lives.

—Colin Evans

Suggestions for Further Reading

Biskupic, Joan. "Court Weighs Immunity for President." *Washington Post* (January 14, 1997): 1.

Taylor, Stuart Jr. "Paula Jones's Case Against Clinton." *The American Lawyer* (November 1996).

FAMILY LAW AND
REPRODUCTIVE
RIGHTS

Martin Guerre Trials: 1560

Defendant: Martin Guerre (Arnaud du Tilh)

Crimes Charged: Defrauding the Guerre family and others and abusing Bertrande Guerre

Defense Lawyer: None

Prosecutors: King's attorneys

Judges: First trial: Firmin Vayssiere; second trial: Jean Coras (and others)

Places: First trial: Rieux, France; second trial: Toulouse, France

Dates of Trials: First trial: January–April 1560; second trial: May–September 12, 1560

Verdicts: Both trials: Guilty

Sentences: First trial: Beheading and quartering; second trial: hanging and burning

SIGNIFICANCE: On one level, this is simply an exciting and curious case that allows everyone to speculate about human conduct and motives, especially those of the wife of Martin Guerre. For historians, however, it presents a unique opportunity to examine how common people of centuries past behaved and thought.

Sanxi Daguerre was a Basque. Basques live on the French-Spanish border. In 1527, Daguerre moved his wife, his young son, Martin, and his brother, Pierre, from the Atlantic coast 170 miles to the east. They settled in the French village of Artigat. The two brothers bought land and began a tile-manufacturing business. In order to blend in with their new neigh-

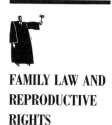

bors they changed their name to Guerre and adopted the French language. A sign of the Guerre family's acceptance came in 1538 when Martin married Bertrande de Rols, the daughter of one of the region's wealthier families.

Martin was only thirteen years old. Bertrande was even younger. Their parents had "arranged" the marriage. This was a common practice so that their families could more easily transfer property from the bride to the groom. During the first eight years of the marriage there were no children. Then in 1547, Bertrande gave birth to a son. By that time Bertrande had matured into a beautiful young woman. Martin, however, was a rather irresponsible young man. His strongest interest was swordplay and acrobatics with other village youths. He either rejected his family responsibilities, or simply wanted to see more of the world. In any event, in 1548, after he was accused of stealing some grain from his father, Martin disappeared.

The villagers considered Bertrande to be married to Martin until she could prove his death. As she could not, she remained financially dependent on his family. After Martin's parents died, Martin's uncle Pierre became the administrator of an estate that would have passed to Martin and his heirs, had Martin not vanished. Then, in 1556, eight years after he disappeared, Martin Guerre returned.

The New Martin Guerre

Perhaps it is more accurate to say that a man claiming to be Martin Guerre came to Artigat in 1556. He said that he had spent his time living in Spain and serving in the French army. However, he appeared to be shorter and stockier than the man who had vanished eight years earlier. What is more, he spoke no Basque. Time, he said, explained these oddities. However, he did seem to recognize his family and his neighbors. He knew many details about their pasts. Furthermore, his sisters accepted him. Most importantly, Bertrande said he was her husband.

Soon, their lives appeared to be perfectly normal. Bertrande gave birth to two more children. Martin increased their wealth by dealing in real estate. In 1559, however, things changed. Martin brought a lawsuit against his uncle, claiming that Pierre, as administrator of the family business, had cheated him and Bertrande. The suit was settled, but Pierre remained so angry that he went around town denouncing Martin as an impostor.

Some villagers agreed with Pierre. Just as many did not. Bertrande said: "He is Martin Guerre my husband or else some devil in his skin. I know him well. Whoever is so mad as to say the contrary, I'll have him killed." For a while, the villagers were satisfied.

Sometime in the fall of 1559, though, a French soldier passing through Artigat said that Martin Guerre was an imposter. The soldier said that he knew the real Martin Guerre had lost a leg in battle two years earlier. Excited by this news, Pierre set about investigating the man who was living with Bertrande.

Very quickly Pierre located several men in the area who confirmed his suspicions. The imposter was really Arnaud du Tilh from the village of Sajas, 150 miles northwest of Artigat. Arnaud had as a youth been "absorbed in every vice," swearing, gambling, drinking, and frequenting prostitutes. His main gifts were his ability to persuade others with smooth talk and an excellent memory. These, of course, are the skills of an actor. After some trouble with the law, the young Arnaud had joined the king's army.

Although Arnaud would later deny it ever happened, it is possible that he met Martin Guerre during their military service in the mid-1550s and saw some resemblance between them. Arnaud claimed, however, that he had never met Martin Guerre. Instead, he declared that he had arrived

The first visual representation of Martin Guerre's case was done by Jacob Cats, Allen de Werken, in Amsterdam in 1568.

at the idea of posing as Guerre after some of the other man's friends mixed the two men up. After he had learned as much as he could about Guerre, Arnaud went to Artigat and began a new life.

The First Trial

Armed with this information, Pierre Guerre personally arrested Arnaud in January 1560. Pierre then took him to the nearby village of Rieux, where the district court was located. What followed was more a judicial hearing than a modern trial. There was no jury, and Arnaud had no defense lawyer. First, the judge called an attorney for the king and court, and statements were taken from witnesses for both sides of the dispute. (Bertrande agreed to Pierre's demand that she join him in charging Arnaud as an imposter. She may also have supplied the names of witnesses who supported Arnaud.) Then the hearing began with the judge questioning Arnaud, Bertrande, and those witnesses who supported Pierre's charges.

Arnaud's cross-examination of the witnesses interested the judge. More people were called to testify. Eventually, some 150 witnesses appeared at the trial. About forty of these insisted that the prisoner was Martin Guerre. About fifty said he was an imposter. The remainder said they could not be sure. The most ambivalent testimony came from Bertrande, who was in effect on trial herself. If this man was an imposter, why had she gone along with him all these years? The defendant finally faced her and said he would accept a death sentence if she would swear under oath that he was not the real Martin Guerre. Bertrande remained silent.

In the end, the judge declared the defendant guilty of fraud and of abusing Bertrande. Bertrande, as one of plaintiffs in the suit, asked only that Arnaud pay a fine and legal fees and ask her pardon in a public ceremony. The judge, however, sentenced the prisoner to be beheaded and his body be quartered (cut up and displayed). Arnaud du Tilh immediately appealed the decision.

The Second Trial

The new trial was before an appeals court of twelve judges. One of them, Jean Coras, acted as the lead judge. (It is his account of the case that serves as the primary source of information about the case.) Martin cross-examined Bertrande and Pierre. He was so convincing that the judges decided "the prisoner was the true husband and that the imposture came from the side of the wife and the uncle." Bertrande and Pierre, too, were placed in prison.

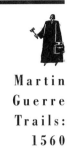

THE OLDEST ETHNIC GROUP IN EUROPE

Martin Guerre was of Basque heritage, which meant that he belonged to what is now the oldest known ethnic group in Europe. The Basques live in an area that today is part of northern Spain and southwest France. Currently, some two million Basques live in Europe. Basque heritage can be traced back to Paleolithic times, with a culture that has remained distinct for several thousands of years. Traditionally, the Basque people have been peasants, fishing people, shepherds, navigators, miners, and metalworkers. In 824, the Basques were united in the kingdom of Navarre. Then, in 1512, Castile (part of present-day Spain) conquered Navarre, and the Basques became far less prosperous. Fifteen years later, Sanxi Daguerre took his family east to the French village of Artigat, where the story of Martin Guerre and his imposter began.

Twenty-five to thirty witnesses appeared during the following weeks. Jean Coras paid close attention to what they had to say. Gradually, he became less certain about the case against the alleged imposter. He became convinced that Pierre had forced Bertrande to turn against her husband. He also decided that Pierre was the true villain, motivated by a desire to get even with his nephew's request for a clear accounting of the family's finances. Coras disregarded claims that the defendant was Arnaud du Tilh. The testimony that Arnaud was "given over to every kind of wickedness" proved that the upstanding individual before the court could not be that man. Finally, because the marriage had produced children, Coras decided that "it was better to leave unpunished a guilty person than to condemn an innocent one."

The Real Martin Guerre

By late July, the court seemed ready to follow Coras's recommendation that Martin be found innocent and Pierre charged with various crimes. Suddenly, out of nowhere came a man with a wooden leg claiming to be

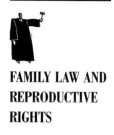

ARREST DV PARLEMENT

de Tolofe, contenant vne hiftoire memorable,
& prodigieufe, auec cent belles & doctes
Annotations, de monfieur maiftre
IEAN DE CORAS, rap-
porteur du proces.

Texte de la toile du proces & de l'arreft.

V moys de Ianuier, mil
cinq cens cinquante neuf,
Bertrande de Rolz, du lieu
d'Artigat, au diocefe de
Rieux, fe rend fuppliant,
& plaintiue, deuant le Iu-
ge de Rieux : difant, que
vingt ans peuuét eftre paf-
fez, ou enuiron, qu'elle eftant ieune fille, de neuf à
dix ans, fut mariee, auec Martin Guerre, pour lors
aufsi fort ieune, & prefque de mefmes aage, que
la fuppliant.

Annotation I.

Les mariages ainfi contractez auant l'aage legitime, ordonné
de nature, ou par les loix politiques, ne peuuent eftre (s'il eft loy-
fible de fonder, iufques aux fecretz, & infcrutables iugemens de
la diuinité) plaifans, ny aggreables à Dieu, & l'iffue, en eft le plus
fouuent piteufe, & miferable, & (comme on voit iournellement
par exemple) pleine, de mille repentances : par tant qu'en telles
precoces, & deuancees conionctions, ceux qui ont tramé, &
proietté le tout, n'ont aucunement refpecté l'honneur, & la
gloire de Dieu: & moins la fin, pour laquelle ce faint, & venera-
ble eftat de mariage, ha efté par luy inftitué du commencement
du monde. ᵃ (qui fut deuant l'offence de noftre premier pere,
pour

ᵃ chap. dernier
au titre de fri-
gid & malefic.
aux Decreta-
les & au ch. vn.
de vot. & vot.
redemp. au Six
iefme.

*The first page of
Arrest Memorable, a
book written on
Martin Guerre by
Jean de Coras in
1561.*

RELATED MOVIES

The Return of Martin Guerre (1982), a French film, starring Gerard Depardieu.
Sommersby (1993), an American version (set during the Civil War) starring Richard Gere and Jodie Foster.

the real Martin Guerre. He said he had gone to Spain after leaving Artigat, where he worked as a servant before joining the Spanish army. He fought with them in Flanders (a region primarily located in Belgium) and lost his leg in the famous battle of Saint-Quentin in 1557. He then returned to Spain, where the military rewarded him with a job. It was not clear why he had returned to France.

The judges began a new round of hearings. At first, the new Martin Guerre seemed less clear on details about Artigat than did the alleged imposter. In the end, the judges were convinced when the Guerre family instantly accepted the newcomer as one of their own. The decisive moment came when Bertrande was brought from her cell. She fell to her knees before the new Martin Guerre, embraced him, and asked his forgiveness.

For Coras and the other judges, the case was over. All that was left was to decide on sentencing. The judges forgave Bertrande. They declared her children by Arnaud legitimate, that is, legally conceived. They also excused Pierre because he had been right in the end. They rebuked Martin for having deserted his family and country. Finally, though, they excused him as well. He had suffered enough. However, the judges sentenced Arnaud du Tilh to be hanged on a gallows to be built in front of Martin and Bertrande Guerre's home. Arnaud's final words urged Martin to be kind to Bertrande, who had truly been deceived.

Nothing more is known of Martin and Bertrande, except that they had two more children. In all the centuries that have passed since the return of Martin Guerre, no one has been able to discover the truth of Bertrande's role in the case.

Suggestions for Further Reading

Coras, Jean de. Arrest memorable du Parlement de Tolose. . . .
  Lyon, France: Antoine Vincent, 1561.

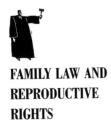

FAMILY LAW AND REPRODUCTIVE RIGHTS

Davis, Natalie Zemon. *The Return of Martin Guerre.* Cambridge, MA: Harvard University Press, 1983.

Lewis, Janet. *The Wife of Martin Guerre.* San Francisco: Colt, 1941.

Praviel, Armand. *L'Incroyable Odyssee de Martin Guerre.* Paris: Librairie Gallimard, 1933.

Packard v. Packard:
1864

Plaintiff: Reverend Theophilus Packard Jr.

Defendant: Elizabeth Parsons Ware Packard

Plaintiff's Claim: That his wife was insane and that he should be able to confine her at home

Chief Defense Lawyers: Stephen Moore and John W. Orr

Chief Prosecutors: No record

Judge: Charles R. Starr

Place: Kankakee, Illinois

Dates of Trial: January 13–18, 1864

Verdict: Elizabeth Packard was declared sane and given her freedom

SIGNIFICANCE: In 1864, Illinois law permitted a man to confine his wife "without the evidence of insanity needed in other cases." Elizabeth Packard's case changed that law and helped to change similar laws in Illinois and Massachusetts (1867), Iowa (1872), and Maine (1874).

In the late fall of 1863, Elizabeth Packard was released from the Illinois State Hospital for the Insane. Her husband, the Reverend Theophilus Packard, had ordered her to be sent there. Soon after she returned home, he locked her away in her children's nursery. During the nineteenth century, most states let husbands decide when their wives needed to be placed in an institution. The law said nothing, however, of a woman's being "put away" in her own home, and Elizabeth responded to her confinement by tossing a letter of protest out her window. Elizabeth's friend, Sarah Haslett, brought the letter to Judge Charles R. Starr.

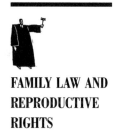
Elizabeth Packard's Sanity Judged

Judge Starr ordered Reverend Packard to bring Elizabeth to him for examination. When the Packards arrived, Theophilus Packard brought along a written document. It explained that Elizabeth had been "discharged [from the Illinois State Hospital for the Insane] . . . and is incurably insane . . . [and] the undersigned [her husband] has allowed her all the liberty compatible with her welfare and safety." The judge was not convinced and set up a jury trial to decide the question of Elizabeth's sanity.

He Says . . .

Reverend Packard was a strict Calvinist minister. He said that his wife's free-spirited, mystical view of religion was clear proof that she was insane. The Reverend stated that his wife refused to be guided by his religious authority. She refused to have faith in the Calvinist belief that mankind is naturally sinful. It claims that God has determined in advance that some will be saved and others will be damned. Elizabeth believed instead in man's free will, which made him answerable to God for his own actions.

She also believed that the Holy Ghost was female, and that she herself might contain it (as might other holy Christian women). Her husband described these thoughts as coming from the devil and proof of his wife's madness. However, the prosecution's witnesses dealt only with the question of Elizabeth Packard's sanity.

Conflicting Testimony

Dr. Christopher Knott had interviewed Elizabeth before her husband had her committed to the Hospital for the Insane. He testified that although she was excitable when it came to the subject of religion, "on all other subjects she was perfectly rational. . . . I take her to be a lady of fine mental abilities. . . . I would say she was insane, the same as I would say Henry Ward Beecher . . . and like persons are insane."

Dr. J. W. Brown, disguised as a traveling sewing machine salesman, had interviewed Elizabeth a few weeks before the trial. In the middle of a sales pitch he had asked about her husband. She had complained about her husband's belief that a man could control his wife. Once religion became the topic of their discussion, Dr. Brown testified, he "had not the slightest difficulty in concluding that she was hopelessly insane."

Dr. Brown confirmed that Elizabeth claimed that she contained the Holy Ghost. She also complained that her husband refused to discuss religion with her, and instead went around telling her friends and his church that she was insane. Her view was that Dr. Brown was a copperhead (a Northern Democrat who liked the South) and she refused to shake his hand when they parted. This, as well as her negative feelings towards her husband, convinced Brown of her insanity.

This nineteenth-century drawing illustrates the house from which Mrs. Packard was kidnapped on June 18, 1860.

When Abijah Dole, Reverend Packard's brother-in-law, took the stand, he testified that Elizabeth had told him she no longer wished to live with her husband—proof that her mind had become confused. He also said that an essay Elizabeth had written was further evidence of her insanity. Finally, he testified that Elizabeth had taken formal steps to leave her husband's church. One of Elizabeth's attorneys, John W. Orr, demanded: "Was that an indication of insanity?" Dole expressed no doubt: "She would not leave the church unless she was insane."

Sybil Dole, the Reverend Packard's sister, also provided "evidence" against her sister-in-law: Elizabeth had accused her husband of not allowing her to think for herself on religious questions because her views differed from his own. Sarah Rumsey, a mother's helper to Elizabeth, testified: "She wanted the flower beds in the front yard cleaned out and tried

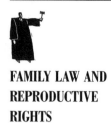
to get Mr. Packard to do it. He would not. She put on an old dress and went to work and cleaned out the weeds . . . until she was almost melted down with heat. . . . Then she went to her room and took a bath and dressed herself and lay down exhausted. . . . She was angry and excited and showed ill-will."

Finally, a certificate given by Dr. Andrew McFarland, supervisor of the Illinois State Hospital for the Insane, said that Elizabeth Packard had been released from the hospital as a hopeless case.

She Says . . .

Elizabeth Packard's lawyers, Orr and Moore, allowed her to read her Bible class essay to the court. Written in 1860 and

A lithograph of Elizabeth Parsons Ware Packard during her trial in 1864.

titled "How Godliness Is Profitable," it argued that a "godly person" may be happier, if not richer, than an "ungodly" one. Several neighbors testified that they had never found any evidence of insanity in Mrs. Packard. Sarah Haslett described Elizabeth's response to the messy home she returned to after she was released from the Hospital for the Insane. She stated, "I called to see her a few days after she returned from Jacksonville. She was in the yard cleaning feather beds. . . . The house needed cleaning. And when I called again it looked as if the mistress of the house was home." Haslett also testified that Reverend Packard had nailed the nursery windows shut in order to confine his wife.

The last witness to testify for the defense was Dr. Duncanson, a doctor of medicine and religion. He said, "I did not agree with . . . her on many things, but I do not call people insane because they differ with me.

WOMEN'S RIGHTS

Legally, U.S. women in 1864 had very few rights, especially if they were married. A married woman had no right to money she earned or property, which were considered to belong to her husband to dispose of as he wished. Also, a married woman could not enter into a contract without her husband's permission. She could not make decisions about her children; a father had the legal right to make whatever arrangements he wished. Even the dying father of an unborn child might decide that someone other than the mother was to serve as the child's guardian. And of course, no woman married or single, had the right to vote.

You might with as much [reason] call Christ insane . . . or Luther, or Robert Fuller. . . . I pronounce her a sane woman and wish we had a nation of such women."

The Verdict

The jury delivered their verdict after only seven minutes of discussion on January 18, 1864. "We, the undersigned, Jurors in the case of Mrs. Elizabeth P. W. Packard, alleged to be insane, having heard the evidence . . . are satisfied that [she] is sane." Starr ordered that she "be relieved of all restraints incompatible with her condition as a free woman."

The Packards did not divorce, but remained apart for the rest of their lives. Elizabeth Packard spoke and wrote in support of rights for women. She also spoke out for people committed to institutions thought to be insane. She helped married women to gain property rights in Illinois (1869) and helped change laws about hospitalization of the insane in Illinois and Massachusetts (1867), Iowa (1872), and Maine (1874).

Suggestions for Further Reading

Burnham, John Chynoweth. "Elizabeth Parsons Ware Packard." *Notable American Women, 1607–1950.* Edward T. James, Janet Wilson James, and Paul S. Boyer, eds. Cambridge, MA: Belknap Press of Harvard University Press, 1971.

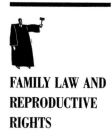

FAMILY LAW AND REPRODUCTIVE RIGHTS

Packard, Elizabeth Parsons Ware. *Great Disclosure of Spiritual Wickedness!! in high places. With an appeal to the government to protect the inalienable rights of married women.* Written under the inspection of Dr. McFarland, Superintendent of Insane Asylum, Jacksonville, Illinois, 4th ed. Boston: Published by the authoress, 1865.

Packard, Elizabeth Parsons Ware. *Marital Power Exemplified in Mrs. Packard's Trial and self-defense from the charge of insanity, or, Three years imprisonment for religious belief, by the arbitrary will of a husband, with an appeal to the government to so change the laws as to afford legal protection to married women.* Hartford, CT: Case, Lockwood & Co., 1866.

Packard, Elizabeth Parsons Ware. *The Mystic Key; or The Asylum Secret Unlocked.* Hartford, CT: Case, Lockwood & Brainard Co., 1866.

Packard, Elizabeth Parsons Ware. *The prisoners hidden life, or Insane asylums unveiled: as demonstrated by the Report of the Investigating Committee of the Legislature of Illinois, together with Mrs. Packards's coadjustors' testimony.* Chicago: The Author; A. B. Case, Printer, 1868.

Sapinsley, Barbara. *The Private War of Mrs. Packard.* New York: Paragon House, 1991.

O'Shea v. Parnell and O'Shea: 1890

Plaintiff: William O'Shea

Defendants: Charles Parnell and Katherine O'Shea

Plaintiff's Claim: Divorce on grounds of adultery

Chief Defense Lawyer: Sir Frank Lockwood, Q.C. (Queen's Counsel)

Chief Prosecutor: Sir Edward Clarke, Q.C.

Judge: Justice Charles Butt

Place: London, England

Dates of Trial: November 15–17, 1890

Decision: Jury found for plaintiff

SIGNIFICANCE: Political scandal, rumors of a duel, rumors of locked rooms and frantic escapes. For Victorian England, these were the ingredients of a notorious divorce trial. For novelists and playwrights, this tale has taken its place as one of the great love stories of all time.

In late nineteenth-century Britain, the most hotly contested political issue was Irish Home Rule, or Irish independence. Leading the struggle for Irish independence was Charles Stewart Parnell. In 1875, he became a member of the British Parliament (MP) for the Irish district of Meath. Within two years, he became the clear leader of the Irish nationalist cause. Parnell was a hero in his homeland and a source of concern to the British government. In 1881, that government put him in jail for dissent. Parnell turned his detention into political gain. After leaving prison the following spring, his political star soared. However, storm clouds were gathering.

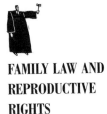

FAMILY LAW AND REPRODUCTIVE RIGHTS

A Passionate Affair

Like Parnell, Captain William O'Shea was an Irish nationalist MP. He was largely responsible for gaining Parnell's release from prison. This development was surprising, since Parnell was involved in a reckless and passionate relationship with O'Shea's beautiful wife, Katherine. (Indeed, before Parnell went to jail, O'Shea had challenged him to a duel. Parnell declined.)

Because both men were politically ambitious, they both kept the affair secret. Parnell went about his job of uniting various Irish political groups. Just as he was on the brink of achieving this goal, O'Shea filed for divorce, naming Parnell as his wife's lover. Most of Parnell's supporters thought that O'Shea filed his divorce suit for political reasons.

Parnell told his friends that O'Shea's claims were untrue. He offered O'Shea 20,000 pounds sterling ($80,000) to withdraw his suit and allow Katherine to be the one to sue for adultery. If Parnell had managed to raise the funds, O'Shea would probably have accepted this offer. However, Parnell did not, so O'Shea pursued his case. Two weeks before the suit was to come to court, Katherine countersued. She claimed that she had evidence that her husband had been unfaithful to her seventeen times.

The jury, with witnesses Harriet Wool and Caroline Pethers, listen to Captain O'Shea present his testimony.

CAPTAIN O'SHEA GIVING HIS EVIDENCE

WITNESSES

HARRIET WOOL

CAROLINE PETHERS.

THE JURY

Extraordinary Surrender

Parnell, who had a reputation as a man of integrity, was expected to fight O'Shea's suit vigorously. Yet when the court met on November 15, 1890, Katherine O'Shea's attorney shocked everyone present. He announced that, after consulting with his client, he did "not intend to cross-examine any witnesses, to call in witnesses, nor to take any part in these proceedings." Parnell was so certain of losing that he did not even hire a lawyer to represent him in court.

O'Shea Takes the Witness Stand

Because juries decided Victorian divorces, Sir Edward Clarke, O'Shea's attorney, was able to make the most of his client's sensational case. However, on November 17, just as Justice Charles Butt was preparing to send the jury out to consider its verdict, one of the jurors rose to address him. How, he asked, could all doubts about the countercharges be eliminated if there were no cross-examination of Captain O'Shea?

The judge allowed O'Shea to be called to the witness stand. O'Shea's attorney agreed that any member of the jury could ask O'Shea questions. Clarke began the questioning by asking his client about neglect and the separate living arrangements in the O'Shea household. O'Shea insisted that he and his wife had been on excellent terms up to the time he had discovered her unfaithfulness.

The juryman was not satisfied with this answer. Why then, he asked, did O'Shea invite Parnell to dinner in 1881, even after he had challenged the other man to a duel? O'Shea first attempted to contradict the juror's assertion; then, caught in a lie, he offered a lame explanation of his actions.

Damaging Testimony

A full public examination of the O'Sheas' marriage followed. The jury learned of their sleeping arrangements, the frequency of Parnell's visits, and Katherine's absences from the house. Clarke produced one list of the many addresses where Katherine and Parnell had been seen together and another of the aliases Parnell had used, such as Smith, Stewart, and Preston. Servants at the O'Shea residence testified that Parnell had stayed in the house at night with Katherine when O'Shea was away.

Far and away the most damaging witness was Caroline Pethers, a servant at the O'Shea's home in Brighton, England. She said that two

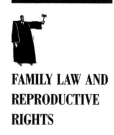
or three days after Captain and Mrs. O'Shea moved into the house, a gentleman appeared, whom she recognized by his photograph. "He went by the name of Mr. Charles Stewart. Sometimes he called when Captain O'Shea was at home, nearly always when he was away and he always came to the house the beach way. . . . He wore a light cloth cap over his eyes. He drove out at night with Mrs. O'Shea, but never during the day."

Parnell Flees House on Rope Fire Escape

Pethers' next revelation sent reporters into a frenzy. Apparently, Captain O'Shea had come home one day and rung the front doorbell while Parnell and Katherine were locked in the darkened drawing room. After being let in by Mrs. Pethers's husband, O'Shea went upstairs. Ten minutes later, Pethers said, Parnell himself rang the front doorbell and asked to see Captain O'Shea. The only way he could have achieved this trick was by using the rope fire escape that hung from the drawing room balcony. The image of the dignified Charles Stewart Parnell sliding down a rope to escape the husband he had wronged kept London newspapers busy for several days.

Parnell's Downfall

Sir Edward Clarke made good use of Parnell's decision not to defend himself. He implied that if Parnell had appeared he would only have added to his problems by lying under oath. Katherine's countersuit for adultery did not help Parnell. Although she cited her own sister, Anna Steele, as one of O'Shea's conquests, Anna successfully refuted Katherine's charges. Again, there was no cross-examination. The jury quickly agreed on the only possible verdict: adultery without connivance (knowledge of wrongdoing). In essence, the jury did not blame Parnell for seducing Katherine away from her husband.

That night, Parnell and Katherine read a copy of her divorce decree. Both were delighted. Parnell, blinded by love, was convinced that the ordeal had not harmed him politically. Initially, his fellow Irishmen supported him. In Britain, however, the public was hostile, as were Roman Catholic authorities in Ireland. They had never trusted the Protestant Parnell, and now they declared him morally unfit for leadership. Parnell attempted to shore up his support with radical appeals to the young. In the end, after a long and angry debate, he was rejected as leader by the Irish Parliamentary Party.

*Charles Stewart
Parnell in 1889.*

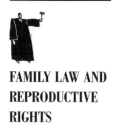

FAMILY LAW AND REPRODUCTIVE RIGHTS

HOME RULE

The political issue of Home Rule was behind the Charles Parnell scandal. Home Rule was the political slogan that Irish nationalists adopted in the nineteenth century to express their desire for self-government. (At that time, all of Ireland was ruled by England.) The modern movement for Home Rule began in 1870. Parnell did a great deal to strengthen the movement: he unified the Irish party in Parliament, creating a strong legislative force for Irish independence. In 1886, he was even able to get a Home Rule bill introduced into Parliament, but the bill failed to pass. The scandal caused by his affair with Katherine O'Shea ended his effectiveness as a political leader. Although other Home Rule bills were introduced in 1893 and 1912, they either did not pass or did not take effect. The Fourth Home Rule Bill, passed in 1920, helped to ratify that the six counties of Northern Ireland would remain under British rule, even as the rest of Ireland was achieving independence.

For the man who had refused to give up the woman he loved, the scandal brought both personal ruin and the loss of hope for Irish home rule. Parnell accepted his fate. Six months after the trial he married his beloved Katie, but their happiness was brief. On October 6, 1891, at the age of forty-six, Charles Stewart Parnell died from a heart attack.

Suggestions for Further Reading

Hickey, D. J. and J. E. Doherty. *A Dictionary of Irish History 1800–1980.* Dublin: Gill & Macmillan, 1980.

Kee, Robert. *The Laurel and the Ivy.* London: Hamish Hamilton, 1993.

Lyons, F. S. L. *Charles Stewart Parnell.* London: Collins, 1977.

O'Shea, K. *Charles Stewart Parnell.* London: Cassell, 1973.

Buck v. Bell:
1927

Appellant: Carrie Buck

Appellee: Dr. J. H. Bell

Appellant's Claim: That Carrie Buck's constitutional rights were violated by Virginia's sterilization law

Chief Lawyers for Appellee: Edmund Ackroyd and Aubrey E. Strode

Chief Lawyer for Appellant: Irving Whitehead

Justices: Louis D. Brandeis, Pierce Butler, Willis Van Devanter, Oliver Wendell Holmes, James C. McReynolds, Edward T. Sanford, Harlan F. Stone, George Sutherland, and Chief Justice William T. Taft

Place: Washington, D.C.

Date of Decision: May 2, 1927

Decision: Upheld Virginia's compulsory sterilization of young women considered "unfit [to] continue their kind"

SIGNIFICANCE: Some fifty thousand Americans were involuntarily sterilized under Virginia's law and under similar laws in thirty states.

The Supreme Court's landmark decision in *Buck v. Bell* received surprisingly little press coverage in 1927. Justice Oliver Wendell Holmes, who wrote the court's opinion, had no second thoughts about the decision to sterilize (cut the Fallopian tubes of) Carrie Buck. He was not concerned that she would never bear more children. He wrote in a letter shortly

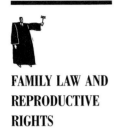

FAMILY LAW AND REPRODUCTIVE RIGHTS

afterward: "One decision . . . gave me pleasure, establishing the constitutionality of a law permitting the sterilization of imbeciles."

However, this ruling had far-reaching and disastrous consequences. Buck was not "feebleminded" or retarded. She was not the only one harmed. Many others also lost their chances to bear children as the result of this decision. The Nazis even used the case as an excuse for the millions of forced sterilizations they performed during World War II.

Carrie Buck's Pregnancy

Carrie's mother, Emma Buck, was a widowed parent of three who supported her family through prostitution. As the children were not well cared for, the state took them away from her. On April 1, 1920, Emma came before Charles D. Shackleford, the Charlottesville, Virginia, Justice of the Peace. Shackleford committed Emma to the Virginia Colony for the Epileptic and Feebleminded, in Lynchburg, Virginia.

J. T. and Alice Dobbs took in the three-year-old Carrie. She did well in school for five years. However, the Dobbs then stopped her education, claiming they needed her help with their housework. Things were peaceful until Carrie turned seventeen. Then, Carrie told the Dobbs that their son had raped her and that she was pregnant.

The Dobbs were horrified. They asked Justice Shackleford to commit Carrie to the Colony for the Epileptic and Feebleminded, as he had done to her mother. In court on January 24, 1924, the Dobbs and two doctors testified that Carrie was feebleminded. The same day, Shackleford signed an order for Carrie's commitment. She entered the institution soon after giving birth to her daughter, Vivian. The Dobbs then raised Vivian as their own child.

Virginia's "Solution"

The first superintendent of the Virginia colony, Dr. Albert Priddy, believed in eugenics (yoo-JEN-icks), or managing human reproduction to "improve" the human race. Eugenics was modeled on the practices used to breed farmyard animals. The method supposedly would eliminate "mental defectives." In the seven years before Carrie Buck arrived at the colony, Priddy had sterilized seventy-five to one hundred young women without their consent. He said he had operated on them to cure "pelvic disease."

In 1924, the Virginia Assembly passed a law making this falsehood unnecessary. The law officially permitted the forced sterilization of "feebleminded" or "socially inadequate person[s]." The law was written by Aubrey Strode. He was a state representative and the chief administrator of the Colony for the Epileptic and Feebleminded. He based his law on the work of Harry H. Laughlin, a well-known eugenicist. Carrie Buck's unhappy fate was to be selected for sterilization under this new law. Dr. Priddy arranged to have Strode's friend Irving Whitehead represent Buck in her fight not to be sterilized.

Carrie Buck As a Test Case

On November 19, 1924, the case of *Buck v. Priddy* came before Judge Bennett Gordon of the Circuit Court for Amherst County. Aubrey Strode represented Dr. Priddy. Priddy had declared Buck feebleminded and a good candidate for forced sterilization. Whitehead represented Buck, but only halfheartedly. The colony paid his fee.

Anne Harris, a Charlottesville district nurse, was the first witness. She testified against Buck. She said that her mother, Emma Buck, had been living in the worst neighborhoods. She said she had not been able to, or would not, work and support her children.

Strode asked, "What about the character of her offspring?"

Harris replied, "Well, I don't know anything very definite about the children, except they don't seem to be able to do any more than their mother."

Strode then asked, "Well, that is the crux of the matter. Are they mentally normal children?"

Harris responded, "No, sir, they are not."

Under cross-examination, Harris admitted, "I really know very little about Carrie after she left her mother [at age three]. Before that time she was . . . too small."

Three teachers testified about Carrie's sister, brother, and cousin, describing one as "dull in her books." An older relative was called "right peculiar." These statements at first did not relate to Carrie herself. Then Caroline Wilhelm, a Red Cross worker contacted by the Dobbs family during Carrie's pregnancy, took the witness stand.

Strode asked Wilhelm, "From your experience as a social worker, if Carrie were discharged from the Colony still capable of child-bearing, is she likely to become the parent of [mentally] deficient offspring?"

Wilhelm replied, "I should judge so. I think a girl of her mentality is more or less at the mercy of other people. . . . Her mother had three il-

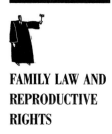

legitimate children, and I should say that Carrie would be very likely to have illegitimate children."

Strode concluded, "So the only way that she could likely be kept from increasing her own kind would be by either segregation or something that would stop her power to propagate [reproduce]."

Wilhelm next testified about Carrie's daughter, Vivian: "It seems difficult to judge probabilities of a child as young as that [eight months], but it seems to me not quite a normal baby."

Then, on cross-examination, Whitehead raised what should have been a crucial issue. "The question of pregnancy is not evidence of feeblemindedness, is it? The fact that, as we say, she . . . went wrong—is that evidence of feeblemindedness?"

Wilhelm replied, "No, but a feebleminded girl is much more likely to go wrong."

"Expert" Witnesses

Arthur Estabrook of the Carnegie Institute of Washington testified about his fourteen years of genetic research. Spode asked, "Would you say that by the laws of heredity [Buck] is a feebleminded person and the probable potential parent of socially inadequate offspring . . . ?"

Estabrook replied, "I would."

Dr. Priddy testified last. Carrie Buck, he said, "would cease to be a charge on society if sterilized. It would remove one potential source of the incalculable number of descendants who would be feebleminded."

Finally, a statement by Harry H. Laughlin, the eugenicist who had never examined Carrie, was read. Priddy had written to him asking for his help. The information in Priddy's letter formed the basis of Laughlin's sworn testimony. Carrie had "a mental age of nine years . . . a record during her life of immorality, prostitution, and untruthfulness; [she] has never been self-sustaining; has one illegitimate child, now about six months old and supposed to be mentally defective. . . . She is . . . a potential parent of socially inadequate or defective offspring."

In February 1925, Judge Gordon upheld the new Virginia law. Carrie Buck would be sterilized. Whitehead appealed to the Virginia Court of Appeals. (The name of the case was now *Buck v. Bell* because Dr. Priddy had died a few weeks earlier. Dr. J. H. Bell had taken his place at the colony.) The appeals court upheld the circuit court decision.

Supreme Court Reviews Case

In the papers he submitted to the U.S. Supreme Court, Whitehead claimed that the Fourteenth Amendment to the Constitution protected a person's "full bodily integrity." He also predicted the "worst kind of tyranny" if there were no "limits of the power of the state . . . to rid itself of those citizens deemed undesirable." Strode, in contrast, said forced sterilization was like forced vaccination. It was good for society.

Justice Oliver Wendell Holmes delivered the nearly unanimous opinion of the court on May 2, 1927:

> It is better for all the world, if instead of waiting to execute offspring for crime, or to let them starve for their imbecility, society can prevent those who are manifestly unfit from continuing their kind. The principle that sustains compulsory vaccination is broad enough to cover cutting the Fallopian tubes.

Only Justice Pierce Butler disagreed with this opinion.

Buck v. Bell: 1927

Carrie Buck languished in the State Epileptic Colony in Lynchburg, Virginia.

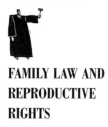

FAMILY LAW AND REPRODUCTIVE RIGHTS

Carrie Buck Eagle and her husband, William Eagle.

SURVIVAL OF THE FITTEST?

After Charles Darwin developed his theory of evolution in 1859, many thinkers tried to apply his ideas to human societies. Nineteenth-century British philosopher Herbert Spencer came up with the notion of "Social Darwinism." This meant that the rich are the most fit human beings, while the poor are the least fit. This idea was carried one step further by people known as "eugenicists." They believed that it was possible to breed humans to develop desirable qualities, such as intelligence. At the same time, they sought to prevent "less desirable" humans from breeding, through such means as forced sterilization. This, they believed, would help the human race "evolve." In fact, both Spencer and the eugenicists were operating on a completely false view of Darwin's theory. According to Darwin, "the survival of the fittest" simply meant the survival of those who were able to produce the most offspring. No moral judgment was involved. By Darwin's logic, poor people, who tended to have more children than the rich, were more "fit," since they produced more children. Moreover, qualities such as intelligence are not necessarily inherited from one's parents. Parents of low intelligence may have highly intelligent children, and vice versa.

Dr. Bell sterilized Carrie Buck on October 19, 1927. Shortly afterward, she was let out of the Virginia colony. She married twice. The letters she wrote to the Virginia colony seeking custody of her mother, as well as the recollections of her minister, neighbors, and health care providers, all make it clear that Carrie Buck was not "feebleminded."

Other Applications Result from *Buck v. Bell*

Sterilization laws similar to Virginia's were passed in thirty other states. As a result, more than fifty thousand people were sterilized against their will. Doris, Carrie Buck's sister, was among them.

Harry H. Laughlin, author of the model sterilization law adapted for Virginia by Aubrey Strode, made his model available to other states, as

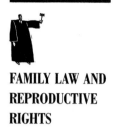

**FAMILY LAW AND
REPRODUCTIVE
RIGHTS**

well as to foreign governments. It resulted in Germany's Hereditary Health Law, adopted in 1933. After World War II, lawyers for Nazi war criminals cited this law as justification for the sterilization of two million people. They pointed out that the U.S. Supreme Court, in *Buck v. Bell,* had declared such laws to be constitutional. The Supreme Court has yet to reverse the case.

Suggestions for Further Reading

Cushman, Robert E. *Cases in Constitutional Law.* 6th ed. Englewood Cliffs, NJ: Prentice Hall, 1984.

Goldstein, Leslie Friedman. *The Constitutional Rights of Women: Cases in Law and Social Change.* Madison: University of Wisconsin Press, 1989.

Smith, J. David and K. Ray Nelson. *The Sterilization of Carrie Buck: Was She Feebleminded or Society's Pawn.* Far Hill, NJ: New Horizon Press, 1989.

Roe v. Wade:
1973

Plaintiff: Norma McCorvey, using "Jane Roe" as an alias, and representing all pregnant women in a class-action suit

Defendant: Dallas County, Texas, District Attorney Henry B. Wade

Plaintiff's Claim: That the Texas abortion law violated the constitutional rights of McCorvey and other women

Chief Defense Lawyers: John Tolle, Jay Floyd, and Robert Flowers

Chief Prosecutors: Sarah Weddington and Linda Coffee

Justices: Harry Blackmun, William J. Brennan, Chief Justice Warren Burger, William O. Douglas, Thurgood Marshall, Lewis Powell, Potter Stewart, William Rehnquist, and Byron White

Place: Washington, D.C.

Date of Decision: January 22, 1973

Decision: Ended all state laws restricting women's ability to have abortions during the first trimester (three months) of pregnancy. Upheld only those second-trimester (three-to-six month) restrictions that protected the health of pregnant women

SIGNIFICANCE: This landmark decision made abortion legal in the United States.

The Supreme Court's landmark decision legalizing abortion aroused more passion than perhaps any before it. Catholics and fundamentalist Protestants thought abortion was murder. However, many others believed that denying

FAMILY LAW AND REPRODUCTIVE RIGHTS

a woman the freedom to choose whether to give birth to a baby was unconstitutional. The 1973 decision triggered a battle between the "right-to-lifers" who opposed the decision and its "pro-choice" supporters.

Support for abortion rights had been growing during the 1960s and 1970s. In 1968, for example, fewer than 15 percent of the participants in a Gallup Poll approved of making abortion more available. The next year, however, that number increased to 40 percent. In 1972, the Gallup Poll released surprising findings. It found that 73 percent of all those questioned and 56 percent of Catholics in particular agreed on one point. The decision about whether or not to abort a fetus should be left to the pregnant mother and her doctor.

Sarah Weddington, attorney for "Jane Roe," on December 13, 1971. The Supreme Court listened that day to oral arguments presented in the Roe v. Wade trial.

Norma McCorvey Tests the Law

The "Jane Roe" whose name would be linked with the decision was Norma McCorvey. By 1969, McCorvey's marriage had ended. Her parents were raising her 5-year-old daughter. In the summer of that year, the twenty-one-year-old McCorvey was working as a ticket seller for a traveling carnival. By the fall, she had lost her job and become pregnant. She wanted

NORMA McCORVEY

Norma McCorvey, commonly known as "Jane Roe," fought for abortion rights in the landmark 1973 *Roe v. Wade* case. In August 1995, McCorvey quit her job at Dallas' A Choice For Women clinic. Within a week she began to volunteer for Flip Benham's antiabortion group, Operation Rescue. This change of heart on McCorvey's part makes her the first volunteer in Operation Rescue's history who supported a woman's right to a first-trimester (within the first three months of pregnancy) abortion.

to end her pregnancy, but in Texas, where she lived, abortion was illegal except in cases where the mother's life was in danger. She was unable to find a person willing to perform an illegal abortion.

McCorvey did, however, find two young lawyers, Linda Coffee and Sarah Weddington. They were interested in challenging the abortion law. There was no chance that McCorvey herself would be helped if Coffee and Weddington succeeded in overturning the law, since McCorvey's baby would be born long before a legal challenge to the laws was concluded. Still, all three wanted to test the law.

Texas had passed its anti-abortion law in 1859. Like the laws in other states, it punished only the people performing abortions. This posed a problem for Coffee and Weddington. The law was written so that a pregnant woman did not have the legal right to challenge the law. If she did get over this hurdle, she would face another one. After giving birth, her case would no longer exist. Linda Coffee prepared and filed the proper legal papers anyway.

Constitutional Issues

Coffee and Weddington decided to attack the Texas abortion law on the grounds that it violated the Fourteenth and Ninth Amendments to the Constitution. The Due Process Clause of the Fourteenth Amendment guaranteed equal protection under the law to all citizens. It also required that

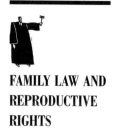

laws be clearly written. Doctors accused of performing illegal abortions usually used the Due Process Clause in their defense. They claimed that the abortion law was not specific enough about when a pregnant woman's life might be endangered, necessitating an abortion.

However, Coffee and Weddington wanted a court decision that rested on a woman's right to decide for herself whether to have an abortion. So they turned to the Ninth Amendment. It states: "The enumeration in the Constitution, of certain rights, shall not be construed to deny or disparage others retained by the people." Before 1965, these words had been interpreted to mean that any rights not specifically granted to the federal government belonged to the states. In 1965, however, the Supreme Court changed that interpretation with *Griswold v. Connecticut.* This decision upheld the right to distribute birth control devices to married couples. Justice William O. Douglas had written the opinion for the court. Coffee and Weddington were especially interested in his discussion of the Ninth Amendment. Rights not spelled out in the Constitution, Douglas said, belonged to individuals, and one of these rights was the right to privacy. This right to privacy, Coffee and Weddington argued, should protect a woman's right to decide for herself whether or not to become a mother.

Trial Court Favors Plaintiff

On May 23, 1970, Coffee and Weddington, together with lawyers for the state, appeared in federal court in Dallas, Texas, before a three-judge panel. Norma McCorvey, or "Jane Roe" as she was listed on the case, was not required to be present.

Coffee and Weddington had changed their case to a "class-action suit." McCorvey was suing not just in her own interest, but in the interests of all pregnant women. It was Coffee's job to argue that McCorvey did indeed have the right to sue. Jay Floyd, representing the state, claimed that "Jane Roe" must certainly have reached the point in her pregnancy where an abortion would be unsafe. Therefore, he said, her case should be dismissed. The judges disagreed. Weddington explained that the Texas abortion law conflicted with the interpretation of the Ninth Amendment. The Ninth Amendment says that the listing of certain rights in the Constitution shall not mean that other rights are denied to "the people." In *Griswold v. Connecticut* (1965) Justice William O. Douglas wrote that a state could not violate a person's privacy. He said that this "right of privacy" under the Ninth Amendment was retained by "the people." The judges agreed.

On June 17, 1970, the panel issued its opinion. "The Texas abortion laws must be declared unconstitutional because they deprive single women and married couples of their right, secured by the Ninth Amendment, to choose whether to have children."

Supreme Court Hears the Case

The Fifth Circuit Court declared the challenged law unconstitutional. This court did not, however, order Texas to stop enforcing its abortion law. For this reason, Coffee and Weddington were entitled to appeal directly to the U.S. Supreme Court, which agreed to hear the case.

On December 13, 1971, Weddington stood before the Supreme Court. She declared that the state's power to force women to have children left women without any power over their own lives. She said an unborn child was not entitled to legal protection. Since there were only seven justices serving on the court at the time, the justices decided that such an important case should be reargued. After two newly appointed justices, William Rehnquist and Lewis Powell, were sworn in on October 10, 1972, Coffee and Weddington repeated their basic arguments to a full nine-member court.

Landmark Decision

On January 22, 1973, Justice Harry Blackmun, speaking for a majority of the justices, read his opinion to a room filled with reporters. He pointed out that laws making abortion a crime were recent in American history. Abortion was legal in the colonial period. However, laws to stop abortion became popular in the nineteenth century. They were designed to protect women against a procedure that was likely to endanger their health. Because modern medical abortions were safer, that reason no longer existed.

Justice Blackmun next said that the court had agreed that there was a "right of personal privacy" in past decisions. Then he delivered the heart of his decision:

> This right of privacy, whether it be founded in the Fourteenth Amendment's concept of personal liberties and restrictions on state action . . . or . . . in the Ninth Amendment's reservations of rights to the people, is broad enough to encompass a woman's decision to terminate her pregnancy.

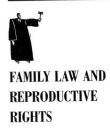

Justice Blackmun disagreed with Texas's claim that it had the right to violate Roe's rights in order to protect the unborn. He discussed the use of the word "person" in the U.S. Constitution and found that it did not apply to the unborn. However, said Justice Blackmun, neither the woman's right to privacy nor the unborn's lack of a right to the state's protection is absolute.

Finally, Justice Blackmun's decision in *Roe v. Wade* provided the states with a formula for balancing these competing interests. During the first three months of a pregnancy, the abortion decision is to be left to the mother and her doctor. During the next three months, the state may "regulate the abortion procedure in ways that are reasonably related to maternal health." During the last three months, the state can regulate and even rule out abortion, except when the mother's life or health is at risk.

More Controversy

Every state was affected. Some, like Texas, had to throw out their abortion laws. Others, like New York, had to extend the period during which abortion was permitted. In the spring of 1973, with support from the Catholic Church, a group calling itself the Committee of Ten Million began a petition drive demanding that a "human rights amendment" be adopted, banning abortion in the United States. Several constitutional amendments were introduced and discussed in Congress. Some proposals banned abortions even when a mother's life was at risk. None of these proposals was adopted. The opponents of *Roe* next tried to organize the legislatures of thirty-four states to call for a constitutional convention. This attempt also failed.

The Republican Party has since adopted the "pro-life" position as part of its political platform. This move gained the party Catholic and fundamentalist members, but it cost Republicans a great deal of support among women voters. The Democratic Party, which supports *Roe v. Wade,* benefitted from the women's vote in the 1992 election, in which Bill Clinton, a supporter of abortion rights, was elected president.

Several of the Supreme Court's more liberal justices have retired since *Roe v. Wade* was decided. The more conservative justices who followed them have indicated a willingness to re-examine the decision. On June 30, 1980, in *Harris v. McRae,* the court ruled that neither the federal government nor state governments are obligated to pay for abortions for women on welfare. More recently, *Webster v. Reproductive Health Services,* decided July 3, 1989, granted states new authority to restrict abortions in tax-supported institutions. *Rust v. Sullivan,* decided May 23,

DOE V. BOLTON

The same day that *Roe v. Wade* was decided, the Supreme Court also issued its opinion on another abortion case, *Doe v. Bolton.* "Doe" in this case was an impoverished Georgia woman, a former mental hospital patient, and the mother of three children— one of whom had already been given up for adoption and two of whom were in foster care. When "Doe" became pregnant again, she tried, on her doctors' advice, to get an abortion. In her case, abortion was unavailable because of the restrictive procedural requirements in her home state of Georgia: that abortions be performed only in hospitals accredited by the Joint Commission on the Accreditation of Hospitals; that the procedure be approved by a hospital abortion committee; that two independent doctors confirm that committee's decision; and that only residents of Georgia could obtain abortions in that state. Justice Brennan, delivering the majority opinion for *Doe v. Bolton,* said that because these requirements were so restrictive, they too were unconstitutional.

1991, upheld federal regulations denying financial support to family planning clinics that provide information about abortion. *Roe v. Wade* remains in force, but its sweep had been diminished.

Suggestions for Further Reading:

Cary, Eve and Kathleen Willert Peratis. *Woman and the Law.* Skokie, IL: National Textbook Co. (in conjunction with the American Civil Liberties Union, New York), 1977.

Cushman, Robert F. *Cases in Constitutional Law,* 6th ed. Englewood, NJ: Prentice Hall, 1984.

Davis, Flora. *Moving the Mountain: The Women's Movement in America Since 1960.* New York: Simon & Schuster, 1991.

Ehrenreich, Barbara and Deidre English. *For Her Own Good: 150 Years of the Experts' Advice to Women.* New York: Doubleday, 1979.

Faux, Marion. *Roe v. Wade.* New York: Macmillan Co., 1988.

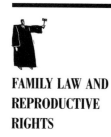

FAMILY LAW AND REPRODUCTIVE RIGHTS

Garrow, David J. *Liberty & Sexuality: The Right to Privacy and the Making of Roe v. Wade.* New York: Macmillan, 1994.

Goldstein, Leslie Friedman. *The Constitutional Rights of Women,* revised edition. Madison: University of Wisconsin Press, 1989.

Guitton, Stephanie and Peter Irons, eds. *May It Please the Court: Arguments on Abortion.* New York: The New Press, 1995.

Petchesky, Rosalind Pollack. *Abortion and Woman's Choice,* revised edition. Boston: Northeastern University Press, 1990.

In the Matter of Baby M: 1988

Plaintiffs: William Stern and Elizabeth Stern

Defendant: Mary Beth Whitehead

Plaintiffs' Claim: That Mary Beth Whitehead should surrender the child she conceived through artificial insemination with William Stern's sperm, according to the terms of a "Surrogate Parenting Agreement" made between Whitehead and Stern before the baby was conceived

Chief Defense Lawyers: Harold Cassidy and Randy Wolf

Chief Prosecutors: Frank Donahue and Gary Skoloff

Justices: Robert Clifford, Marie L. Garibaldi, Alan B. Handler, Daniel O'Horn, Stewart G. Pollock, Gary S. Stein, and Chief Justice Robert N. Wilentz

Place: Trenton, New Jersey

Date of Decision: February 3, 1988

Verdict: The court ended Mary Beth Whitehead's parental rights and gave Elizabeth Stern the right to adopt William Stern's and Whitehead's daughter. The New Jersey Supreme Court overturned this verdict in part on February 2, 1988. It restored Whitehead's parental rights and canceled Elizabeth Stern's adoption, while granting William Stern custody of the infant

SIGNIFICANCE: This was the first widely followed trial to wrestle with the ethical questions raised by "reproductive technology."

FAMILY LAW AND REPRODUCTIVE RIGHTS

Mary Beth Whitehead (left) speaks to supporters outside the New Jersey courthouse.

Melissa Stern's life began under an agreement signed at Noel Keane's Infertility Center of New York on February 5, 1985. On that day Richard Whitehead gave his consent for his wife, Mary Beth Whitehead, to have a doctor implant William Stern's sperm in her uterus. The process is called "artificial insemination." In addition, since any child born to Mary Beth Whitehead would legally be her husband's child, Richard Whitehead agreed to surrender his custody rights, as well as his parental rights.

Mary Beth Whitehead also agreed not to form a "parent-child relationship" with the baby. In addition, she would also surrender her parental rights to William Stern.

Stern agreed to pay $10,000 to Whitehead. Their contract stated that the fee was not "a fee for termination of parental rights or a payment in exchange for a consent to surrender the child for adoption." It would, however, change hands only when Whitehead surrendered a living infant to Stern. Stern also paid $10,000 to Noel Keane for arranging the agreement with the Whiteheads.

Stern's wife, Elizabeth, was not part of the agreement. The contract referred to her only as Stern's wife. Should William die before the baby was born, the contract stated that Elizabeth would adopt it.

The Birth

Events did not go as planned. On March 27, 1986, Whitehead gave birth to a daughter. She named the infant "Sara Elizabeth Whitehead." She took her home, and turned down the $10,000. On Easter Sunday, March 30, the Sterns took the infant to their home. The baby was back at the Whitehead home on March 31. In the second week of April, Mary Beth Whitehead told the Sterns she would never be able to give up her daughter. The Sterns responded by hiring attorney Gary Skoloff to fight for their rights under the contract.

The police arrived to remove "Melissa Elizabeth Stern" from the Whitehead's custody, but when they saw a birth certificate for "Sara Elizabeth Whitehead," they left. When the police returned, Whitehead passed her daughter through an open window to her husband, telling him to make a run for it.

The Trial Begins

The trial opened on January 5, 1987. By then, the court had appointed a representative to protect the interests of "Baby M," which stood for Melissa. The court gave the Sterns temporary custody. Whitehead, whom the judge had ordered to stop breast-feeding the child, could make short, closely watched visits.

Attorney Skoloff said that the issue to be decided was "whether a promise to make the gift of life should be enforced." He stated that Elizabeth Stern suffered from multiple sclerosis, which made her "as a practical matter, infertile . . . because she could not carry a baby without significant risk to her health."

Harold Cassidy, the attorney for Whitehead, said that the reason the Sterns had not attempted to have a child together was that Mrs. Stern did not want to interrupt her career with a pregnancy. Her multiple sclerosis, he said, was very mild. The doctors had only diagnosed it after the legal case began. "We're here," Cassidy summed up, "not because Betsy Stern is infertile but because one woman stood up and said there are some things that money can't buy."

The Custody Issue

Skoloff stated the infant's best interests meant that the Sterns should have custody. Baby M's representative, Lorraine Abraham, took the stand to make her own recommendation. She told the court that she had relied on

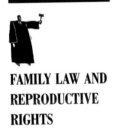
the opinions of three experts in reaching the conclusion that the Sterns deserved custody of Baby M and that Whitehead should not visit her. Experts then testified. Backing up this recommendation, they pointed to the contract, Baby M's "best interests," and Mary Beth Whitehead's qualities as a mother.

"By These Standards, We're All Unfit Mothers"

Outside the courtroom, 121 prominent women were protesting. They disagreed with the experts' opinion that Whitehead's flight to Florida with Baby M shortly after the infant's birth proved she was an "unfit" mother. On March 12, 1987, they issued a document titled "By These Standards, We Are All Unfit Mothers," which argued that Whitehead did not need to behave perfectly to deserve her child.

Finally, Cassidy warned that a decision for the Sterns would allow the rich to exploit the poor, because the rich could pay the poor to bear their children. "And it will always be the wife of the sanitation worker who must bear the children of the pediatrician," he said. Nevertheless, on March 31, 1987, the court read its decision: "The parental rights of the defendant, Mary Beth Whitehead, are terminated. Mr. Stern is formally judged the father of Melissa Stern." Then, in the judge's chambers, Elizabeth Stern adopted Baby M as her daughter.

Judgment Overruled

The Supreme Court of New Jersey overturned the lower court's decision on February 2, 1988. The state supreme court ruled that the contract was not valid. It canceled Elizabeth Stern's adoption of Baby M, and restored Whitehead's parental rights. All of the justices agreed with this judgment. Writing for the court, Chief Justice Robert N. Wilentz said:

> We do not know of, and cannot conceive of, any other case where a perfectly fit mother was expected to surrender her newly born infant, perhaps forever, and was then told she was a bad mother because she did not.

The justices then dealt with the case as a difference between "the natural father and the natural mother, [both of whose claims] are entitled to equal weight." As in the case of a divorce, both parents sought custody of the child. The justices gave custody of Baby M to William Stern. How-

DEBATES OVER BABY M

The Baby M case raised three major questions among the public. Should women be allowed to enter into "surrogate-parent" contracts like the one in the Baby M case? Should both a mother and father have equal rights to their child as well as responsibilities for its upbringing? Could the practice of allowing a woman to bear a child for another couple lead to rich people paying poorer ones to bear their children? While none of these questions have been answered, one important change has occurred since the Baby M case. Throughout the United States surrogate parenting is becoming more heavily regulated.

ever, Mary Beth Whitehead still had parental rights to Melissa as well. The court allowed her to visit Melissa regularly. However, since the Sterns lived in New Jersey and Whitehead lived on Long Island in New York, it was difficult for Whitehead to follow the visitation schedule set by the court. Years after the New Jersey Supreme Court decision, Whitehead gave an interview to the press. She said she would either ask the court to revise the terms under which she could see Melissa, or move the rest of her family closer to Melissa's home.

The Outcome

The New Jersey Supreme Court decision outlawed surrogate agreements in that state unless the mothers gave birth without payment and had the right to change their minds. At least seventeen states now have similar rules. Women have reacted in different ways to the decision. Some agree that a mother's right to her child is most important. Others feel the right to undo a Baby M type of agreement could become a restriction on a woman's right to control her own body.

Suggestions Further Reading

Brennan, Shawn, ed. *Women's Information Directory.* Detroit, MI: Gale Research, 1993.

Chesler, Phyllis. *Sacred Bond: The Legacy of Baby M.* New York: Times Books, 1988.

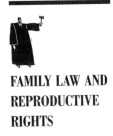

FAMILY LAW AND REPRODUCTIVE RIGHTS

Cullen-DuPont, Kathryn. *Encyclopedia of Women's History in America.* New York: Facts On File, 1996.

Davis, Flora. *Moving the Mountain: The Women's Movement in America Since 1960.* New York: Simon & Schuster, 1991.

Evans, Sara M. *Born for Liberty: A History of Women in America.* New York: The Free Press, 1989.

Sack, Kevin. "New York is Urged to Outlaw Surrogate Parenting for Pay." *The New York Times* (May 13, 1992): B5.

Squire, Susan. "Whatever Happened to Baby M?" *Redbook* (January 1994): 60.

Whitehead, Mary Beth with Loretta Schwartz-Nobel. *A Mother's Story: The Truth About the Baby M Case.* New York: St. Martin's Press, 1989.

FREEDOM OF SPEECH

John Peter Zenger Trial: 1735

Defendant: John Peter Zenger

Crime Charged: Seditious libel

Chief Defense Lawyers: Andrew Hamilton and John Chambers

Chief Prosecutor: Attorney General Richard Bradley

Judge: Chief Justice James De Lancey

Place: New York, New York

Date of Trial: August 1735

Verdict: Not guilty

SIGNIFICANCE: This trial laid the foundations of freedom of the press in America.

The most important political trial in American history took place in New York City in 1735, long before the Revolutionary War (1775–1783). The defendant was a printer, John Peter Zenger. The British government charged him with the crime of criticizing the royal governor in the *New York Weekly Journal*. At this time, criticism of officials was interpreted as a threat to law and order. Some found it to be treason.

Zenger's Attack on the Royal Governor

Zenger was an ordinary man whose career only became notable when he was middle-aged. Born in what is now Germany, he emigrated to the American colonies in 1710 as a boy of thirteen. The next year he went to work as an apprentice (person who studies a trade) to William Bradford,

FREEDOM OF SPEECH

On November 2, 1734, Royal Governor Cosby issued an order to burn four issues of Zenger's Weekly Journal.

the royal printer for the British colony of New York. By 1725, Zenger had become Bradford's partner in the colony's official newspaper, *New York Gazette*. That year Zenger decided to go into business for himself. Until 1733, he made a living printing religious pamphlets.

Zenger's success began when a new royal governor, William Cosby, arrived in New York. Cosby was greedy. He demanded that the New York colonial council pay him large sums of money for his services as governor. He even tried to force his predecessor, Rip Van Dam, to turn over half the salary he had been paid. When Van Dam refused, Cosby sued him. Most of the colony's wealthy gentlemen supported Van Dam.

These wealthy gentlemen wanted to make their dislike for Cosby publicly known. Because the British government had appointed Bradford, they knew better than to ask him for help. Instead, they turned to Zenger. They offered him money to produce a newspaper of his own. Zenger's *Weekly Journal* first appeared on November 5, 1733. Unlike Bradford's official publication, which published nothing controversial, the *Weekly Journal* contained scorching editorials written by a Van Dam supporter, attorney James Alexander, and was filled with political satire (ridicule). Much of this was aimed at Cosby and his friends. Included were fake advertisements making fun of people such as Francis Harrison, who was de-

John Peter Zenger Trial: 1735

Andrew Hamilton's defense of John Peter Zenger.

scribed as "a large Spaniel, of about five feet five inches high." The sheriff was characterized as a "monkey . . . lately broke from his chain and run into the country." Both Harrison and the sheriff were Cosby's friends. None of this pleased the governor.

Cosby Strikes Back

Cosby had Zenger arrested and charged with libel (attacking a person's reputation). The governor also charged Zenger with sedition, which then meant urging people to hold their government in contempt. Zenger landed in the dungeon in the old city hall. His bail was 400 pounds (British currency), an amount two or three times larger than the annual income from his newspaper. (It was Zenger's penalty that prompted the adoption of the prohibition against excessive bails and fines in the Eighth Amendment to the U.S. Constitution.)

Crowds acclaim Andrew Hamilton after John Peter Zenger's acquittal.

Zenger's lawyers, William Smith and James Alexander, challenged the authority of Chief Justice James De Lancey, whom Cosby had appointed. Cosby had the two attorneys banned from practicing law. He then appointed John Chambers to defend Zenger.

The jury included seven New Yorkers of Dutch heritage. These jurors were anti-British. Even so, the prosecution was sure it would win. The jury's only role was to decide if Zenger was "guilty" of publishing the articles in question. Since the printer never denied this, there was little doubt about the jury's verdict. Also legal opinion at the time held that printed words that attacked an individual's reputation were libelous, regardless of whether the claims made were true or false. The judge, another Cosby appointee, was responsible for deciding whether they were also seditious.

Zenger's friends recruited Andrew Hamilton of Philadelphia, the most famous trial lawyer in the colonies, to defend Zenger. It was Hamilton's role in the Zenger trial that gave rise to the saying, "When in trouble, get a Philadelphia lawyer."

The appointed defense lawyer, Chambers, happily turned the job of defending Zenger over to Hamilton. From the start, Hamilton admitted that Zenger had printed the papers. He also said, though, that they could not libel the governor unless they were also malicious (mean-spirited) and false. Prosecutor Richard Bradley argued this, insisting that libel consisted of words that were scandalous and upset people. The chief justice ruled in Bradley's favor, preventing Hamilton from calling witnesses who would testify as to the truth of the *Weekly Journal*'s articles.

John Peter
Zenger
Trial: 1735

Hamilton's Appeal for Press Freedom

Since he was unable to present his evidence, Hamilton's only chance to acquit (find not guilty) his client came at the end of the trial as he was summing up. He began by pointing out that keeping information from the jury "ought always to be taken for the strongest evidence." He scolded "corrupt and wicked magistrates [judges]." He condemned the Star Chamber, a secret English court where trial by jury was not allowed. Liberty, he declared, is our "only bulwark [defense] against lawless power." Closing his argument, Hamilton declared:

> Gentlemen of the jury . . . it is not the cause of a
> poor printer, nor of New York alone, which you are
> now trying. No! It may in its consequences affect
> every freeman that lives under British a government
> on the main of America. It is the best cause. It is
> the cause of liberty.

FREEDOM OF THE PRESS GUARANTEED

John Peter Zenger established the principle that freedom of the press is an important American liberty. The First Amendment of the U.S. Constitution protects this right, along with guarantees of freedom of religion, speech, and assembly, and of the right of people to take their complaints to the government. Although the language is simple, it is powerful: "Congress shall make no law respecting an establishment of religion, or prohibiting the free exercise thereof; or abridging the freedom of speech, or of the press; or the right of the people peaceably to assemble, and to petition the government for a redress of grievances."

This summation, one of the most famous in legal history, gave courage to the jury as well as the spectators in the courtroom. Shortly after retiring, the jurors returned with a verdict of not guilty. The crowd erupted in cheers.

Zenger Verdict's Legal Impact

Zenger quickly published the transcript (record of what is said during court) of the trial. News of its drama and its outcome spread quickly throughout the American colonies and to England. Although both Americans and British approved the verdict, it took many years before the *Zenger* decision became an accepted legal principle. In 1792, however, the British Parliament adopted the Fox Libel Act. It gave juries the right to consider truth as well as publication in deciding such cases.

Freedom of the press was formally adopted in the United States in the Bill of Rights. But political rivalry (competition) between the Federalist Party and the Republicans after American independence resulted in more similar cases against newspapers. In the 1803 prosecution of a Federalist editor, Harry Croswell, for libeling President Thomas Jefferson, the Republican justice Morgan Lewis banned evidence that might demonstrate the truth of the newspaper's claims. Alexander Hamilton, a Federalist, appealed to the New York Supreme Court to overturn its guilty verdict. He pointed to the Zenger case. Although the court split 2–2, the eloquence of Hamilton's argument won the day. The case against Croswell was dropped. The legal principles Hamilton argued were finally incorporated into the New York State Constitution in 1821.

The powerful arguments put forward by the two Hamiltons—Andrew and Alexander—established the rights of free speech and freedom of the press. The importance of the right to trial by jury was also affirmed as a protection against oppressive government rule.

Fifty years after the Zenger trial, American statesman Gouverneur Morris described the verdict in this case as "the morning star of liberty which subsequently revolutionized America." Morris helped to write into the Constitution the basic freedom for which Zenger and his allies fought.

John Peter
Zenger
Trial: 1735

Suggestions for Further Reading

Buranelli, Vincent. *The Trial of John Peter Zenger.* Westport, CT: Greenwood, 1975.

Fleming, Thomas J. "A Scandalous, Malicious and Seditious Libel." *American Heritage* (December 1967): 22–27, 100–106.

Hopkins, W. Wat. "John Peter Zenger." *A Biographical Dictionary of American Journalism.* Joseph P. McKerns, ed. Westport, CT: Greenwood, 1989.

Konkle, B. A. *The Life of Andrew Hamilton, 1676–1741.* Philadelphia: National Publishing Co., 1941.

Rutherford, Livingston. *John Peter Zenger, His Press, His Trial, and a Bibliography of Zenger Imprints.* New York: Arno, 1904.

Alien and Sedition Acts: 1798

Defendants: Twenty-four people, including Matthew Lyon, Anthony Haswell, William Duane, Thomas Cooper, and James Thompson Callender

Crime Charged: Seditious libel

Chief Defense Lawyers: Lyon acted for himself, advised by Israel Smith; David Fay and Israel Smith (Haswell); Thomas Cooper and Alexander Dallas (Duane); Cooper acted for himself; and William B. Giles, George Hay, and Philip Nicholas (Callender).

Chief Prosecutors: Charles Marsh (Lyon, Haswell); William Rawle (Duane, Cooper); and Thomas Nelson (Callender).

Judges: William Paterson and Samuel Hitchcock (Lyon, Haswell); Samuel Chase and Richard Peters (Cooper); Bushrod Washington and Peters (Duane); and Samuel Chase (Callender)

Dates of Trials: October 8, 1799 (Lyon); May 5, 1800 (Haswell); April 16, 1800 (Cooper); June 3, 1800 (Callender); June 11, 1800 (Duane court appearance)

Place: Rutland, Vermont (Lyon); Windsor, Vermont (Haswell); Norristown, Pennsylvania (Duane); Philadelphia, Pennsylvania (Cooper); and Richmond, Virginia (Callender)

Verdict: Guilty (Lyon, Haswell, Cooper, and Callender)

Sentences: $1,000 fine, $60.96 court costs, four months in jail (Lyon); $200 fine, two months in jail (Haswell); $400 fine, six months in jail, a $2,000 surety bond upon leaving prison (Cooper); and $200 fine, nine months in prison, a $1,200 bond for good behavior (Callender)

SIGNIFICANCE: On paper only, the terms of the Sedition Act, punishing rebellion against the government, were an improvement over traditional unwritten common law. But the very fact that the federal government would enact a sedition law was a blow to freedom of the press.

P ower struggles often lead to bad laws. One example of bad laws were the Alien and Sedition Acts in 1798. Congress passed these laws fearing war with France. The Federalist administration of President John Adams introduced them in order to keep its enemies, the Jeffersonian Republicans (followers of Vice President Thomas Jefferson), from winning at the polls. The fact that the laws could be used against the French living in the country, who backed the Republicans, was icing on the cake for the Federalists.

Alien and Sedition Acts: 1798

Background

Congress passed several of these laws. The act passed on June 18 declared that foreigners must live in America for fourteen years, instead of five years, before they could become citizens. Foreigners must also declare their intent to become citizens five years before applying for citizenship. (In 1802, the Jeffersonian Republicans would repeal this law.)

The June 25 act allowed the president to deport any aliens he thought were "dangerous." (This law would expire, or end, in 1800.)

This caricature depicts the first fight in Congress—between Matthew Lyon and Roger Griswold. Officials later charged Lyon with seditious libel under the Sedition Act.

The July 6 act allowed the president to arrest, jail, or banish foreigners from countries with whom the United States was at war. In the two years that this law was in force, the president never used it. However, clearly, he had too much power.

Finally, the Sedition Act of July 14 made it a crime to oppose the government. It became unlawful to interfere with an officer doing his duty. One could not encourage a riot or "unlawful assembly" (a meeting). The penalty for violating this law was $5,000 and five years in jail. The law also made it a crime to publish "any false, scandalous and malicious [mean-spirited] writing" against the federal government, the Congress, or the president. Fines were as high as $2,000 for this crime and jail time as long as two years. (This law would remain in effect until 1801.)

As president of the Senate, Thomas Jefferson signed the contempt warrant that led to the arrest of William Duane, publisher of the Aurora.

The Federalists unfairly used the laws to punish Republicans. They especially hated editors who criticized President Adams. But they ignored the insults of Federalists against Vice President Thomas Jefferson. Ten Jeffersonian Republicans were arrested and fined under the Act. The most famous was Dr. Thomas Cooper, who later became a college president. He spent six months in prison and paid $400 for mildly criticizing President Adams. Federalist judges, such as Samuel Chase, showed hateful prejudice against the Republican defendants. Soon the public began to see the victims as heroes. In 1798 and 1799, for example, two states voiced their protests. The Virginia and Kentucky Resolutions, written by James

Madison and Thomas Jefferson, strongly protested the passage of the Alien and Sedition Acts by the Federalists.

First Victim of the Sedition Act

Under the Sedition Act, truth was a defense against libel. If someone were libeled by a newspaper, that person had to prove the paper bore ill will against him or her to win in court. In practice, courts ruled by Federalist judges ignored these rules. The government did not have to prove that the defamatory statements were false. Instead, the defendant had to prove they were true.

The first man to face charges under the new Sedition Act was a member of Congress, Matthew Lyon. He had published a letter written by Joel Barlow. Commenting on a speech made by President Adams, Barlow wondered why Congress had not sent the president "to a mad house."

Lyon tried to defend himself on grounds that the Sedition Law was unconstitutional. The court ignored this defense. Found guilty, Lyon still wrote, published, and was reelected to Congress from his jail cell.

Anthony Haswell, a supporter of Lyon, faced charges when he wrote that Lyon was a victim of "the oppressive hand of usurped power."

The William Duane Trial

William Duane, the new publisher of the *Aurora,* also faced charges under the Sedition Act. Duane, a Republican, claimed that the British bribed federal officials, spending a fortune to do so. He also wrote that there was a secret alliance (partnership) between England and America against France.

Duane was arrested. But his trial was postponed for several months. The court gave a technical reason for the delay. The true reason rested with a letter Tench Coxe had sent to Duane. Coxe had been an assistant to the secretary of the treasury, Alexander Hamilton. John Adams had written the letter years earlier to Coxe. In it he had claimed the British were helping the Pinckney family of South Carolina win federal jobs. The letter showed evidence of British influence on the federal government.

While awaiting a new trial, Duane criticized a Senate bill. Then he refused to answer the senators' questions about his claims because his lawyers would not appear with him. They felt Senate rules prevented them

AN UNPOPULAR PRESIDENT

John Adams, America's second president, was not nearly as popular as George Washington had been. At that time, America had two political parties. The Federalists believed in a strong central government and rule by men of property. The Democratic Republicans upheld the principle of expanding democracy and voting rights. John Adams, a Federalist, had narrowly defeated Thomas Jefferson, a Democratic Republican, in the first true American presidential campaign in 1796. The Democratic Republicans disliked Adams intensely, and their newspapers frequently criticized him. Partly as a result, Congress passed the Alien and Sedition Acts. They made it criminal to publish "false, scandalous and malicious writing" about the president or his government.

from defending Duane. Duane was arrested again, this time for contempt of Congress. The charges were signed by Thomas Jefferson, then Senate president.

After Congress went home, the administration indicted Duane for libeling the Senate. When Jefferson became president, he dismissed that suit. In order to preserve the Senate's rights, Jefferson ordered a new suit to begin. However, a grand jury, called to determine evidence of Duane's guilt, refused to indict (bring charges against) him.

Others Charged

Because he was one of Duane's lawyers, Thomas Cooper faced charges for publishing a handbill months earlier. Prosecutor William Rawle treated the handbill as if it were meant to cause a rebellion. Cooper maintained that the statements he made in the handbill were true, that he held no malicious motives, and that he had attributed none of the statements to Adams. The judge, Samuel Chase, blocked Cooper's defense at every turn.

James Thompson Callender, who had faced charges for his writings about Adams, went before Justice Chase. Callender had no regard for truth or decency; Chase had little regard for truth or law. Chase struck down every reasonable defense request made, harassing Callender's lawyers until they withdrew from the case.

Callender's sentence ended the day the Sedition Act expired. The new Jefferson administration did not seek to renew the Act. It had proven to be poor law and poor politics. However, it would take an 1882 decision of the Supreme Court to determine once and for all that the Sedition Act was unconstitutional.

Suggestions for Further Reading

Miller, John C. *Crisis in Freedom.* Boston: Little, Brown and Co., 1951.

Smith, James Morton. *Freedom's Fetters, The Alien and Sedition Laws and American Civil Liberties.* Ithaca, NY: Cornell University Press, 1956.

Schenck v. U.S. Appeal: 1919

Appellant and Defendant: Charles T. Schenck

Appellee and Plaintiff: The United States of America

Appellant Claim: Not guilty, as convicted, of conspiracy to violate the Espionage Act of 1917

Chief Defense Lawyer: John Lord O'Brian

Chief Lawyers for Appellant: Henry J. Gibbons and Henry John Nelson

Justices: Louis D. Brandeis, John H. Clarke, William R. Day, Oliver Wendell Holmes, Charles Evans Hughes, Joseph McKenna, James C. McReynolds, Willis Van Devanter, and Chief Justice Edward D. White

Place: Washington, D.C.

Date of Decision: March 3, 1919

Decision: Guilty verdict unanimously affirmed

SIGNIFICANCE: This case marked the first time the Supreme Court ruled directly on the extent to which the U.S. government may limit speech. It produced, in the opinion written by Justice Oliver Wendell Holmes, two of that famous justice's most memorable and most often quoted statements on the law.

On June 15, 1917, just after the United States entered World War I, Congress passed the Espionage Act. This made it a federal crime to hinder the nation's war effort. The law followed on the heels of the Conscription Act of May 18, which enabled the government to draft men for military service.

At this time a political organization existed in America called the Socialist Party. It pushed for government ownership of factories, railroads, iron mines, and such. At a meeting at the party's headquarters in Philadelphia, Pennsylvania, in 1917, its leaders decided to print 15,000 leaflets to go to new draftees. The pamphlets included the words of the Thirteenth Amendment to the Constitution, which states: "Neither slavery nor involuntary servitude, except as a punishment for crime whereof the party shall have been duly convicted, shall exist within the United States or any place subject to their jurisdiction." The leaflets went on to read that a draftee was like a criminal convict. Drafting men (called conscription) was oppression. "Do not submit to intimidation," read the leaflets, urging readers to petition the government to repeal the Conscription Act.

Charles T. Schenck

As general secretary of the Socialist Party, Charles T. Schenck was in charge of the Philadelphia headquarters that mailed the leaflets. Officials quickly arrested him. They charged him with conspiring to cause a rebellion in the armed forces and getting in the way of the recruitment and enlistment of troops. Congress had made these acts crimes under various "sedition" laws. (Sedition means any illegal action that attempts to disrupt or overthrow the government.)

The government, however, produced no evidence that Schenck had influenced even one draftee. Instead, the prosecutors assumed that publication of the pamphlets was itself proof of his guilt.

The defense presented a simple argument: Schenck had exercised a right guaranteed by the First Amendment. This is the right to speak freely on a public issue. Nonetheless, the court found him guilty. Schenck then appealed to the federal courts and finally to the U.S. Supreme Court. All along he insisted on his right to freedom of speech.

At the Supreme Court in Washington, D.C., Schenck's defense lawyer argued that there was not enough evidence to prove that Schenck mailed out the leaflets. Reviewing the testimony in the case, Justice Oliver Wendell Holmes pointed out that Schenck was the general secretary of the Socialist Party. He was in charge of the headquarters that mailed the pamphlets. The general secretary's report of August 20, 1917, Holmes noted, had read, "Obtained new leaflets from printer and started work addressing envelopes." Holmes also pointed out that "there was a resolve that Comrade Schenck be allowed $125 for sending leaflets through the mail."

"No reasonable man," concluded Holmes, "could doubt that the defendant Schenck was largely instrumental in sending the circulars about."

"Clear and Present Danger"

Justice Holmes wrote the opinion that all of the justices signed. Noting that prosecutors had not shown that the leaflets had caused any revolt, he commented:

> Of course the document would not have been sent unless it had been intended to have some effect, and we do not see what effect it could be expected to have upon persons subject to the draft except to influence them to obstruct the carrying of it out.

Holmes agreed with the defense that the leaflets deserved First Amendment protection, but only in peacetime—not in war.

> We admit that in many places and in ordinary times the defendants in saying all that was said . . . would have been within their constitutional rights. But the character of every act depends upon the circumstances in which it is done. The most stringent

The 1919 Supreme Court. Until Schenck v. U.S. Appeal was heard, the Supreme Court judges had allowed the government to limit any speech that displayed a "dangerous tendency."

THE GREAT DISSENTER

Justice Oliver Wendell Holmes, who wrote the majority opinion on the Charles Schenck case, frequently disagreed with his more conservative colleagues on the court. Thus, he won the nickname "The Great Dissenter." Holmes even dissented from his own opinions—or at least, from the way his fellow justices sometimes applied them. In 1917, in *Abrams v. United States,* a Russian-born American named Jacob Abrams was found guilty of violating the Espionage Act when he scattered leaflets protesting the sending of U.S. troops into the Soviet Union to help suppress the Russian Revolution. Although seven of his colleagues upheld the conviction on the grounds that Abrams presented a "clear and present danger"—Holmes's own words—Holmes disagreed. He insisted that Abrams had a right to his opinion under the first Amendment, and that since Abrams had acted during peacetime, his actions posed no danger. In 1927, the court upheld the conviction of Socialist Benjamin Gitlow, who had supported an overthrow of the government. Again, Holmes dissented from those who had cited his own words, saying that there was "no present danger" of an attempt to overthrow the government by force.

[strongest] protection of free speech would not protect a man in falsely shouting fire in a theater and causing a panic.

Next came the justice's other memorable phrase:

The question in every case is whether the words used are used in such circumstances and are of such a nature as to create a clear and present danger that they will bring about the substantive evils that Congress has a right to prevent.

The "clear and present danger," said Holmes, is a question of "proximity and degree."

FREEDOM OF SPEECH

> When a nation is at war things that might be said in time of peace are such a hindrance [obstacle] to its effort that their utterance will not be endured so long as men fight and that no court could regard them as protected by any constitutional right.

Finally, the justice observed, it made no difference that Schenck and his associates had failed to get in the way of military recruiting. "The statute," he said, "punishes conspiracies to obstruct as well as actual obstruction."

> If the act [speaking or circulating a paper], its tendency and the intent with which it is done are the same, we perceive no ground for saying that success alone warrants making the act a crime.

With that, the Supreme Court upheld the judgment of the lower court. Charles T. Schenck faced ten years in prison on each of three counts. (However, he would serve them at the same time, so that he would actually spend a total of ten years in jail.)

The Schenck case, in establishing the "clear and present danger" test, marked a turning point in First Amendment (free speech) cases. Until then, Chief Justice Edward White and other judges had permitted the government to silence any speech that displayed a "dangerous tendency."

Suggestions for Further Reading

Burton, David H. *Oliver Wendell Holmes Jr.* Boston: Twayne Publishers, 1980.

Commager, Henry Steele and Milton Cantor. *Documents of American History.* Englewood Cliffs, NJ: Prentice Hall, 1988.

Friedman, Leon and Fred L. Israel, eds. *The Justices of the United States Supreme Court 1789–1969: Their Lives and Major Opinions.* New York: Chelsea House, 1969.

Novick, Sheldon M. *Honorable Justice: The Life of Oliver Wendell Holmes.* Boston: Little, Brown and Co., 1989.

Schnayerson, Robert. *The Illustrated History of the Supreme Court of the United States.* New York: Harry N. Abrams, 1986.

Witt, Elder, ed. *The Supreme Court and Individual Rights.* Washington: Congressional Quarterly, 1980.

Ulysses Trial: 1933

Defendant: "One Book Entitled *Ulysses* by James Joyce"

Crime Charged: Obscenity

Chief Defense Lawyers: Morris L. Ernst and Alexander Lindey

Chief Prosecutors: Nicholas Atlas, Samuel C. Coleman, and Martin Conboy

Judge: John M. Woolsey

Place: New York, New York

Dates of Trial: November 25–26, 1933

Verdict: The book was ruled not obscene

SIGNIFICANCE: Judge John Woolsey's decision in the *Ulysses* case marked a notable change in the policies of the courts and legislative bodies of the United States toward obscenity (something considered vulgar or offensive). Before this decision, it was universally agreed that a) laws banning obscenity were not in conflict with the First Amendment of the U.S. Constitution and b) the U.S. Post Office and the U.S. Customs Service held the power to determine obscenity. *Ulysses* became the major turning point in reducing government prohibition of obscenity.

James Joyce's novel *Ulysses* was in trouble from the moment it was published. When parts of it appeared in a magazine called the *Little Review* in 1919 and 1920, the U.S. Post Office seized three issues of the magazine and burned them. The publishers were then convicted of publishing obscene material, fined $50 each, and nearly sent to prison.

After that decision, several American and British publishers backed away from plans to publish the entire book. Joyce lost hope of finding a publisher. His friend Sylvia Beach, owner of the Shakespeare and Company bookstore in Paris, France, asked if her store might "have the honor" of bringing out the Irish novelist's book. In this way, *Ulysses* was first published in 1922 in Paris and instantly became a valuable collector's item—when it could be smuggled past British and American customs officials. By 1928, the U.S. Customs Court officially listed *Ulysses* among the obscene books to be kept from the hands and eyes of the American public.

James Joyce, author of Ulysses.

Meanwhile, such important literary figures as the novelist Virginia Woolf and the poets T. S. Eliot and Ezra Pound had already applauded Joyce's novel, labeling it a classic. In Paris, Bennett Cerf, founder of the Modern Library division of the American publisher Random House, told Joyce he would publish the book if he could do so legally.

2 Percent for Life

Cerf hired Morris L. Ernst, America's leading lawyer in obscenity cases. Ernst's fee, which depended on winning the case, was 5 percent of the sales price from the first 10,000 published copies of *Ulysses*. He also received 2 percent for life on all copies sold from subsequent printings of the book.

Ernst and his associate, Alexander Lindey, carefully planned their strategy. Early in 1932, they had a copy of the book mailed across the Atlantic from Paris. They fully expected U.S. Customs agents to seize it. However, it arrived untouched.

"So we had a friend bring a copy in," wrote Random House publisher Donald Klopfer many years later, "and we went down to the dock to welcome him! The Customs man saw the book and didn't want to do anything about it, but we insisted and got his superior over, and finally they took the book and wouldn't allow us to bring it into the U.S. because it was both obscene and sacrilegious [religious disrespect]." That copy was sent by Customs to the U.S. attorney in charge of libel cases. One meaning of the word "libel" is "the publication of blasphemous, treasonable, seditious [anti-government], or obscene writings or pictures."

Ernst then got the U.S. attorney to agree to have the case tried before a single judge, rather than a jury. Ernst managed to keep putting the case off until it came before one particular judge, John M. Woolsey. Woolsey was known to be a cultured gentleman who wrote elegant legal opinions and who loved old books and furniture.

The judge further postponed the case to give himself time to read *Ulysses* and the other books that had been written about it. At last, on November 25, 1933, the hearing began in a small, crowded court room that seated fewer than fifty people. One of the prosecuting attorneys turned and said to Ernst, "The government can't win this case." Ernst asked why. "The only way to win," said the prosecutor, "is to refer to the great number of vulgar four-letter words used by Joyce. But I can't do it." Ernst asked why not.

"Because there is a lady in the courtroom."

"But that's my wife," said Ernst. "She's a schoolteacher. She's seen all these words on toilet walls or scribbled on sidewalks by kids who enjoy them because of their being taboo."

Trial Begins

The government's case against Joyce's book made two clear objections to its publication. First, four-letter words could not be used in polite company. To combat that point, Ernst set out to prove that standards of obscenity change, and that by the standards of 1933, Joyce's choice of words did not make *Ulysses* obscene. To support his point, Ernst traced the roots and developing meanings of several four-letter words. Of one particularly

FREEDOM OF SPEECH

offensive word, he said, "Your Honor, it's got more honesty than phrases that modern authors use to connote [mean] the same experience."

"For example, Mr. Ernst?"

"Oh—'they slept together.' It means the same thing."

"That isn't usually even the truth," said Judge Woolsey.

Ernst later remarked that at that moment he knew "the case was half won."

The prosecution's second objection was to the openness of the stream of thought Joyce portrayed in his rendering of such characters as Molly Bloom. This was—as Ernst later put it—Joyce's dramatic "attempt to record those thoughts and desires which all mortals carry within themselves."

After the government appealed Judge Woolsey's decision to the Circuit Court of Appeals, Judge Learned Hand (pictured here) and his cousin, Judge Augustus Hand, affirmed the judgment.

The judge asked Ernst if he had read through Joyce's entire novel. "Yes, Judge," he replied. "I tried to read it in 1923 but could not get far into it. Last summer, I had to read it in preparation for this trial. And while lecturing in the Unitarian Church in Nantucket on the bank holiday . . ."

Judge Woolsey interrupted, "What has that to do with my question— have you read it?"

"While talking in that church I recalled after my lecture was finished that while I was thinking only about the banks and banking laws, I was in fact, at that same time, musing about the clock at the back of the church, the old woman in the front row, the tall shutters at the sides. Just

GREAT WRITERS ON JOYCE

Although James Joyce's *Ulysses* is generally considered to be one of the great novels of the twentieth century, it is not a book that everyone enjoys. The humorist and essayist E. B. White, for example, author of the children's books *Charlotte's Web* and *Stuart Little,* wrote: "It is a matter of some embarrassment to me that I have never read Joyce and a dozen other writers who have changed the face of literature. But there you are. I picked up *Ulysses* the other evening when my eye lit on it, and gave it a go. I stayed with it only for about twenty minutes, then was off and away. It takes more than a genius to keep me reading a book." Even more famously, Joyce's wife Nora, the basis for the famous character Molly Bloom within the book, is supposed to have asked her husband, "Why don't you write books people can read?"

as now, Judge, I have thought I was involved only in the defense of the book—I must admit at the same time I was thinking of the gold ring around your tie, the picture of George Washington behind your bench and the fact that your black judicial robe is slipping off your shoulders. This double stream of the mind is the contribution of *Ulysses.*"

The judge rapped on the bench before him. "Now for the first time I appreciate the significance of this book. I have listened to you as intently as I know how. I am disturbed by the dream scenes at the end of the book, and still I must confess, that while listening to you I have been thinking at the same time about the Hepplewhite furniture behind you."

"Judge," said Ernst, "that's the book."

An Artistic Decision

On December 6, Judge Woolsey delivered his opinion in *United States v. One Book Called Ulysses:*

> I hold that *Ulysses* is a sincere and honest book.
>
> . . . The words which are criticized as dirty are old Saxon words known to almost all men, and, I ven-

FREEDOM OF SPEECH

ture, to many women, and are such words as would be naturally and habitually used, I believe, by the types of folk whose life, physical and mental, Joyce is seeking to describe. In respect of the . . . theme of sex in the minds of his characters, it must always be remembered that his locale was Celtic and his season Spring. . . .

Ten minutes after the judge had declared that the novel was not obscene, Random House had its typesetters (workers who set type for printed material) at work on *Ulysses.*

The government appealed Woolsey's decision to a three-judge panel at the Circuit Court of Appeals, where Judge Learned Hand and his cousin, Judge Augustus Hand, affirmed the judgment (let the original decision stand). Judge Martin Manton dissented.

Suggestions for Further Reading

Arnold, Bruce. *The Scandal of Ulysses: The Sensational Life of a Twentieth-Century Masterpiece.* New York: St. Martin's Press, 1992.

Budgen, Frank. *James Joyce and the Making of "Ulysses" and Other Writings.* London: Oxford University Press, 1989.

Esterow, Milton. "Perspective: United States of America v. One Book Called *Ulysses.*" *Art News* (September 1990): 189–190.

Moscato, Michael and Leslie LeBlanc. *The United States of America v. One Book Entitled Ulysses by James Joyce.* Frederick, MD: University Publications of America, 1984.

Sultan, Stanley. *The Argument of Ulysses.* New York: Harper & Row, 1987.

Hollywood Ten Trials: 1948–1950

Defendants: Alvah Bessie, Herbert Biberman, Lester Cole, Edward Dmytryk, Ring Lardner Jr., John Howard Lawson, Albert Maltz, Sam Ornitz, Robert Adrian Scott, and Dalton Trumbo

Crime Charged: Contempt of Congress

Chief Defense Lawyers: Bartley Crum, Charles J. Katz, Robert W. Kenny, and Martin Popper

Chief Prosecutor: William Hitz

Judges: Edward M. Curran, Richmond B. Keech, and David A. Pine

Place: Washington, D.C.

Dates of Trials: April 12–19, 1948 (Lawson); May 3–5, 1948 (Trumbo); June 22–29, 1950 (Biberman, Cole, Dmytryk, Lardner, and Scott); June 23–29, 1950 (Bessie, Maltz, and Ornitz)

Verdicts: Guilty

Sentences: One year imprisonment and $1,000 fine (Bessie, Cole, Lardner, Lawson, Maltz, Ornitz, Scott, and Trumbo); six months and $500 fine (Biberman and Dmytryk)

SIGNIFICANCE: The Hollywood Ten case was one of the lowest points in the history of American civil liberties. It made political beliefs a reason for not hiring job applicants.

Respected author E. B. White once wrote, "Ten men have been convicted, not of wrong-doing but of wrong thinking; that is news in this country

FREEDOM OF SPEECH

and if I have not misread my history, it is bad news." He was referring to the trials of the Hollywood Ten.

During the 1930s and 1940s many people supported the American Communist Party. This was especially true in Hollywood. A number of writers, producers, actors, and directors in the film business felt the party was humane and progressive (forward thinking). By 1946, however, they began to change their minds. But they were too late to escape the wrath of the government and their own colleagues.

Hollywood Divided

The "Hollywood Ten," May 29, 1950.

At this time, two major unions were at war. They were the International Alliance of Theatrical Stage Employees and Motion Picture Machine Operators (IATSE) and the Conference of Studio Unions (CSU). In 1945, the CSU called a strike. The American Communist Party supported them. The IATSE leader Roy Brewer believed the Communists were trying to take over the movie business. As the strike dragged on for six months, he persuaded the heads of major studios to accept his ideas.

The Communists began losing support. Organizations formed to oppose them. One was led by Ronald Reagan (the future U.S. President). By 1947, the film capital seemed divided into two camps.

In Washington, D.C., a committee of Congress called the House Committee for the Investigation of Un-American Activities (HUAC) was following these events. The committee sent investigators to Hollywood where they interviewed anti-Communists belonging to the Motion Picture Alliance for the Preservation of American Ideals. These interviews led to public hearings in Washington.

"Friendly witnesses," all members of the Alliance, testified first. They included producer Jack L. Warner, novelist Ayn Rand, and actors Gary Cooper, Robert Montgomery, Ronald Reagan (then-president of the Screen Actors Guild), Robert Taylor, and Adolphe Menjou. Each described a Hollywood at the mercy of militant Communists whose orders came directly from Moscow.

Next, the committee called nineteen people, identified by the friendly witnesses as Communists, from a list of seventy-nine suspects. All were known as radicals. Most were writers. To HUAC, it seemed likely that they would use the movies to spread Communist propaganda to the American people at large. But no one knows why these particular individuals were called.

Hollywood
Ten Trials:
1948–1950

The Right to Remain Silent

HUAC chairman J. Parnell Thomas called eleven of the nineteen witnesses to testify. Some in the Hollywood community supported them. They formed a Committee for the First Amendment. Its sponsors included four U.S. senators, author Thomas Mann, and film producer Jerry Wald. It believed the First Amendment to the Constitution guaranteed not only the right to free speech but the right to remain silent.

Also supporting them were famous stars Humphrey Bogart, Lauren Bacall, Danny Kaye, Gene Kelly, Jane Wyatt, and Sterling Hayden, as well as director John Huston. The first witness, screenwriter John Howard Lawson, asked to read a statement. Each of the friendly witnesses had done so. However, when Chairman Thomas looked at the first line of the statement he said no. The line read, "For a week, this Committee has conducted an illegal and indecent trial of American citizens. . . ." It went on to accuse the committee of publicly smearing them. Thomas immediately denied Lawson permission to read it. The chairman then demanded an answer to the question, "Are you now, or have you ever been a member of the Communist Party of the United States?"

FREEDOM OF SPEECH

"The question of Communism is in no way related to the inquiry," Lawson replied. He went on to say that the committee was trying to "invade the basic rights of American citizens in all fields." The chairman turned to a nine-page single-spaced memo on Lawson's career. The committee's investigators had prepared it. Thomas had it read into the written record of the hearing, but he did not let Lawson respond. Soon the questions and answers developed into a shouting match. The committee repeatedly asked Lawson about his Communist membership. Finally, the chairman, pounding his gavel for quiet, ordered that the witness leave. Because he had refused to answer HUAC's questions about his Communist Party affiliations, the committee charged Lawson with contempt of Congress.

"I Would Hate Myself in the Morning"

The committee then questioned the other suspect witnesses. They were writers Dalton Trumbo, Albert Maltz, Alvah Bessie, Samuel Ornitz, Herbert Biberman, Lester Cole, Ring Lardner Jr., producer Robert Adrian Scott, and director Edward Dmytryk. All had to answer the same questions. None could read their statements. They would be known with Lawson as "The Hollywood Ten." Congress issued a citation (similar to a summons to appear in court) to all ten. This meant they could face charges of contempt of Congress. Asked repeatedly if he were a Communist, Lardner simply responded, "I could answer, but if I did, I would hate myself in the morning."

Soon after, a private meeting in New York's Waldorf-Astoria Hotel brought together Hollywood's top studio heads. They issued a statement saying they would fire any of the Hollywood Ten who worked for them. They would not hire the person back until "until such time as he . . . declares under oath that he is not a Communist." The group also said it would not hire a Communist or anyone that tried to topple the government by force.

The Blacklist Is Born

This was the origin of the famous Hollywood "blacklist." No artist in show business on the list could work without turning in the names of other suspects. To be on the list one had to have been accused of Communist Party membership, or called to testify before HUAC.

In November 1947, a special session of Congress met to allot (distribute) funds to fight the spread of Communism in Europe. In that session, Representative Thomas brought the citations for contempt given to the Hollywood Ten. The House voted in favor of the citations 346 to 17.

On April 12, 1948, John Howard Lawson was brought to trial, followed three weeks later by Trumbo. In each brief trial, the jury found the defendant guilty of contempt of Congress. Lawson's and Trumbo's sentences were then suspended while they appealed their convictions.

Supreme Court Refuses Review

As Lawson's and Trumbo's attorneys filed appeals, the eight other members of the Hollywood Ten surrendered their right to trial by jury, saying that they would stand on the records of the jury trials of the first two defendants. However, they reserved the privilege of appealing (a legal method for obtaining a new trial or reversal of conviction) any sentence they might receive to a higher court. All ten were confident that the Supreme Court would clear them. But in the summer of 1949, two liberal justices, Frank Murphy and Wiley Rutledge, died. Their successors, Tom Clark and Sherman Minton, shifted the court majority to the conservative side. That majority refused to review the convictions of Lawson and Trumbo.

On June 9, 1950, Lawson and Trumbo began their jail terms. The trials of the remaining eight opened on June 22 before Judges Edward M. Curran and David A. Pine and Judge Richmond B. Keech. By June 29, all were found guilty. Six received one-year sentences and $1,000 fines. Dmytryk and Biberman, however, for reasons never explained, were fined $500 each and jailed for only six months.

Defense lawyers Robert W. Kenny and Martin W. Popper introduced motions for acquittal (suspension of sentence), and release on bail pending appeal. The judges denied them all. Since the remaining eight had agreed to stand on the records of the jury trials of the first two, and the Supreme Court had denied any review, these eight were sentenced and jailed at once.

Aftermath

From their prison cells, all ten men sued their employers for breach of contract. The studios finally settled out of court for $259,000, to be shared—but not equally—by all the defendants, who had by that time been released from prison.

Some returned to their professions but had to write in the "black market"—using pen names—for years. Trumbo wrote scripts under other

McCARTHY AND McCARTHYISM

The Hollywood Ten testified before the House of Representatives. Meanwhile, in the Senate, another anti-Communist leader was gaining a reputation. He was Senator Joseph McCarthy (1909–1957), a Republican from Wisconsin. Ironically, McCarthy had shown no particular concern over Communism before 1950. But in February of that year he told a women's club in Wheeling, West Virginia, that he held, "here in my hand," a list of 205 employees in the State Department who were Communist Party members. He claimed they were part of a spy ring. The press picked up this dramatic statement, and McCarthy's career as a Communist hunter took off. The number of Communists McCarthy claimed were employed by the government changed almost every day. Still he never produced any evidence. He continued to make headlines, and the word "McCarthyism" came to mean "patriotic anti-Communism," even though a Senate committee had investigated and dismissed his charges. Eventually, McCarthy went too far, however. In 1954, he claimed that the U.S. Army was also full of Communists. The journalist Edward R. Murrow showed excerpts on live television of the "Army-McCarthy hearings" held to investigate this charge. Although the hearings came to no strong conclusion, McCarthy lost his credibility and was eventually censured by the Senate.

names for ten years, winning an Oscar for Best Motion Picture Story in 1957. Lardner's blacklisting ended in 1964; he won an Oscar in 1971 for writing the screenplay for *M*A*S*H*. Maltz wrote novels while remaining on the blacklist for twenty years. Cole taught screenwriting and reviewed films. Lawson moved from creating plays and films to writing about them and teaching. Bessie wrote novels.

In 1951, Dmytryk appeared before HUAC and retracted his former testimony, naming twenty-six individuals as Communists. Over the next twenty-five years, he directed one film each year. Ornitz wrote a best-selling novel. Scott wrote and produced for television. Biberman formed an independent production company and produced a prize-winning film.

In 1948, HUAC Chairman J. Parnell Thomas was convicted of conspiracy to cheat the government by taking payoffs from his staff. By the time two of the Hollywood Ten—Cole and Lardner—were imprisoned in the federal penitentiary at Danbury, Connecticut, in 1950, Thomas was already there serving his sentence.

Suggestions for Further Reading

Aaron, Daniel. *Writers on the Left.* New York: Harcourt, Brace & World, 1961.

Belfrage, Cedric. *The American Inquisition.* New York: Bobbs-Merrill Co., 1973.

Bessie, Alvah. *Inquisition in Eden.* New York: Macmillan Co., 1965.

Biberman, Herbert. *Salt of the Earth.* Boston: Beacon Press, 1965.

Cook, Bruce. *Dalton Trumbo.* New York: Charles Scribner's Sons, 1977.

Dick, Bernard F. *Radical Innocence.* Lexington: University Press of Kentucky, 1989.

Donner, Frank J. *The Un-Americans.* New York: Ballantine, 1961.

Goodman, Walter. *The Committee.* New York: Farrar, Straus & Giroux, 1969.

Kahn, Gordon. *Hollywood on Trial.* New York: Boni & Gaer, 1948.

Kanfer, Stefan. *A Journal of the Plague Years.* New York: Atheneum, 1973.

Kempton, Murray. *Part of Our Time.* New York: Simon & Schuster, 1955.

Lardner, Ring Jr. *The Lardners.* New York: Harper & Row, 1976.

Navasky, Victor S. *Naming Names.* New York: Viking, 1980.

Taylor, Telford. *Grand Inquest.* New York: Simon & Schuster, 1955.

Vaughn, Robert. *Only Victims.* New York: G. P. Putnam's Sons, 1972.

New York Times Company v. Sullivan: 1964

Appellant: The New York Times Company

Appellee: L. B. Sullivan

Appellant Claims: That when the Supreme Court of Alabama upheld a libel judgment against *The New York Times,* it violated the newspaper's free speech and due process rights. These rights are defined by the First and Fourteenth Amendments of the Constitution and certain Supreme Court decisions. Also, that an advertisement published in the *Times* was not libelous and that the Supreme Court should reverse the decision of the Alabama trial court

Chief Defense Lawyers: Sam Rice Baker, M. Roland Nachman Jr., and Robert E. Steiner III

Chief Lawyers for Appellant: Herbert Brownell, Thomas F. Daly, and Herbert Wechsler

Justices: Hugo L. Black, William J. Brennan Jr., Tom C. Clark, William O. Douglas, Arthur J. Goldberg, John M. Harlan, Potter Stewart, Earl Warren, and Byron R. White

Place: Washington, D.C.

Date of Decision: March 9, 1964

Decision: The Alabama courts' decisions were reversed

SIGNIFICANCE: The U.S. Supreme Court greatly expanded Constitutional guarantees of freedom of speech and the press. It halted the rights of states to award damages in libel (attacking a person's reputation) suits according to state laws.

On March 9, 1964, Supreme Court Justice William J. Brennan Jr. defined actual malice as "knowledge that it was false or with reckless disregard of whether it was false or not."

On March 23, 1960, the "Committee to Defend Martin Luther King and the Struggle for Freedom in the South" paid *The New York Times* to publish a full-page advertisement. It called for public support and money to defend Reverend Martin Luther King Jr. Reverend King was struggling to gain equal rights for African Americans. Bearing the title "Heed Their Rising Voices" in large, bold print, the ad ran in the March 29, 1960, edition of the *Times*.

The ad criticized several Southern areas, including the city of Montgomery, Alabama, for breaking up civil rights demonstrations. It mentioned no one by name as responsible. Instead, the ad declared that "Southern violators of the Constitution" were determined to destroy King and his civil rights movement. The reference was to the entire South, not just to Montgomery or other specific localities.

Sullivan Sues

Over 600,000 copies of the March 29, 1960, *Times* edition appeared. Only a couple hundred went to Alabama subscribers. Montgomery City Commissioner L. B. Sullivan learned of the ad through an editorial in a local newspaper. On April 19, 1960, an angry Sullivan sued the *Times* in the Circuit Court of Montgomery County, Alabama. He claimed that the *Times* had defamed (libeled) him and that the ad's reference to Montgomery and to

FREEDOM OF SPEECH

"Southern violators of the Constitution" had the effect of attacking him and abusing his reputation. He demanded $500,000.

On November 3, 1960, the Circuit Court found the *Times* guilty. It awarded Sullivan the full $500,000 in damages. The Alabama Supreme Court upheld the Circuit Court judgment on August 30, 1962. In its opinion, the Alabama Supreme Court gave an extremely broad definition of libel. It said libel occurs when printed words injure a person's reputation, profession, trade, or business; charge him with an illegal offense; or bring contempt upon that person.

Supreme Court Protects the Press

The advertisement published in The New York Times *on March 29, 1960, asked for public support and money to defend Martin Luther King Jr. (pictured here) and the civil rights struggle in the South.*

The *Times*'s chief lawyers took the case to the U.S. Supreme Court. On January 6, 1964, the two sides appeared at a hearing in Washington, D.C., before the court. On March 9, 1964, the Supreme Court unanimously reversed the Alabama court decisions. The court held that Alabama libel law violated the *Times*'s First Amendment rights to freedom of the press.

The court was recognizing what Alabama's own newspapers had been writing. Alabama's libel law was a powerful tool in the hands of anti-civil rights officials. The court's decision canceled out Alabama's overly broad libel law so that politicians could not use it anymore to threaten freedom of the press.

MONTGOMERY DEMONSTRATIONS

Montgomery was the site of much civil rights activity, largely because of the events set off by Rosa Parks. In 1955, Parks, then a forty-three-year-old seamstress working at a Montgomery department store, was on her way home from work. At that time, Montgomery city buses were segregated. Whites sat up front, blacks sat in the back. When Parks could not find a seat there, she sat in the middle of the bus. The driver told her to move to make room for new white passengers. Parks refused—and was arrested. She had been a civil rights activist for some time, working with the local chapter of the National Association for the Advancement of Colored People (NAACP). Now she worked with local civil rights leaders who decided to use her case to end segregation on public transportation. Parks's pastor, the twenty-seven-year-old Martin Luther King Jr. led a boycott of Montgomery city buses. The boycott lasted for over a year, ending with a November 1956 Supreme Court decision against the bus segregation. Meanwhile, local officials bitterly resisted the boycott. Police arrested Parks a second time for refusing to pay her fine. They also arrested King first on a drunk-driving charge, then for conspiring to organize an illegal boycott. Montgomery continued to be a center of civil rights activity throughout the early 1960s.

Next, Justice William J. Brennan stated that a new federal rule was needed. It would prohibit a public official from recovering damages for a defamatory falsehood (lie) about his official conduct unless he proved that the statement was made with actual malice (ill will).

Sullivan had not proven that the *Times* acted with ill will. What constitutes malice? The court defined it as knowing that a printed statement was false or making it "with reckless disregard of whether it was false or not."

Court Broadens Freedom of Speech and Press

After *New York Times Company v. Sullivan,* the court continued to advance freedom of speech and press. They decided that for any "public fig-

FREEDOM OF SPEECH

ure" to sue for libel successfully, she or he would have to prove "actual malice." Public figures include anyone widely known in the community. This requirement protects anyone accused of libel, not just a newspaper. The *Sullivan* case was a tremendous advance for freedom of speech. It prevented genuine criticism from being silenced by the threat of damaging and expensive libel lawsuits. *Sullivan* has not, however, become a license for the newspapers to print anything that they see fit to print. Defendants who do act with ill will can receive severe penalties.

Suggestions for Further Reading

Bain, George. "A Question of Honor, Malice and Rights." *Maclean's* (October 1984): 64.

Friedman, Robert. "Freedom of the Press: How Far Can it Go?" *American Heritage* (October–November 1982): 16–22.

Hopkins, W. Wat. *Actual Malice: Twenty-Five Years After Times v. Sullivan.* New York: Praeger, 1989.

Lewis, Anthony. *Make No Law: The Sullivan Case and the First Amendment.* New York: Random House, 1991.

Winfield, Richard N. *New York Times v. Sullivan: The Next Twenty Years.* New York: Practicing Law Institute, 1984.

Chicago Seven Trial: 1969–1970

Defendants: Rennard C. Davis, David Dellinger, John R. Froines, Thomas H. Hayden, Abbott Hoffman, Jerry C. Rubin, Bobby G. Seale, and Lee Weiner

Crimes Charged: Incitement to riot and conspiracy

Chief Defense Lawyers: William Kunstler and Leonard Weinglass

Chief Prosecutors: Roger Cubbage, Thomas A. Foran, and Richard G. Shultz

Judge: Julius J. Hoffman

Place: Chicago, Illinois

Dates of Trial: September 24, 1969–February 20, 1970

Verdict: Dellinger, Davis, Hayden, Hoffman, Rubin: guilty; Froines and Weiner: not guilty; Seale: mistrial

Sentence: Five years in jail, $5,000 fine

SIGNIFICANCE: This was the most hotly debated—and certainly the most chaotic—political trial in American history.

The 1968 Democratic National Convention marked a turning point in America. Anti-Vietnam War protesters of every political belief flocked to Chicago, Illinois. They wanted to stop the conference and provoke authorities. They succeeded beyond their wildest expectations. Battles in the streets between police and protesters led to grand jury charges against eight left-wing radicals: Rennie Davis, David Dellinger, John Froines, Tom Hayden, Abbie Hoffman, Jerry Rubin, Bobby Seale, and Lee Weiner. Officials

charged each with having crossed state lines to start a riot. This offense had been on the law books less than nine months. However, the government wanted to put a stop to the anti-war protests. That determination led to what amounted to an attack on every type of political dissent.

Trial Opens

Rarely does a judge achieve or desire the celebrity that this trial gave Judge Julius Hoffman. From day one—September 24, 1969—he displayed a hostile attitude that seemed improper. Seventy–three years old, humorless, and with a reputation for handing down rulings that favored the government, Hoffman's hostility toward the defendants that was obvious.

On opening day U.S. Attorney Thomas Foran angrily objected because four of the lawyers who represented the defendants were missing. All four had sent telegrams withdrawing from the case. Judge Hoffman immediately issued warrants for the arrest of the absent attorneys. He then made matters worse by temporarily jailing two of them for contempt of court—an act that obstructs or interferes with the orderly ad-

Jerry Rubin, one of the members of the "Chicago Seven," displays a note from fellow defendant Bobby Seale, who had been gagged and manacled during the previous day's trial session.

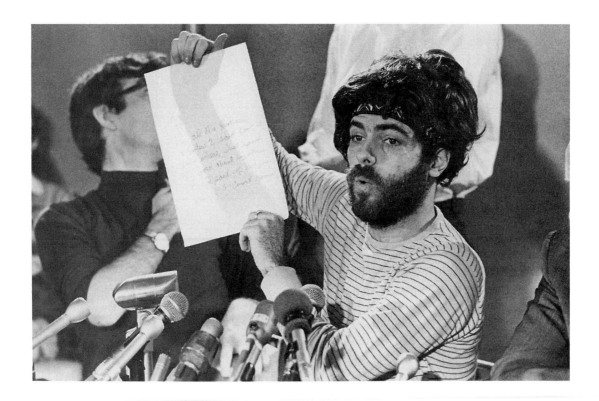

ministration of justice. Law professors and lawyers protested these actions so strongly that Hoffman canceled the order and allow the lawyers to withdraw.

William Kunstler and Leonard Weinglass ended up sharing the responsibilities of defending the accused. Neither had an easy task. Besides battling the judge, they had Bobby Seale to control. Seale, a militant black activist, refused to accept either one as his attorney. On September 26, he submitted a handwritten note to the court. It read: "I submit to Judge Julius Hoffman that the trial be postponed until a later date when I, Bobby G. Seale, can have the 'legal council [sic] of choice who is effective. . . .'" He went on, "And if my constitutional rights are not respected by this court then other lawyers on record here . . . do not speak for me . . . I fire them now." Judge Hoffman, taking offense at being characterized in the note as "a blatant racist," angrily denied Seale's request.

Seale Bound and Gagged

Seale would not be quiet. He continued to disrupt the trial, yelling "pig" at Hoffman and comparing him to a plantation slave owner. Finally, on October 29, Hoffman's patience ran out, and he ordered guards to gag Seale and tie him to a chair. As Seale struggled to free himself, guards strong-armed him. This brought Kunstler to his feet in loud protest. He shouted: "Your Honor, are we going to stop this medieval torture that is going on in this courtroom? I think this is a disgrace."

Judge Hoffman declared a mistrial with regard to Seale, severing his case from that of the other seven defendants. He also found Seale guilty of sixteen counts of contempt and jailed him for four years.

Trial of Other Defendants Proceeds

The prosecution had a strong case against the remaining defendants, yet the chaos surrounding Seale nearly overshadowed it. The main witnesses against the others were police officers, who testified that the defendants had tried to provoke them. Robert Murray, an undercover police sergeant, described being in Lincoln Park, the scene of a particularly violent clash between police and demonstrators. There he saw defendant Jerry Rubin talking to a television news reporter. When the reporter indicated that he was about to leave, Murray claimed, Rubin called the reporter back, saying, "Wait, don't go right now. We're going out in the ball field. We want to see what these pigs [police officers] are going to do about it."

**FREEDOM OF
SPEECH**

Murray carefully watched Rubin's behavior throughout the night:

> I saw him walking through the park, walking up to
> small groups, having a conversation with them and
> leaving . . . I heard him say that 'we have to fight
> the pigs in the park tonight . . . we're not going to
> let them take the park.'

Crucial evidence of an "intent to riot" came with the testimony of newspaper reporter Dwayne Oklepek. He spoke of attending a meeting on August 9, 1968, at which defendants Hayden, Davis, and Froines were present. Oklepek told the court how Davis produced a street map of Chicago and plans for a march on August 28, 1968. Oklepek said: "Mr. Davis felt that the separate groups should form up and then attempt to move their way south to the Loop area. . . . He went on to say that he thought these groups should try to disrupt traffic, should smash windows, run through stores and through the streets."

"Do you recall anything else that was discussed?" asked Foran.

"Someone asked Mr. Davis what would occur if it were impossible for the demonstrators to get out of Lincoln Park . . . and Mr. Davis said, 'That's easy, we just riot.'"

The prosecution had a strong case against some of the defendants. However, whether their words and actions constituted the crime outlawed by the recent anti-riot law remained in doubt. Under that law, to be guilty, the defendants had to cross a state line.

Star Witnesses Appear

First, defense attorney William Kunstler brought character witnesses to the stand. The list included many celebrities. Writer Norman Mailer and civil rights leader Reverend Jesse Jackson testified. So did poet Allen Ginsburg, novelist William Styron, and popular singers Arlo Guthrie, Country Joe McDonald, Judy Collins, and Phil Ochs. Even a British Member of Parliament, Anne Kerr, took the stand.

Apart from the publicity value lent by their names, there was little that these witnesses could offer in court. The defendants did not help themselves, either. All seemed more interested in presenting their anti-war views than in defending themselves. Abbie Hoffman's opening remarks set the tone. Asked to identify himself for the record, he said, "My name is Abbie. I am an orphan of America. . . . I live in Woodstock Nation." (He was referring to the massive rock concert that took place at Woodstock, New York, earlier that year.) When defense counsel Leonard Weinglass asked for more, Hoffman eagerly seized his opportunity. "It is a nation of alienated young people. We carry it around with us as a state of mind." Weinglass concluded his examination with a simple question:

"Did you enter into an agreement with [the other defendants] to come to the city of Chicago for the purpose of encouraging and promoting violence during the Convention week?"

"An agreement?"

"Yes."

"We couldn't agree on lunch!"

Cross-examination by prosecutor Richard Schultz was less friendly but equally insignificant. Hoffman and his fellow defendants refused to recognize the court's authority. Their crude, childlike antics exasperated Judge Hoffman. The judge vented his anger with a series of improper remarks directed toward the defendants and their lawyers.

After months of confusion and much rambling testimony, closing arguments began on February 10, 1970. Thomas Foran had the last word. Describing the defendants, he said, "They are not kids. Davis, the youngest one, took the witness stand. He is twenty-nine. These are highly sophisticated, educated men and they are evil men." Laughter greeted this remark.

Judge Hoffman's final charge to the jury was remarkably subdued. On February 14 the jury withdrew to deliberate.

Guilty Verdicts Multiply

While the jury was out, Judge Hoffman dealt with the numerous contempt of court citations he had handed down during the trial. He found all seven defendants and their attorneys guilty, for a total of 159 counts. He then imposed sentences. They ranged from more than two months for Weiner to four years for Kunstler.

On February 18, 1970, the jurors declared that Davis, Dellinger, Hayden, Hoffman, and Rubin were guilty. The jury found Froines and Weiner innocent. Two days later Judge Hoffman passed sentence. Each defendant received the maximum penalty of five years in prison and a $5,000 fine.

A long round of appeals followed. On May 11, 1972, the Seventh Circuit Court of Appeals reversed all the contempt of court convictions. Because Judge Hoffman had been the target of the defendants' attacks,

FREEDOM OF SPEECH

OPPOSITION TO THE VIETNAM WAR

The events leading to the Chicago Seven trial grew out of anger at the fact that U.S. soldiers were fighting in Vietnam. Anti-war protests had begun as early as 1963, when President Lyndon B. Johnson sent some 16,300 U.S. military advisors to South Vietnam. Johnson had run for re-election in 1964 on a promise not to "widen" the war. Still, he continued to send money and troops, and protests mounted. In 1968, Senator Eugene McCarthy challenged Johnson by announcing his intention to seek the Democratic Presidential nomination. On March 12, in a stunning upset, the relatively unknown McCarthy nearly defeated Johnson in the New Hampshire primary. Four days later, the more well-known Senator Robert F. Kennedy also declared his intention to challenge Johnson. On March 31, Johnson announced that he would not run again. His vice president, Hubert H. Humphrey, became the mainstream Democratic contender for the nomination. When Robert Kennedy was assassinated in June, McCarthy, a much weaker candidate, stood as the lone challenger to Humphrey. By the time of the Democratic convention in August, it seemed clear that the party would nominate Humphrey, who was associated with Johnson and the war. The stage was set for the anti-war protests that led to the arrests of Bobby Seale and the Chicago Seven.

the appellate court ruled, he should not also have been the one to decide the contempt charges he had imposed to punish his attackers.

In November 1972 the appellate court overturned all five incitement to riot convictions, citing numerous errors by Judge Hoffman and the prosecution attorneys. In particular, they criticized Judge Hoffman's "deprecatory and often antagonistic attitude toward the defense." Seale, too, had his conviction overturned.

The government dropped its incitement to riot case, but it did press the contempt charges. In November 1973, a jury again found Dellinger, Kunstler, Hoffman, and Rubin guilty of this offense. However, Judge Edward Gignoux, who heard the retrial of these charges, declined to impose further jail sentences.

The Chicago Seven trial was a low point in the history of American justice. Nobody emerged from the conflict looking good. The only real victor, perhaps, was the legal system itself. Mocked and derided by the defendants, it ultimately came to the assistance of those who criticized it most loudly.

Suggestions for Further Reading

Belknap, Michael P. *American Political Trials.* Westport, CT: Greenwood Press, 1981.

Clavir, Judy and John Spitzer. *The Conspiracy Trial.* Indianapolis: Bobbs-Merrill, 1970.

Epstein, Jason. *The Great Conspiracy Trial.* New York: Random House, 1970.

Goldberg, Stephanie Benson. "Lessons of the 60's." *ABA Journal* (May 15, 1987): 32ff.

Shultz, John. *Motion Will Be Denied.* New York: William Morrow, 1972.

Peter Wright (Spycatcher) Trials: 1986–1988

Defendant: Peter Wright

Crimes Charged: Breach of confidence, violation of Official Secrets Act

Chief Defense Lawyer: Michael Turnbull (Australia)

Chief Prosecutor: Theo Simos (Australia)

Judges: Australia: Justice Phillip Powell; Australian appeal: Justice Michael Kirby, presiding; House of Lords, London: Lord Bridge, presiding

Places: Sydney, Australia; London, England

Dates of Trials: Sydney: November 17–December 10, 1986; London: July 28–30, 1987; Sydney (appeal): July 27–September 24, 1987; London (appeal): November–December 1987; London (appeal): February 11–October 12, 1988

Verdicts: First trial: Injunction to suppress publication denied; Australian appeal trial: injunction denied; House of Lords: injunction against quoting from *Spycatcher* lifted October 12, 1988

SIGNIFICANCE: The trials brought public attention to the claims by Peter Wright that Roger Hollis, director general of the British Security Service (known as MI-5) from 1956–1965, had been a possible Soviet agent and that MI-5 had worked in 1974–1976 to oust Prime Minister Harold Wilson because the agency suspected he was a possible Soviet agent of influence. The effort of the British government to suppress publication of a memoir, *Spycatcher,* by Wright detailing these charges resulted in the book becoming an international bestseller and in discrediting the British effort at censorship.

Chapman Pincher was a British journalist who wrote about spies. In September 1980, he went to the home of Lord Victor Rothschild to meet with Peter Wright. Wright had been an official with the British Security Service called MI-5. In 1980, however, he was living in Australia on a small pension. He suggested to Pincher that they work together on a memoir about Wright's career with the spy agency. The two men entered into an agreement that Pincher would interview Wright and then write a long, revealing account of the Security Service. They would call the book *Their Trade Is Treachery*. Under this agreement, Wright would receive half of the income from the book.

On September 25, 1987, Peter Wright talks to reporters about his candid autobiography, Spycatcher, and his court struggle to have this book published in Australia.

Their Trade Is Treachery

In the book, Pincher wrote about Kim Philby, Guy Burgess, Donald Maclean, and Anthony Blunt—MI-5 agents who were Soviet spies. He also wrote that the former director of MI-5, Roger Hollis, was suspected of being a double agent at the Security Service. In other words, some thought he was really working for the Soviet Union. Hollis had never been fully cleared. If the charges against Hollis were true, this would mean that the Soviets had completely infiltrated the British Security Service during the cold war (the term used to describe the struggle for power and prestige between the Western powers and the Communist bloc from the end of World War II until 1989.)

Wright had joined the Security Service in 1955. He was the service's first scientific officer, using electronic methods of spying. Earlier, he had worked with the U.S. Central Intelligence Agency (CIA). He was still in contact with James J. Angleton, the head of the CIA unit charged with combating Soviet spying. Wright was for a short time the assistant director of MI-5 before he retired in 1976.

In addition to revealing MI-5's suspicions about Roger Hollis, Wright told Pincher another shocking story. He said that MI-5 also suspected the former Labour party leader and British Prime Minister Harold Wilson of being a Soviet agent. Wright said Angleton agreed with this view, and that MI-5 had tried to remove Wilson from office. Wright also told Pincher that during 1974–1976, MI-5 had bugged several meetings of Wilson's cabinet. The agency had hoped to force several of his advisors to resign.

In 1980, Pincher and his publisher, through a third person called "the arbiter," contacted MI-5 and MI-6 (the British Secret Intelligence Service specializing in spying abroad). They wanted them to read what Pincher had written before they published it. Officials at both MI-5 and MI-6 decided not to interfere with the publication of Pincher's book. Pincher's story came out as a book and as a newspaper series. As a result, Conservative Prime Minister Margaret Thatcher admitted to Parliament that Hollis had been under investigation. She indicated, however, that MI-5 had cleared him of suspicion.

British Seek to Block Publication of Next Book

Five years later, Peter Wright worked with another author, Paul Greengrass, on *Spycatcher: The Candid Autobiography of a Senior Intelligence Officer* (1987). It also referred to the Hollis investigation and the MI-5 plot against Wilson. If Wright had been living in Britain, the government could have prosecuted him under the Official Secrets Act for revealing confidential information. They could have blocked the publication of his book. However, Australia would not send him to Britain to be tried under the act.

The British government tried to prevent publication of the book in Australia by saying that Wright's revelations were a breach of confidence. The government filed a case in March 1986 that went to trial in November 1986. The decision of the trial court was appealed several times. As a result, the book's release was delayed in Australia. In the United States, however, Viking Press published the book in mid-1987.

Appeals by the British government to courts in Australia and to the House of Lords in Britain failed. Much of the material in *Spycatcher* had already appeared in *Their Trade Is Treachery,* which had been published without any attempt to censor it. The British government could not now claim that Wright was violating the confidentiality of the security agencies. *Spycatcher* had already been published in the United States, and books were on sale in Britain by the time of the court appeals. British newspapers also fought the government's attempts to stop the book on grounds of freedom of the press. The newspapers claimed that the government was attempting not to protect national security, but to cover up evidence of a scandal. This was an argument that carried a great deal of weight with the British public and with international public opinion.

The first trial in Australia was named *HM Attorney General v. Heinemann (Australia) and Another* [Peter Wright]. The judge ruled that the British government had given up any claims of confidentiality by giving in to the original publication. The British government could not, therefore, claim that confidentiality was breached by the proposal by Heinemann to publish the book in Australia. The judge dismissed a claim made by Wright's defense lawyer that there had been a conspiracy to publish Pincher's book as a means of damage control. The judge added that it was to Australia's benefit to publish the book there because it revealed information about Roger Hollis, who had helped to set up Australia's own Security Intelligence Organization.

Chapman Pincher later wrote a book about the trials called *The Spycatcher Affair* (published in Britain as *A Web of Deception*). In it he pointed out several reasons for Britain's failure in the Australian courts. One problem was that Sir Robert Armstrong, the British government's primary witness, was not familiar with Australian court practices and did not know all the details of the case. He did not know that MI-5 and MI-6 had reviewed *Their Trade Is Treachery.* He also did not realize that they could

easily have stopped the book from being published by passing a message through "the arbiter." Pincher argued in *The Spycatcher Affair* that it was just such practices of confidentiality and secrecy that prevented the British government from making a good case before the Australian courts.

Courts Reject All Government Appeals

The British government filed an appeal of the trial judge's decision with the appeals court of the Australian state of New South Wales in March 1987. Before the hearing began, the Viking Press edition of *Spycatcher* appeared in the United States. At the same time, a high court of the British House of Lords took up the British case, which it heard July 28–30, 1987. The lords serving as judges ruled 3–2 to continue the ban on publication of *Spycatcher* in Britain during the course of a trial involving two newspapers, the *Guardian* and the *Observer,* that was also in progress. In February 1988, judges in the newspaper case ruled against the government. After a final appeal to the House of Lords, the ban on newspaper reporting on *Spycatcher* was lifted on October 12, 1988.

The New South Wales appeals court met in late July 1987. The court did not, however, issue an opinion until that September. It then ruled that although the British government had tried to sue on grounds of breach of confidentiality, in fact it had attempted to use the Australian courts to enforce the Official Secrets Act. The case was then appealed to the high court in Canberra (the Australian equivalent of the U.S. Supreme Court). In the meanwhile, the Australian ban on publication was lifted on the grounds that any continuation was pointless because so much of the book had already been released. The book was published in Australia by Heinemann in October 1987.

Peter Wright's defense attorney, Michael Turnbull, accused Sir Robert Armstrong of having been sent to Australia to lie for the British government. Although the court rejected this charge, Armstrong admitted that his position called for him to be "economical with the truth." It was a remark that made him an object of ridicule in the Australian press.

Aftermath

Publicity surrounding the trials and appeals made *Spycatcher* a best seller. Although sales approaching one million helped to solve Wright's financial problems, he was widely criticized as a man who had sold his government's secrets. Follow-up works by Pincher, Turnbull, and journalist

BRITAIN'S PRIME MINISTER

Sir (James) Harold Wilson was Britain's prime minister from 1964 to 1970 and from 1974 to 1976. His political career began in 1945 when, as an economist, he was elected to Parliament as a Labour party member. Wilson soon became the spokesperson for the Labour Party's left wing, and he became party leader in 1963. The following year, he was elected prime minister. Wilson used his position to try to establish closer ties between Britain and Europe, as well as to mend the ailing British economy.

David Leigh generally concluded that Wright's memory was not always accurate and that he built up his own role. However, both Pincher and Leigh reported that the information regarding the investigation of Roger Hollis and the plot against Harold Wilson had been confirmed by others.

Altogether, the disclosures in books by Pincher, Wright, and Leigh caused great embarrassment to both of Britain's political parties, the Conservative Party and the Labour Party. The books left important questions unanswered. If the charges against either Hollis or Wilson were true, then the Labour Party's leaders were Soviet pawns (those that can be used to further the purposes of another). If the charges were false, then the Conservatives had revealed their contempt for British democracy by using MI-5 to investigate left-of-center politicians and drive them from office. British voters were left only with a sense of unease. On thing was, however, absolutely clear in the aftermath of the "spycatcher affair:" censoring former spies' memoirs, even when publishing them would violate British law, is pointless when publication begins abroad.

Suggestions for Further Reading

Leigh, David. *The Wilson Plot.* New York: Pantheon, 1988.

Pincher, Chapman. *The Spycatcher Affair.* New York: St. Martin's Press, 1988.

Wright, Peter. *Spycatcher: The Candid Autobiography of a Senior Intelligence Officer.* New York: Viking, 1987.

HUMAN RIGHTS

Anne Hutchinson's Trials: 1637 and 1638

Defendant: Anne Hutchinson

Crimes Charged: Traducing the ministers and their ministry (attacking church leaders and their authority) and heresy

Chief Defense Lawyer: None

Chief Prosecutors: Civil trial: John Winthrop; religious trial: the Reverend John Davenport

Judges: Civil trial: John Winthrop and the Magistrates of Massachusetts; religious trial: John Wilson and the ministers of the Church of Boston

Places: Civil trial: Newtown (Cambridge); religious trial: Boston, Massachusetts

Dates of trials: Civil trial: November 7–8, 1637; religious trial: March 22, 1638

Verdicts: Guilty

Sentences: Banished from the colony and excommunicated (deprived of church membership) from the Church of Boston

SIGNIFICANCE: Anne Hutchinson became the most famous of the women who rebelled against the religious authority of the Massachusetts Bay Colony's male leadership.

When the Puritans established the Massachusetts Bay Colony, they wanted to be free of the religious prejudice they had experienced in England. As founding governor John Winthrop described it, they wanted a perfect "citty [sic] upon a hill." However, their model of proper Christian behavior did not include religious liberty for those with different beliefs.

HUMAN RIGHTS

This nineteenth century painting shows Anne Hutchinson preaching at her home in Boston.

Good Works Versus God's Grace

A n n e
H u t c h i n s o n ' s
T r i a l s : 1 6 3 7
a n d 1 6 3 8

Most Puritan ministers preached that a person's "good works"—obedience to the laws of church and state—proved that God had chosen that person for salvation. Anne Hutchinson (1591–1643), midwife and herbal healer, disagreed. Her father had gone to prison in England for criticizing the bishops for ordaining unfit men. Anne followed his rebellious example by attacking the sermons of Massachusetts ministers who preached that people could help bring about their own salvation by doing good works. She agreed with minister John Cotton and John Wheelwright (her brother-in-law) that only God's grace could save people from damnation.

So Hutchinson held weekly meetings for the religious improvement of women. Her front room held sixty to eighty people. Soon wives started bringing their husbands, so Hutchinson had to hold extra meetings. Many of the attendees were merchants. They agreed with her criticisms of the church and state, who had placed wage and price limits on their businesses. Authorities quickly became alarmed.

An Uppity Woman

In November 1637, Hutchinson was called to civil trial by Governor Winthrop, who charged her with crimes. "Mrs. Hutchinson," he said, "you are called here as one of those that have troubled the peace . . . you have spoken of divers[e] things . . . very prejudicial to the honour of the churches and ministers thereof." He continued, "You have maintained a meeting . . . that hath been condemned . . . as a thing not tolerable nor comely in the sight of God nor fitting for your sex."

Hutchinson demanded to know where she had been wrong. Winthrop finally accused her of supporting Wheelwright. The colony had banished Wheelwright following his conviction for rebellion and contempt. He had stubbornly refused to bow to the wishes of church and state authorities. Anne had both signed and encouraged others to sign a petition on his behalf.

Winthrop persisted in his exploration of Anne's support for Wheelwright and his followers, until she asked, "What breach of law is that, Sir?"

"Why dishonoring of parents," Winthrop quickly replied, implying that the colony's judges and governor were "parents" to those they led, including Hutchinson.

She asked: "But put the case Sir that I do fear the Lord and my parents, may I not entertain them that fear the Lord because my parents will not give me leave?"

Winthrop shifted the questioning to Hutchinson's conduct in holding religious meetings. Hutchinson asked Winthrop in turn how he could give himself permission to preach while condemning her for the same thing. She reminded Winthrop of the apostle Paul's letter to Titus. In it Paul stated that "the elder women should instruct the younger." Winthrop insisted that older women should only instruct the younger "about their business and to love their husbands." Hutchinson answered by saying such instruction "is meant for some publick [sic] times." Winthrop then took her to task for distracting women from their homemaking duties and therefore wasting their time. He also accused her of attacking the leaders and their authority.

Despite his charges, the next day Hutchinson seemed close to being acquitted. However, she announced that she had had an immediate revelation from God and that she knew her inquisitors would be destroyed. No further proof of heresy was required, and she was "banished . . . as a woman not fit for our society." She was allowed, however, to stay in the colony until the end of winter.

Banned from the Church

Despite her legal conviction, Anne continued to preach. Finally, the Elders of Boston held a second, religious trial on March 22, 1683. Even John Cotton testified against Anne. He told the female members of the church to disregard Anne's teachings, and he cautioned, "[Y]ou see she [Anne] is but a Woman and many unsound and dayngerous principles are held by her."

At the trial's conclusion, the elders banned Anne from the church as well as the colony. She was not without her supporters, however. Mary Dyer—who would herself be hanged in 1660 for religious crimes—boldly walked to Anne's side and took her hand. Before the two persons exited the church, Anne had the last word: "The Lord judgeth not as a man judgeth, better to be cast out of the Church than to deny Christ."

During the eighteen-month period directly following the trials, other women experienced similar punishments. Judith Smith was excommunicated in April 1638 for "sundry Errors." Katherine Finch was whipped on October 10, 1638, as punishment for having "spoke[n] against the magistrates, against the churches, and against the Elders." Afterward, when she failed to behave "dutifully to her husband," she was forced to make a public promise of obedience to him. In 1639, Phillip[a] Hammond was excommunicated for "sins." These included her public declaration that Anne Hutchinson did not deserve her punishment.

ANNE HUTCHINSON IN RHODE ISLAND

Anne Hutchinson was banished from Massachusetts in 1638. Two years earlier, Roger Williams had also been banned from the Puritans' colony for religious dissent. Williams went on to found the city of Providence, where he preached the radical idea of the separation between church and state. He even claimed that Native Americans should be paid for their land. When Hutchinson was banned from Massachusetts, she went to settle near Williams' Providence, founding the city of Portsmouth. At about the same time, the city of Newport was also founded. Some six years later, in 1644, these three new towns became part of the colony of Rhode Island, which received a royal colonial charter in that year.

The Church of Boston clergy were sure they had acted properly. Indeed, they interpreted later events as divine signs of her guilt: Mary Dyer and Hutchinson both gave birth to what the clergy described as stillborn "monster[s]." When a local Native American tribe in what would later be New York State killed Hutchinson in 1643, the church's final verdict was harsh. "Let her damned heresies shee fell into . . . and the just vengeance of God, by which shee perished, terifie all her seduced followers from having any more to doe with her leaven."

Suggestions for Further Reading

Battis, Emery. "Anne Hutchinson." *Notable American Women, 1607–1950.* Edward T. James, Janet Wilson James, and Paul S. Boyer, eds. Cambridge, MA: Belknap Press of Harvard University Press, 1971.

Dailey, Barbara Ritter. "Anne Hutchinson." *A Reader's Companion to American History.* Eric Foner and John A. Garraty, eds. Boston: Houghton Mifflin, 1991.

Evans, Sara M. *Born for Liberty: A History of Women in America.* New York: The Free Press, A Division of Macmillan, Co. 1989.

Flexner, Eleanor. *Century of Struggle.* Cambridge, MA: Belknap Press of Harvard University Press, 1959.

HUMAN RIGHTS

Hutchinson, Thomas. "The History of the Colony and Province of Massachusetts Bay." *Roots of Bitterness: Documents of the Social History of American Women.* Nancy Cott, ed. New York: E. P. Dutton, 1972.

Koehler, Lyle. "The Case of the American Jezebels: Anne Hutchinson and Female Agitation during the Years of the Antinomian Turmoil, 1636–1640." *Women's America: Refocusing the Past.* Linda K. Kerber and Jane DeHart Mathews, eds. New York: Oxford University Press, 1991.

Morgan, Edmund S. *The Puritan Dilemma: The Story of John Winthrop.* Boston: Little, Brown and Company, 1958.

Stanton, Elizabeth Cady, Susan B. Anthony, and Matilda Joslyn Gage, eds. *History of Woman Suffrage.* (Reprint.) Salem, NH: Ayer Co., 1985.

Winthrop, John. *Winthrop's Journal, "History of New England," 1630–1649.* New York: Charles Scribner's Sons, 1908.

Mary Dyer Trials: 1659 and 1660

Defendant: Mary Dyer

Crime Charged: Quakerism

Chief Defense Lawyer: None

Chief Prosecutor: No record

Judge: Governor John Endecott

Place: Boston, Massachusetts Bay Colony

Dates: October 19, 1659 and May 31, 1660

Verdicts: Guilty

Sentences: First trial: death by hanging, changed to banishment from the colony and hanging if she returned; second trial: death by hanging

SIGNIFICANCE: Mary Dyer, convicted and executed in 1660 for practicing her Quaker faith, is an important "Witness for Religious Freedom" in American history.

In 1638, the Church of Boston forced Anne Hutchinson to leave the church for preaching in her home. Her friend Mary Dyer walked by her side as she left, extending her hand in support. Twenty-two years later, Dyer once again acted without hesitation to live up to her own principles.

The Puritan founders of the Massachusetts Bay Colony had established the colony to guarantee their religious freedom. They did not, however, extend this religious freedom to those with different beliefs. Frequently they expelled dissenters (those with differing opinions) from the colony. In 1658, they identified the Quakers, or members of the Society of Friends,

MARY DYER

QUAKER

WITNESS FOR RELIGIOUS FREEDOM

HANGED ON BOSTON COMMON 1660

"MY LIFE NOT AVAILETH ME
IN COMPARISON TO THE
LIBERTY OF THE TRUTH"

ART COMMISSION OF
LTH OF MASSACHUSETTS
Y OF ZENAS ELLIS
ERMONT

ILY, 1959

as a particularly dangerous religious group. The colony therefore passed a law on October 19, 1658, that banished Quakers on pain of death.

In 1659, Dyer learned that two of her Quaker friends, Marmaduke Stephenson and William Robinson, were in a Boston jail. As she visited her friends, jailers promptly imprisoned her as well. Officials then banished the three from the colony, threatening them with death should they return. The three left the colony, but within a few weeks they decided to return. They would "looke [the] bloody laws in the face."

Quakers Tried for Rebellion

Authorities quickly jailed the three Quakers. The charges were rebellion, sedition (revolutionary activity), and undermining the government. The General Court tried them on October 19, 1659. Governor John Endecott pronounced the same sentence on all three defendants: death by hanging.

Dyer remained calm and said simply, "The will of the Lord be done." In contrast, her husband, William Dyer, sought more immediate help for his wife. On August 30, 1659, he wrote to the court in Boston to protest the violation of his wife's religious freedom. He compared the General Court's members to the inquisitors of the Spanish Inquisition who had been responsible for persecuting thousands of non-Catholics. He pointed out that they, too, had acted as "judge and accuser both." Finally, he expressed fury that the Puritans, who had fled oppression in England, should in turn victimize Quakers. Among the others who protested Dyer's sentence were Dyer's son William, Governor John Winthrop Jr. of Connecticut, and Governor Thomas Temple of Nova Scotia.

Mary Dyer's Martyrdom

Finally the day of their expected hanging arrived. Dyer, Stephenson, and Robinson walked to drum beats to the scaffold. Then Dyer, like her fellow convicts, stood on the gallows, with a rope around her neck. Stephenson and Robinson were hanged. Dyer, to her surprise, did not feel the noose tighten. Officials set her free, giving her forty-eight hours to leave the colony, or else face death.

After seven months Dyer returned to the Massachusetts Bay Colony to test the decision. Arrested, she came before the General Court and Governor Endecott on May 31, 1660. The court sentenced her to death.

Dyer was hanged on June 1, 1660. Nearly three centuries later, in 1959, the Massachusetts General Court honored Mary Dyer by ordering

OPPOSITE PAGE

In honor of Mary Dyer's missionary efforts for the Quakers, the citizens of Boston erected a statue of her on the grounds of the State House in 1959.

HUMAN RIGHTS

BELIEVING IN AN INNER LIGHT

George Fox founded the Society of Friends around 1650. Fox propounded the radical idea that no minister was needed to interpret the word of God or to help human beings worship. Rather, he believed, each human being could find the word of God in his or her own soul. Instead of holding formal church services that relied upon quotations from the Bible and long-established prayers, the society had meetings, in which members sat silently meditating until they experienced an "inward light," a direct spiritual connection with God. Because receiving this spiritual message caused believers to tremble or "quake," they became known as "Quakers." In America, the only colony that did not pass anti-Quaker laws was Roger Williams' Rhode Island. Finally, in 1682, the Quaker William Penn founded the colony of Pennsylvania, based on the idea of religious tolerance for all.

that a seven-foot statue of her be placed on the Boston State House lawn. It bears the inscription "Witness for Religious Freedom."

Suggestions for Further Reading

Chu, Jonathan M. *Neighbors, Friends, or Madmen: The Puritan Adjustment to Quakerism in Seventeenth-Century Massachusetts Bay.* Westport, CT: Greenwood Press, 1985.

Cullen-DuPont, Kathryn. *Encyclopedia of Women's History in America.* New York: Facts On File, 1996.

Dyer, William. *Mary Dyer, Quaker: Two Letters of William Dyer of Rhode Island, 1659–1660.* Printed for Worthington C. Ford by the University Press, Cambridge, n.d.

Frost-Knappman, Elizabeth. *The ABC-CLIO Companion to Women's Progress in America.* Santa Barbara, CA: ABC-CLIO, 1994.

McHenry, Robert, ed. *Famous American Women: A Biographical Dictionary from Colonial Times to the Present.* New York: Dover Publications, 1983.

Shurtleff, Nathaniel B., ed. *Records of the Governor and Company of the Massachusetts Bay in New England.* Boston: From the Press of William White, Printer to the Commonwealth, 1854.

Tolles, Frederick B. "Mary Dyer." *Notable American Women, 1607–1950.* Edward T. James, Janet Wilson James, and Paul S. Boyer, eds. Cambridge, MA: Belknap Press of Harvard University Press, 1971.

Mary Dyer Trials: 1659 and 1660

The "Great Negro Plot" Trial: 1741

Defendants: More than 170 people prosecuted, including: Caesar, Prince, John Hughson, Sarah Hughson, Sarah Hughson (daughter), Margaret Sorubiero (alias Kerry), Quack, Cuffee, and John Ury

Crimes Charged: Entering, theft (Caesar, Prince); receiving stolen goods, conspiracy to commit arson (John Hughson, Sarah Hughson, Sorubiero); conspiracy to commit arson (Sarah Hughson, daughter); arson, conspiracy to murder inhabitants of New York (Quack, Cuffee); conspiracy to commit arson and being a Catholic priest (Ury)

Chief Defense Lawyer: None

Chief Prosecutors: James Alexander, Richard Bradley, John Chambers, Abraham Lodge, Joseph Murray, Richard Nicolls, and William Smith

Judges: James De Lancey, Daniel Horsmanden, and Frederick Philipse

Dates of Trials: May 1, 1741 (Caesar, Prince); May 6 (John Hughson, Sarah Hughson, and Sorubiero for receiving stolen goods); May 29 (Quack, Cuffee); June 4 (John Hughson, Sarah Hughson, Sarah Hughson, daughter, and Sorubiero, for conspiracy with Quack and Cuffee); July 29 (Ury)

Place of Trials: New York, Colony of New York

Verdicts: Guilty

Sentences: Hanging (Caesar, Prince, John Hughson, Sarah Hughson, Margaret Sorubiero, Ury); hanging, but pardoned in exchange for testimony, particularly against Ury (Sarah Hughson, daughter); burning at the stake (Quack, Cuffee)

SIGNIFICANCE: This case served as a vivid example of the consequences of panic, when legal procedures can be brushed aside.

The panic over the "Great Negro Plot" was like the madness of the Salem Witchcraft Trials. People thought that "plotters" were trying to stage an uprising of enslaved Africans. Once aroused, the blacks would burn New York and murder the white citizens. The crime of conspiracy (an agreement to commit a crime) is separate from the actual crime that is carried out. The key question of the "Great Negro Plot" is what kind of conspiracy existed, if any. True, a few people conspired to burn and loot some buildings. It is possible that some enslaved workers discussed revolt. Beyond that, the conspiracy was a delusion (false belief) that grew out of fear.

The "Great Negro Plot" Trial: 1741

Roots of the "Plot"

In February 1741, someone broke into Robert Hogg's tobacco shop. An investigation of the burglary led to the arrest of two slaves, Caesar and Prince. They had often been customers of a tavern owned by John Hughson. Following these arrests, Mary Burton, a sixteen-year-old servant in Hughson's tavern, dropped hints about the burglary. When questioned, Burton claimed that the Hughson family bought and sold stolen property, assisted by a woman living at the tavern, possibly Margaret (Peggy) Kelly or Sorubiero. After a search, police found the goods stolen from Hogg's shop, arrested Hughson, and held the other three as accomplices (partners-in-crime).

Soon after the arrests, New York suffered several mysterious fires. They started with the city's fortress, Fort George. During some of the fires, goods were stolen. This made many suspect that the fires had been started on purpose. Suspicion fell on two slaves men, Quack and Cuffee. Police soon arrested them.

On Trial

Quack and Cuffee denied everything, even when convicted. When faced with the prospect of being burned at the stake, though, they tried to save themselves by confessing. The sheriff, however, could not fight the mob that came to see them die.

When Burton testified before the grand jury investigating the fires, she said that John Hughson led a conspiracy that included Caesar, Prince, and Cuffee. They supposedly met at Hughson's to plan the fires and the massacre of the white population. Burton went on, speaking in the third person (referring to herself as "she"):

THE RIGHT TO A LAWYER

Although more than 170 people faced prosecution in the "Great Negro Plot" Trial, none had a lawyer. As a result, the prosecution could bring in evidence that the law would not normally accept. One example was the testimony of a convicted thief who claimed that some of the accused had admitted their guilt to him in prison. Today, no person accused of a felony (serious crime) stands trial without a lawyer. However, this change to the legal system is relatively recent. Only in 1963, with the second trial of Clarence Earl Gideon, did the U.S. Supreme Court rule that every defendant for a felony must have a lawyer. The Gideon trial also established that if the defendant cannot afford a lawyer, the court will appoint and pay for one.

Caesar should be governor, and Hughson . . . king . . . that she has seen twenty or thirty negroes at one time in her master's house . . . the three aforesaid negroes . . . were generally present . . . that the other negroes better not refuse to do what they commanded them . . . That she never saw any white person . . . when they talked of burning the town, but her master, her mistress, and Peggy.

Burton's testimony became wilder as the number of people she accused grew. Prosecutor Richard Bradley used testimony that a judge would not usually have accepted as evidence. It came from convicted thief Arthur Price. He swore that several of the accused confessed to him while he was in jail with them. The defendants denied these admissions. Bradley also used illegal hearsay evidence (information someone tells the witness). He also used testimony of frightened defendants trying to win mercy or to cast suspicion on others. The court permitted these violations of proper trial rules. Since no lawyer in New York would agree to defend any of the accused, no one objected.

Next, Governor James Oglethorpe of Georgia wrote authorities in other colonies, warning them to beware of Spanish plots and spies. This led New York authorities to link their suspected conspiracy to Spain and, eventually, to English schoolmaster John Ury.

Ury, skilled in Latin and theology, faced weak testimony from people trying to prove he was a Catholic priest and the real head of the conspiracy. This testimony contradicted (opposed) earlier claims that Hughson was the leader. Ury produced witnesses who knew where he was during so-called plotting sessions. Nevertheless, he was hanged.

There were no more grand jury indictments, but Judge Daniel Horsmanden's obsession with the conspiracy led to one last death, that of a slave named Tom.

Suggestions for Further Reading

Davis, T. J. *A Rumor of Revolt.* New York: The Free Press, 1985.

Horsmanden, Daniel. *The New York Conspiracy.* Boston: Beacon Press, 1971.

The "Great Negro Plot" Trial: 1741

U.S. v. Cinque:
1839–1840

Defendants: Joseph Cinque and others

Crimes Charged: Murder and piracy

Chief Defense Lawyers: John Quincy Adams, Roger S. Baldwin, Joshua Leavitt, and Seth Staples

Chief Prosecutor: William S. Holabird

Judges: Andrew T. Judson and Smith Thompson

Place: New Haven, Connecticut

Dates of Trial: November 19, 1839–January 13, 1840

Verdict: Not guilty

SIGNIFICANCE: An American court refused to convict enslaved men from the schooner (ship) *Amistad* after they had killed their captors in order to free themselves. This decision was a victory for the cause of abolition.

By the 1830s, many countries were trying to limit slavery. Slavery was legal in the United States, however. Still, it was illegal to bring new slaves into the country. The abolitionist (anti-slavery) movement, which sought to do away with slavery altogether, was gaining support. Great Britain wanted an end to the practice. It had used its naval power to pressure Spain to make it illegal to bring new captives into any territory controlled by Spain.

The Slave Trade in the Spanish New World

Spanish power in the New World was declining at this time. The government in Madrid lacked the power to enforce its will. Wealthy landowners in Cuba and throughout the Spanish New World needed people to work their lands. If they obeyed the law against importing captive Africans, they would have to wait for the children of existing slaves to grow up. Under a weak government, an illegal slave trade soon developed. Slavetraders went to the west coast of Africa, bought or captured healthy young black men and women, and brought them back to Cuba for resale. The colonial authorities did nothing to stop this trade. In 1839, slavers brought back a cargo of slaves from what is now Sierra Leone. Among the slaves was a young man they named Joseph Cinque.

Cinque Leads Slave Mutiny

In June 1839, Jose Ruiz and Pedro Montes bought forty-nine captured Africans in Havana, including Cinque. The owners intended to take the men to their estates in the Cuban town of Puerto Principe. Ruiz and Montes put the captives aboard the schooner *Amistad,* intending to sail from Havana up the Cuban coast to Puerto Principe. The Spanish crew taunted their cargo, telling them wild stories, such as that their new owners would kill and eat them when they arrived. On the night of July 1, Cinque led

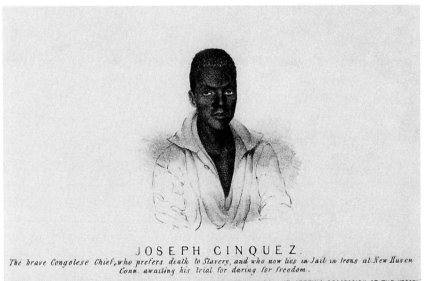

JOSEPH CINQUEZ.

The brave Congolese Chief, who prefers death to Slavery, and who now lies in Jail in Irons at New Haven Conn. awaiting his trial for daring for freedom.

SPEECH TO HIS COMRADE SLAVES AFTER MURDERING THE CAPTAIN &C. AND GETTING POSSESSION OF THE VESSEL AND CARGO

"Brothers, we have done that which we purposed, our hands are now clean for we have Striven to regain the precious heritage we received from our fathers. We have only to persevere, Where the Sun rises there is our home, our brethern, our fathers. Do not seek to defeat my orders, if so I shall sacrifice any one who would endanger the rest, when at home we will kill the Old Man, the young one shall be saved he is kind and gave you bread, we must not kill those who give us water. Brothers, I am resolved that it is better to die than be a white man's slave, and I will not complain if by dying I save you. Let us be careful what we eat, that we may not be sick. The deed is done and I need say no more."

On March 9, 1840, the U.S. Supreme Court upheld the ruling of Andrew T. Judson of the U.S. District Court for Connecticut. His verdict was that Joseph Cinque, leader of the Amistad rebellion, and his followers "were born free, and . . . of right are free and not slaves."

his fellow slaves in a successful rebellion to seize control of the ship. The captives killed several members of the crew in the struggle, but they let Ruiz and Montes live. Cinque then ordered Ruiz and Montes to take the ship back to Sierra Leone.

The Spaniards sailed east for Africa by day, but secretly reversed course by night. For nearly two months the *Amistad* wandered back and forth. Eventually winds and currents drove it north to the coast of the United States. On August 26, the U.S.S. *Washington* spotted the *Amistad* off the coast of New York. It seized the ship and brought it into New London, Connecticut.

One of the defense lawyers hired by the abolitionists was ex-president of the United States John Quincy Adams.

Cinque On Trial

In New London Ruiz and Montes described the slave rebellion to the American authorities. They pressed for the return of the *Amistad* with its human cargo. Despite the fact that the capture of the Africans was illegal, the Spanish government backed Ruiz's and Montes' claim of ownership. With the approval of President Martin Van Buren's administration, District Attorney William S. Holabird charged Cinque and the others with committing murder and piracy aboard the *Amistad*.

The trial took place in the U.S. District Court for Connecticut. The abolitionists who supported Cinque hired lawyers to fight back. This team included John Quincy Adams, the former president of the United States.

The trial began on November 19, 1839. The defense lawyers declared that the defendants had the right to free themselves from the hor-

A COMMITTED ABOLITIONIST

One of Cinque's lawyers, John Quincy Adams, was unusually dedicated to the cause of abolitionism—the complete elimination of slavery—in the United States. After Adams lost the 1828 Presidential election, he ran for Congress as a representative from Massachusetts. When he won that election, he became the only ex-President ever to serve in Congress, where he led the antislavery forces right up until his death in 1848.

rible conditions of slavery. In support of this position, the defense lawyers introduced as a witness Dr. Richard R. Madden. He had traveled widely in Cuba and was an expert on slave conditions. Dr. Madden testified about the inhumanity of slavery. He said, "So terrible were these atrocities, so murderous the system of slavery, so transcendent the evils I witnessed, over all I have ever heard or seen of the rigour of slavery elsewhere, that at first I could hardly believe the evidence of my senses."

If the court returned Cinque and the others to Cuba, the slavers would kill them. In addition, since the men had originally been captured in Africa in violation of Spanish law, the abolitionists argued that the blacks were not legally slaves and therefore not "property" belonging to Ruiz and Montes.

The judge felt pressure from the Van Buren administration, which wanted to avoid diplomatic tension with Spain. However, on January 13, 1840, he ruled in favor of the enslaved men. The *Amistad,* with its goods, would be returned to Ruiz and Montes. Judge Judson declared that Cinque and the others "were born free, and ever since have been and still of right are free and not slaves." He added that because their captors had illegally kidnapped them, the men were innocent of murder and piracy. They had only acted to free themselves.

Supreme Court Upholds Freedom for Cinque

The prosecution appealed Judson's decision to the Supreme Court. The abolitionists had anticipated this move. They knew that five Supreme Court justices, including Chief Justice Roger B. Taney, were Southerners

HUMAN RIGHTS

and had owned slaves. The defense turned to John Quincy Adams to present their case, relying on his prestige as much as on his legal ability to win Cinque's case. On February 22, 1840, the Supreme Court heard both sides' legal arguments. On March 9, the court issued its opinion upholding Judson's decision. Cinque and the others were free and would return to Africa.

Technically, the Supreme Court's decision did not condemn slavery. It only held that people who were not legally "slaves" were not property. Still, the courts could just as easily have turned the rebels over to the Spanish authorities or returned them to Cuba. The case was a victory for the abolitionist cause, and it was a landmark in the quest for the total end of slavery.

Suggestions for Further Reading

Adams, John Quincy. *Argument in the Case of U.S. v. Cinque.* New York: Arno Press, 1969.

Cable, Mary. *Black Odyssey: the Case of the Slave Ship Amistad.* New York: Penguin Books, 1977.

"Cinque." *Jet* (March 1984): 21.

Jones, Howard. *Mutiny on the Amistad: the Saga of a Slave Revolt and its Impact on American Abolition, Law, and Diplomacy.* New York: Oxford University Press, 1987.

Owens, William A. *Slave Mutiny: the Revolt on the Schooner Amistad.* New York: J. Day Co., 1953.

U.S. v. Susan B. Anthony: 1873

Defendant: Susan B. Anthony
Crime Charged: Unlawful voting
Chief Defense Lawyers: Henry R. Selden and John Van Voorhis
Chief Prosecutor: Richard Crowley
Judge: Ward Hunt
Place: Canandaigua, New York
Dates of Trial: June 17–18, 1873
Verdict: Guilty

SIGNIFICANCE: Susan B. Anthony's casting of her ballot almost fifty years before the Nineteenth Amendment was ratified—giving true citizenship to American women—was both an act of political defiance and an attempt to test whether the recently adopted Fourteenth Amendment would be interpreted as expanding or protecting women's rights.

During the 1870s, American women tried to gain their full rights as citizens by using the judicial system. Most of these attempts, including the trial of Susan B. Anthony, failed. If they had succeeded, women would not have had to wait for the slow, state-by-state campaign to pass laws giving women the right to vote. In addition, it took more than one hundred years for the Equal Protection Clause of the Fourteenth Amendment to the Constitution to be applied to sex discrimination cases.

The states adopted the Fourteenth Amendment in July 1868. This was exactly twenty years after American women had publicly demanded voting rights at Seneca Falls, New York. Section 2 of the amendment was meant to encourage states to permit African American men to vote. Not surprisingly, women's rights leaders objected to it. Not only did it exclude women, it introduced the word "male" into the Constitution and possibly cast doubt on the status of women as citizens. Francis Minor, a lawyer who was the husband of Virginia Minor, president of the Woman Suffrage Association of Missouri, thought women were worrying about the wrong section of the Fourteenth Amendment. Section 1, he pointed out, confirmed women's citizenship and made state denials of the vote for women unconstitutional.

Susan B. Anthony cast her ballot in the 1872 presidential election to test women's right to vote.

Women's rights leaders Susan B. Anthony and Elizabeth Cady Stanton published Francis Minor's remarks in their newspaper, the *Revolution,* and urged women to go to the polls. In 1871 and 1872, women did so in at least ten states. Most were not permitted to vote, but a few managed to do so anyway.

Female Voters Arrested

One of those who voted in 1872 was Susan B. Anthony. Before she registered to vote, she talked to Judge Henry R. Selden. He agreed that Section 1 of the Fourteenth Amendment gave women the right to vote. When she went to the polls, Anthony carried the judge's written opinion with her. She threatened to sue if she were not allowed to register. The tactic worked. On November 5, Anthony and fourteen other women who had managed to become registered cast their ballots. On November 28, the fifteen women, as well as the officials who had registered them, were all arrested.

The courts offered each of them the opportunity to go free if they paid $500 bail. Only Anthony refused the offer. Henry Selden, acting as her attorney, filed a document stating that Anthony had been illegally detained (a writ of *habeas corpus*). A U.S. district court judge denied the writ on January 21, 1873. He set new bail at $1,000. Again, Anthony refused to pay. Selden, who said that he "could not see a lady I respected put in jail," paid the bail. Anthony went free. However, because her writ of *habeas corpus* had been denied, she had lost her right to appeal her case to the U.S. Supreme Court. Her trial had to go forward.

Stumping before the Trial

Before her trial began, however, Anthony tried to present her side of the case to people who might serve as jurors. She gave the same speech in all twenty-nine postal districts in her county, arguing her cause. Because it was said that Anthony's speech had "prejudiced any possible jury," her trial was moved from her own Monroe County to Canandaigua, a town in Ontario County, New York, and rescheduled for June 17. By June 16, Anthony had spoken in every village in Ontario County, arguing her case.

Trial Begins June 17

The trial opened before Judge Ward Hunt on June 17, 1873. U.S. District Attorney Richard Crowley presented the government's case: "Miss Susan B. Anthony . . . upon the 5th day of November, 1872 . . . voted. . . . At that time she was a woman."

Beverly W. Jones, one of the officials who had registered Anthony, testified that he had indeed registered her and had received her election ballot on November 5. Crowley introduced as evidence the list of voters including Anthony's name as proof. Then the government rested its case.

Henry Selden tried to call Anthony to the witness stand. Crowley objected: "She is not competent as a witness in her own behalf." (Women were not permitted to testify in federal court in the nineteenth century.) The judge agreed. Selden then took the witness stand and testified that he

agreed with Anthony's reading of the Fourteenth Amendment. He also said that he had advised her to vote.

After the lawyers had delivered their final arguments, Judge Hunt then directed the jury to deliver a guilty verdict. Hunt said that he had decided, as a matter of law, that the Fourteenth Amendment did not protect Anthony's right to vote. "I therefore direct you to find a verdict of guilty," he said again. Hunt then asked the clerk of the court to record the jury's verdict.

The next day, Selden requested a new trial, but Judge Hunt refused. Hunt then asked Anthony to stand to receive her sentence: "The sentence of this Court is that you pay a fine of $100.00 and the costs of prosecution."

Anthony replied: "May it please your honor, I will never pay a dollar of your unjust penalty. . . . 'Resistance to tyranny is obedience to God.' " She never paid the fine.

Supreme Court Reviews Women and the Fourteenth Amendment

In 1873, the Supreme Court heard the case of Myra Bradwell. Bradwell claimed that the state of Illinois had violated her rights under the Fourteenth Amendment when it prevented her from practicing law in that state. The court found otherwise, because the right to practice law, or to perform any job, was not guaranteed to women as citizens. Justice Samuel F. Miller, writing for a majority of the justices, stated the view of many men at this time:

> The paramount destiny and mission of woman are
> to fulfill the noble and benign offices of wife and
> mother. This is the law of the Creator. And the rules
> of civil society must be adapted to the general con-
> stitution of things.

In a later lawsuit, *Minor v. Happersett* (1875), the Supreme Court ruled unanimously that the right to vote was also not a right of citizenship guaranteed to women. Although the rights of women as citizens of the United States were protected by the Fourteenth Amendment, the amendment did not cover activities, such as voting, that were controlled by individual state governments. If state governments chose not to grant women the vote, the Fourteenth Amendment was beside the point.

"ONE HALF OF THE PEOPLE OF THIS NATION"

Before Susan B. Anthony's trial on May 13th, she traveled throughout New York State, arguing her case and defending women's right to vote:

> One half of the people of this Nation today are utterly powerless to blot from the statute books an unjust law, or to write a new and just one. . . . this form of government, that enforces taxation without representation—that compels them to obey laws to which they have never given their consent—that imprisons and hangs them without a trial by a jury of their peers— that robs them, in marriage of the custody of their own persons, wages, and children—are . . . left wholly at the mercy of the other half.

The first successful challenge to this reading of the Fourteenth Amendment did not come until 1971 with *Reed v. Reed*. When Idaho resident Sally Reed's son died without leaving a will, the state automatically put her husband in charge of the boy's estate. Reed, who was separated from her husband, challenged this. However, her petition to control the estate was rejected because of her gender. She took her case to the Supreme Court, where she won. More than a century after the adoption of the Fourteenth Amendment in 1868, women were granted equal protection under the laws of the United States.

Suggestions for Further Reading

Barry, Kathleen. *Susan B. Anthony: A Biography.* New York: New York University Press, 1988.

Flexner, Eleanor. *Century of Struggle.* Cambridge, MA: The Belknap Press of Harvard University Press, 1975.

HUMAN RIGHTS

Frost, Elizabeth and Kathryn Cullen-DuPont. *Women's Suffrage in America: An Eyewitness History.* New York: Facts On File, 1992.

Harper, Ida Husted. *Life and Work of Susan B. Anthony.* (Reprint.) Salem, NH: Ayer Company, 1983.

Stanton, Elizabeth Cady, Susan B. Anthony, and Matilda Joslyn Gage. *History of Woman Suffrage,* Vol. II. (Reprint). Salem, NH: Ayer Company, 1985.

Oscar Wilde Trials: 1895

Defendant: Oscar Wilde

Crimes Charged: Sodomy, indecency

Chief Defense Lawyers: Sir Edward Clarke, Q.C. (Queen's Counsel), Charles Mathews, and Travers Humphreys

Chief Prosecutors: First trial: Charles Gill, Horace Avory, and Arthur Gill; second trial: Sir Frank Lockwood, Q.C., and Charles Gill

Judges: First trial: Justice Arthur Charles; second trial: Justice Alfred Wills

Place: London, England

Date of Trials: April 26–May 1, 1895; May 22–26, 1895

Verdicts: First trial: mistrial; second trial: guilty

Sentence: Two years hard labor

SIGNIFICANCE: What began with a libel (defamation) suit ended in the downfall of Britain's finest contemporary playwright.

On February 18, 1895, the Marquess of Queensberry, a British nobleman who wrote the rules for boxing that still bear his name, entered London's Albemarle Club. His plan was to end a feud that had been going on for three years. As he expected, the person he was mad at was not at the club. So Queensberry left his calling card, on which he wrote, "To Oscar Wilde posing as a Somdomite [sic]." The meaning of the note was that Wilde was a homosexual.

HUMAN RIGHTS

At age forty, Oscar Wilde, dramatist, wit, storyteller, and comic master, was at the peak of his popularity. Two of his plays, *The Importance of Being Earnest* and *An Ideal Husband,* were being performed in both Europe and the United States. He was at the time also closely associated with Queensberry's twenty-two-year-old son, Lord Alfred Douglas. The two had met in 1892. Since then rumors had spread about their love affair.

Queensberry at first watched the growth of the relationship with grief, then with anger. He tried everything in his power to come between his son and Wilde. He even threatened to shoot the playwright if Wilde did not end this "most loathsome and disgusting relationship." When even this attempt failed, he decided to attack Wilde publicly. He knew that the note on the calling card left at the Albemarle Club would be read and repeated by many before it reached Oscar Wilde.

Oscar Wilde published his first volume of poetry in 1881.

Wilde Sues for Libel

In Victorian England, homosexuality was a serious crime. Queensberry knew that after reading the card, Wilde would have only one choice. He must sue him for libel in order to argue the charge that he was homosexual. Queensberry's defense would be that what he stated was true. He would claim that the public needed to be protected from homosexuals. The scandal brought by the trial would ruin the playwright. Against the advice of friends and urged on by Lord Alfred, Wilde sued.

When the case opened in court in London on April 3, 1895, Wilde used the opportunity to display his sense of humor. Some of his responses to questions rank among the finest, most amusing remarks ever heard. However, Wilde's cleverness began to work against him as Edward Carson, Q.C., questioned certain ambiguities (expressions with more than one meaning) in his writings. Then, on the third day of the trial, Carson surprised the court. He said that he intended to call young men to testify that Wilde bought sexual services from them. Immediately, Wilde's attorney, Sir Edward Clarke, Q.C., withdrew his client's libel suit against Queensberry.

The Tables Turn

Most expected this to be the end of the matter, but Queensberry had other plans. He promptly sent copies of the witnesses' statements to the director of public prosecutions. As a consequence, Wilde soon became the object of a lawsuit, charged with numerous acts of indecency and sodomy (illegal sex acts). Also accused was Alfred Taylor, who was widely suspected of having obtained sexual partners for Wilde.

Testimony in the trial began on April 26, 1895. The witnesses Queensberry had rounded up for the earlier libel trial now took the stand. They painted a dirty picture. Charles Parker, a twenty-one-year-old servant, described how Taylor had taken him and his brother to a restaurant, where Wilde looked them over.

Parker went on. "Subsequently, Wilde said to me, 'This is the boy for me! Will you go to the Savoy Hotel with me?' I consented, and Wilde drove me in a cab to the hotel. At the Savoy he committed the act of sodomy upon me."

"Did Wilde give you any money on that occasion?" asked chief prosecutor Charles Gill.

"Before I left, Wilde gave me 2 pounds (British currency), telling me to call at the Savoy Hotel in a week," Parker said. Later, Wilde visited Parker in his own rooms. "I was asked by Wilde to imagine that I was a woman, and that he was my lover. . . . I had to sit on his knee."

Wood, an unemployed clerk, claimed he had been introduced to Wilde by Lord Douglas. Again the meeting had taken place in a restaurant.

"What happened next?" asked Gill.

"After dinner I went with Mr. Wilde to [Wilde's home]. There was no one in the house to my knowledge. Mr. Wilde let himself in with a latchkey. We went up to his bedroom where he had [wine] and seltzer.

Here an act of the grossest indecency occurred. Mr. Wilde used his influence to induce me to consent. He made me nearly drunk."

Further evidence came from a Savoy Hotel chambermaid who claimed that she had seen a youth, sixteen-year-old Edward Shelley, in Wilde's bed at the hotel.

Wilde took the stand to deny every claim. Gill then turned to letters exchanged by Wilde and Douglas. In particular, Gill asked for clarification of a line from a poem, "Two Loves," included in one of these letters: "I am the Love that dare not speak its name." Gill asked, "Is it not clear that the love described relates to natural love and unnatural love?"

"No," said Wilde.

"What is 'the Love that dare not speak its name'?"

Wilde answered this question with a speech describing the spiritual affection between an older and a younger man, an affection as old as time. The speech was so eloquent and persuasive that it brought an ovation from onlookers in court. It also planted seeds of doubt among the members of the jury. On May 1, 1895, the jury declared that it was unable to reach a verdict. Judge Arthur Charles had no choice but to declare a mistrial. Wilde left the courtroom a free man, but his freedom was short-lived: he was

Soon after Oscar Wilde's first trial, the Marquess of Queensbury had a heated argument with his oldest son just outside the courthouse.

immediately arrested again and charged with yet another fifteen counts of impropriety (indecency).

Freedom Short-Lived

Three weeks later, on May 22, Wilde again stepped into court to face his accusers. This time he was alone (Alfred Taylor, his co-defendant in the first trial, had been convicted but not sentenced). For some reason, the string of young male prosecution witnesses failed to make the same impact as before, but Alfred Wood again revealed the dark side of his nature.

"You have met Lord Alfred Douglas?" prosecutor Charles Gill asked Wood.

"Yes . . . he gave me a suit of clothes."

"And you found four letters in one of the pockets?"

"Yes."

"From who?"

"From Mr. Wilde to Lord Alfred."

"What happened to the letters?"

"Allen [a friend] stole them. He kept one of them, saying, 'This one's quite hot enough for me.'"

"You went to Mr. Wilde and asked him for money?"

"Yes. I told him I was tired of life, tired of those big dinners, and tired of mixing with people like Wilde and Douglas and those people."

Blackmail Ring

What happened next had already been described by Wilde at the libel trial. He had paid Wood 15 pounds for the letter, only then to receive a visit from someone called William Allen. Wilde knew what to expect. "I suppose you have come about my very beautiful letter to Lord Alfred Douglas," he said. "I consider it to be a work of art."

Allen replied, "A very curious construction can be put on that letter."

Wilde sighed, "Art is rarely intelligible to the criminal classes."

To which Allen said, "A man offered me 60 pounds for it."

Wilde seemed pleased. "If you take my advice you will sell my letter to him for 60 pounds. I myself have never received so large a sum for

"ART FOR ART'S SAKE"

At the time of his trial, Oscar Wilde was one of the most successful playwrights in England. He was also known for developing the doctrine (belief) of "Art for art's sake," which held that art did not need to be justified on the grounds that it made people more virtuous (strengthened their moral values) or taught them anything. Rather, Wilde believed that beauty was its own justification, and that if good art brought beauty into the world, it needed no other defense.

any prose work of that length; but I am glad to find that there is someone in England who considers a letter of mine worth 60 pounds." When Allen underwent a change of heart and complained that he was completely broke, Wilde gave him the equivalent of $2, and he left.

Allen then gave the letter to yet another young man, Robert Clibborn. He, too, showed up on Wilde's doorstep. He, too, left with just a half sovereign (gold coin used as British currency) in his pocket. Between them the three blackmailers had gotten only 16 pounds from their victim.

Wilde Sentenced to Hard Labor

By the end of the third trial, Wilde's defenses were gone. In his final address to the jury, Edward Clarke gave this description of his client: "Broken as he is now, as anyone who saw him at the first trial must see he is, by being kept in prison without bail."

Unlike the jury who had heard the case against Wilde just one month earlier, this jury had no doubts about the defendant's guilt. On May 26, 1895, Wilde wept as he heard Justice Alfred Wills pass sentence: two years' hard labor. It was a brutal sentence, the maximum permitted by the law. Still Wilde's troubles were not over. Seeking more revenge, Queensberry decided to sue Wilde for the money he had spent during the libel trial. Wilde, brought from his cell manacled (handcuffed) and helpless, stood in court and heard himself declared bankrupt.

Wilde served his complete sentence. He left prison a shattered man. He knew there was no place for him in England, so he decided to live the rest of his life in exile elsewhere in Europe. He finally settled in Paris, where, on November 30, 1900, he died of a brain infection at the age of forty-six.

Suggestions for Further Reading

Ellmann, Richard. *Oscar Wilde.* New York: Random House, 1988.

Fido, Martin. *Oscar Wilde.* New York: Viking Press, 1973.

Montgomery Hyde, H. *Oscar Wilde.* New York: Farrar, Straus, and Giroux, 1975.

The Trials of Alice Paul and Other National Woman's Party Members: 1917

Defendants: Gertrude Crocker, Gladys Greiner, Alice Paul, and Dr. Caroline Spencer

Crime Charged: Obstructing a sidewalk

Chief Defense Lawyer: Dudley Field Malone

Chief Prosecutor: Mr. Hart (first name unavailable)

Judge: Alexander Mullowney

Place: Washington, D.C.

Date of Decision: October 22, 1917

Verdicts: Guilty

Sentences: Alice Paul and Caroline Spencer: seven months imprisonment; Gertrude Crocker and Gladys Greiner: five dollar fine or thirty days imprisonment

SIGNIFICANCE: Police arrested nearly 500 suffragists (people who support voting rights) during their picketing of the White House in 1917 and 1918. National Woman's Party chair Alice Paul and 167 other women were tried, convicted, and jailed for up to seven months for blocking pedestrian traffic on a sidewalk. The women, protesting that they were jailed for their political beliefs, became the first U.S. citizens to claim that their government was holding them as political prisoners.

Women first demanded the right to vote in 1848, at what became known as the Seneca Falls Convention, held in New York State. In 1917, after sixty-nine years of effort, women still did not have the right to vote. Members of the National Woman's Party, led by Alice Paul, decided to try a new tactic. On January 10, 1917, they began picketing (marching with signs of protest) President Woodrow Wilson and the White House.

Picketers Arrested

Before the United States entered World War I, the government largely ignored the picketers. After the U.S. entered the war on April 6, 1917, however, the District of Columbia police chief told Alice Paul that the picketers would be arrested. Paul replied that her lawyers had "assured us all along that picketing was legal." And, she added, it was "certainly . . . as legal in June as in January."

Police arrested the first two protesters anyway on June 22, 1917. The government charged them with blocking a sidewalk, but then released and never tried them. The same thing happened to twenty-seven other women over the next four days. This process of arrest and release

The Trials of
Alice Paul
and Other
National
Woman's
Party
Members:
1917

Alice Paul and Lucy Burns organized the National Woman's Party picket of the White House that began in January 1917.

MR.PRESIDENT HOW LONG MUST WOMEN WAIT FOR LIBERTY

U of MO

LELAND STANFORD

MR.PRESIDENT WHAT WILL YOU DO FOR WOMAN SUFFRAGE

did not put an end to the picketing, however. On June 27, six women stood trial for blocking traffic. The judged found them guilty and fined them twenty-five dollars. Because they refused to pay the fine, they spent three days in jail.

The Marching Goes On

Still, the picketing continued. On July 14, police arrested sixteen women. They included Florence Bayard Hilles, the daughter of a former U.S. ambassador to Great Britain, and Allison Turnbull Hopkins, the wife of one of President Wilson's campaign officials. All the women stood trial the same day before Judge Alexander Mullowney.

Alice Paul and other group members celebrate the 1920 ratification of the Nineteenth Amendment at the National Suffrage Association Headquarters in Washington, D.C.

Mullowney had already discussed with the U.S. attorney the possibility of trying the picketers under the Espionage Act of 1917. Passed in June 1917, the act prohibited, among other things, making false statements that might interfere with the war effort. Mullowney said that the banners worn by the marchers contained words that were "treasonous and seditious [meant to cause rebellion]." In fact, the words on the banners merely quoted speeches made by President Wilson. One such line was taken from the President's War Message Speech of April 2: "We shall fight for the things which we have always held nearest our hearts—for democracy, for the right of those who submit to authority to have a voice in their own governments."

As Paul had known, the president's own words could not possibly be used as a basis for trial under the Espionage Act. Also picketing was clearly a legal activity when performed in front of the White House. Once again, therefore, police arrested the women, who were charged with the crime of obstructing traffic. All sixteen spent sixty days in the Occoquan Workhouse.

Dudley Field Malone, a friend of President Wilson and a government official, happened to see the women's trial. Outraged by the verdict, he took a taxi to the White House and gave Wilson his resignation. He planned, he told the president, to offer his services as a legal advisor to the women demanding the vote. Wilson refused to accept his resignation. On July 20, the president pardoned the sixteen suffragists serving time in Occoquan.

The picketing continued and in August more arrests followed. Malone offered his resignation again on September 7. This time he sent copies of his resignation letter to major newspapers as well as to the president. The letter said, in part: "I think it is high time that men in this generation, at some cost to themselves, stood up to battle for the national enfranchisement [right to vote] of American women." This time, the president accepted Malone's resignation.

The Trials of Alice Paul and Other National Woman's Party Members: 1917

Alice Paul Arrested

On October 4, police arrested Paul, along with ten other women. In court on October 8, the women refused to be sworn in to testify and refused to accept the court's authority. They felt that women, unable to vote, had not made the laws under which they were tried. Although the charge against them was not dismissed, the women went free.

Police arrested Paul again on October 20 with Dr. Caroline Spencer, Gladys Greiner, and Gertrude Crocker. The four women went to trial on October 22 before Judge Mullowney.

Police Sergeant Lee testified: "I made my way through the crowd that was surrounding them, and told the ladies they were violating the law by standing at the gates, and would not they please move on."

When Assistant District Attorney Hart asked Lee about the women's response, Lee replied: "They did not [move on], and they did not answer either . . . [I] placed them under arrest."

Paul and Spencer, who had been carrying banners, would spend seven months in prison. Greiner and Crocker had a choice of five dollar fines or thirty days' imprisonment. They chose to go to jail.

THE FIRST POLITICAL PRISONERS

Alice Paul and the women imprisoned with her were the first U.S. citizens who maintained that the U.S. government was holding them as political prisoners (prisoners whose only crime was holding certain unpopular political beliefs). Although in some countries, it actually is illegal to promote certain beliefs, the First Amendment of the U.S. Constitution guarantees freedom of speech. Thus, no U.S. citizen can officially be charged for political reasons. In fact, Paul and her fellow picketers went to jail for blocking a sidewalk. Paul argued that this charge was made up, and that the real reason she and her fellow suffragists were sent to jail was because they were trying to win the vote for women. She was the first of many activists, including the Hollywood Ten, the Chicago Seven, and Angela Davis, to call themselves political prisoners.

Prisoners Strike

Lucy Burns was one of the first women arrested and released on June 22. Police arrested her again in September. Imprisoned in Occoquan after her conviction, Burns organized the other women's rights activists confined there. They smuggled out a petition requesting that District of Columbia officials grant them the status of political prisoners, rather than common criminals. Each of the women who had signed the petition was immediately placed in solitary confinement (kept in a prison cell alone). When Paul and the recently sentenced Rose Winslow arrived at Occoquan, they announced they would go on a hunger strike. Their goal was to receive "treatment accorded political prisoners in every civilized country but our own."

Guards force-fed by a tube Paul, Winslow, and others who had joined the hunger strike. Paul first spent time in solitary confinement, then was sent to a psychiatric hospital. Malone finally managed to get her released to a regular hospital.

On November 27 and 28, 1917, all of the protesters were released without explanation. On March 4, 1918, the District of Columbia Court of Appeals ruled on an appeal that Malone had filed earlier. Each one of the activists, the court said, had been "illegally arrested, illegally convicted, and illegally imprisoned."

The Nineteenth Amendment, granting women the right to vote, was finally adopted on August 26, 1920.

Suggestions for Further Reading

Frost, Elizabeth and Kathryn Cullen-DuPont. *Women's Suffrage in America: An Eyewitness History.* New York: Facts On File, 1992.

Irwin, Inez Hayes. *The Story of Alice Paul and the National Woman's Party.* Fairfax, VA: Denlinger's Publishers, 1964.

Lunardini, Christine A. *From Equal Suffrage to Equal Rights: Alice Paul and the National Woman's Party, 1910–1928.* New York: New York University Press, 1986.

Stevens, Doris. *Jailed for Freedom.* (Reprint.) Salem, NH: Ayer Co., 1990.

The Trials of Alice Paul and Other National Woman's Party Members: 1917

The Scottsboro Trials: 1931–1937

Defendants: Olin Montgomery, Clarence Norris, Haywood Patterson, Ozie Powell, Willie Roberson, Charles Weems, Eugene Williams, Andy Wright, and Roy Wright

Crime Charged: Rape

Chief Defense Lawyers: Stephen R. Roddy, Milo Moody, George W. Chamlee, Samuel S. Leibowitz, Joseph Brodsky, and Clarence Watts

Chief Prosecutors: H. G. Bailey, Wade Wright, Thomas G. Knight Jr., Melvin Hutson, and Thomas Lawson

Judges: Alfred E. Hawkins, James Edwin Horton Jr., and William Washington Callahan

Places: Scottsboro, Alabama; Decatur, Alabama

Dates of Trials: April 6–9, 1931; March 27–April 9, 1933; November 20–December 6, 1933; January 20–24, 1936; July 12–24, 1937

Verdicts: All but Roy Wright: guilty; Roy Wright: mistrial

Sentences: Death by electrocution, later reduced

SIGNIFICANCE: Such trials as the Scottsboro case gave America harsh and unforgettable lessons in the procedures of Southern courts. The opportunism of American Communists, the prejudice against blacks and Jews in the South, and the hypocrisy then rampant among Southern whites marked an era.

On a March morning in 1931, seven young white men entered a railroad stationmaster's office in northern Alabama. They claimed that while they were riding the rails, a "bunch of Negroes" threw them off the train. The stationmaster phoned ahead to a location near Scottsboro. There a deputy sheriff made deputies of every man with a gun. When the train stopped, the posse (group of legally authorized people used to keep the peace) rounded up nine young black men and two young white women. The women were dressed in men's caps and overalls.

While the females chatted, the deputy sheriff tied the black youths together and started asking questions. Five of the nine were from Georgia. Twenty-year-old Charlie Weems was the oldest. Clarence Norris was nineteen. Ozie Powell was sixteen. Olin Montgomery, seventeen, looked "sleepy-eyed" because he was blind in one eye and had only 10 percent of his vision in the other eye. Willie Roberson, seventeen, suffered from the sexually-transmitted diseases syphilis and gonorrhea, which made him walk with a cane. The other four boys came from Chattanooga, Tennessee. Haywood Patterson and Andy Wright were nineteen. Eugene Williams was thirteen. Wright's brother, Roy, was twelve.

The Scottsboro Trials: 1931–1937

Defendant Haywood Patterson holds a horseshoe for good luck while defense attorney Samuel Leibowitz (left) looks on.

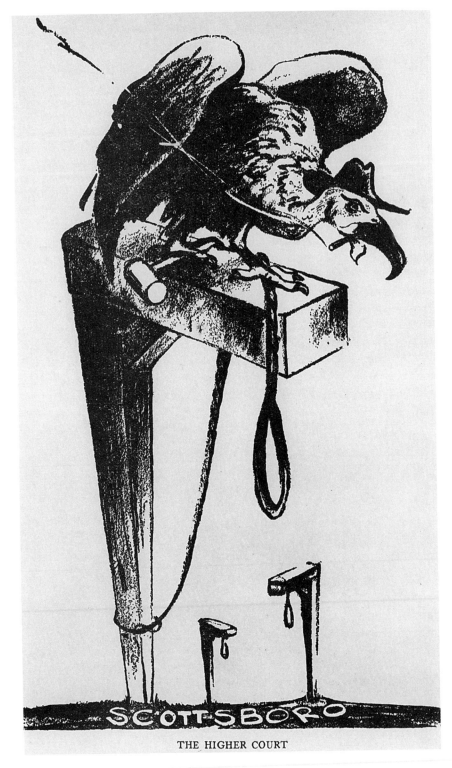

A cartoon from the Scottsboro trials depicts a judge holding a gavel and a noose. The cartoon inferred that the state was like a vulture trying to string up the defendants in an unfair trial.

SCOTTSBORO

THE HIGHER COURT

Accused of Rape

The deputy sheriff loaded his prisoners onto a truck. Then one of the women, Ruby Bates, from Huntsville, Alabama, spoke up. She told the deputy sheriff that she and her friend, Victoria Price, had been raped by the nine black youths.

In Scottsboro, the sheriff sent the women off to be examined by two doctors. Meanwhile, news of the rape had spread throughout the county. By nightfall, a mob of several hundred people stood outside the Scottsboro jail, promising to lynch (mob) the prisoners. The sheriff, barricaded inside, telephoned the governor. The governor sent out twenty-five National Guardsmen, but by the time they arrived at the jail, the mob had broken up.

The Trial Begins

Judge Alfred E. Hawkins offered the job of defending the nine black youths to anyone who would take it. He selected attorney Stephen R. Roddy, a resident of Chattanooga who admitted he did not know much about Alabama law. On the day the trial opened, Roddy, who already had a prison record for public drunkenness, was drunk by nine in the morning.

Prosecutor H. G. Bailey tried Norris and Weems first. Victoria Price described how she and Ruby Bates had hopped freight trains to Chattanooga to look for jobs. When they found none, they turned around to go home. Back on board the train, they met the nine black boys. After throwing seven white youths off the train, Price said, the blacks turned on she and her friend. She described how she was "beaten up" and "bruised up" as she was raped time after time. Then, she claimed, she lost consciousness.

Dr. R. R. Bridges testified that he saw no evidence of violence when he examined the girls. A second doctor agreed with him that while both girls showed signs of having had sexual intercourse recently, it had occurred at least twelve hours before he examined them.

Nonetheless, all of the defendants except twelve-year-old Roy Wright were found guilty of rape. Because of Roy Wright's age, the prosecution had asked that he be given a life sentence rather than death. When the jury could not agree on his sentence, the judge declared a mistrial in Roy Wright's case. The other eight were sentenced to die in the electric chair.

A "Legal Lynching"

Nationwide, those on the political left reacted to the sentences. The Central Committee of the Communist Party of the United States called the sentences "legal lynching." Its International Labor Defense (ILD) section pushed the National Association for the Advancement of Colored People (NAACP) to help them take the case to the U.S. Supreme Court. In Harlem (a section of New York City), 300,000 blacks and whites marched in the streets declaring "The Scottsboro Boys shall not die."

The ILD hired prominent Chattanooga lawyer George W. Chamlee. He requested a new trial for the Scottsboro boys. To support this request, he offered statements from various Chattanooga blacks. They said they had seen Victoria Price "embracing Negro men in dances in Negro houses," and that Ruby Bates had bragged that she could "take five Negroes in one night." The local press declared these statements false, but a Huntsville detective confirmed that both women were prostitutes.

"You Can't Mix Politics with Law"

The court denied the request for a new trial. The defendants looked for help, first to the NAACP, then to the ILD. Celebrated attorney Clarence Darrow turned down the NAACP's request that he argue an appeal before the Supreme Court. "You can't mix politics with law," he said. The NAACP then withdrew its support from the case.

In March, the Alabama Supreme Court upheld the convictions of all but Eugene Williams. As a juvenile, he was granted a new trial. In November, the U.S. Supreme Court ruled that seven of the defendants had been denied "due process" of law under the Fourteenth Amendment. When Judge Hawkins had appointed the unqualified Stephen Roddy to defend the Scottsboro boys, he had in effect prevented them from having a fair trial. A new trial would take place.

For the retrial, the ILD turned to noted New York criminal lawyer Samuel Leibowitz. Leibowitz succeeded in having the trial transferred to Decatur, Alabama. Patterson was tried first. Leibowitz produced several surprises. Bates took back her earlier testimony, saying she had lied to avoid being arrested for vagrancy (wandering without money or work). The defendants had not been seized all at once; instead, the arresting posse had found them in various areas of the forty-two-car train that carried them toward Scottsboro. Roberson's medical condition made it impossible for him to engage in sexual activity, and Montgomery's blindness also made him an unlikely rapist. Victoria Price, who was married, had served time for adultery.

Dr. Bridges repeated his earlier testimony that the girls had not been raped. The second doctor took Judge Horton aside to tell him that he, too, knew there had been no rape. But, he added, if he testified for the boys, "I'd never be able to go back into Jackson County." The judge believed the defense would prove Patterson innocent, so he said nothing.

Defense attorney Leibowitz now lived with National Guardsmen to protect him against threats of lynching. Prosecutor Wade Wright added to the tense atmosphere surrounding the trial when he told the jury, "Show them that Alabama justice cannot be bought and sold with Jew money from New York."

The jury found Patterson guilty. He was sentenced to death. When the defense requested a new trial, however, Judge Horton granted it. Then, under pressure from Attorney General Thomas Knight, he withdrew from the case.

Another New Trial

Opening the new trial, Judge William Washington Callahan, seventy, dismissed the National Guard and banned cameras inside and outside the courtroom. He rejected Leibowitz's motion to dismiss Patterson's indictment because blacks were not allowed to serve on the jury. He ran a twelve-hour day in the courtroom. He refused to allow in testimony about Victoria Price's sexual activity two nights before the train ride to Scottsboro. When he gave the jury its instructions before they retired to consider their verdict, he told them that any intercourse between a black man and a white woman is rape. Until Leibowitz reminded him to do so, Judge Callahan neglected to give the jury instructions on how to acquit the defendant if they found him not guilty.

Again Patterson was found guilty and sentenced to death. Clarence Norris was also found guilty. Then Leibowitz discovered that two ILD attorneys were trying to bribe Victoria Price to change her testimony. Price had hinted that she was willing to do so, and the attorneys told Leibowitz that a changed story would be good for their cause. Furious, Leibowitz threatened to withdraw from the case "unless all Communists are removed from the defense."

Supreme Court Overturns Convictions

The U.S. Supreme Court overturned all the convictions because the state of Alabama excluded African Americans from all juries at the time. In

LABOR ACTIVITIES IN THE SOUTH

The arrest and trial of the "Scottsboro boys" took place against a background of interracial labor organizing in the South. In 1932, the Sharecroppers Union was seeking to organize both black and white sharecroppers—tenant farmers who worked other people's land in exchange for a percentage of the crop. Ralph Gray, African American leader of that union in Alabama, was lynched after the union passed resolutions in support of the Scottsboro boys.

November 1935, a grand jury of thirteen whites and one black brought new indictments. At the fourth trial, in January 1936, a jury again found Patterson guilty. Sentenced this time to seventy-five years in jail, he said, "I'd rather die."

The next trial was delayed until July 1937. Then the court found Norris guilty and sentenced him to death. It also found Wright guilty and gave him ninety-nine years in jail. Weems was also declared guilty and given seventy-five years' imprisonment. The rape charge against Powell was dropped when he pleaded guilty to stabbing a deputy sheriff and was sentenced to twenty years. The charges against Montgomery, Wright, Roberson, and Williams were suddenly dropped.

"All were Guilty or All should be Free"

The U.S. Supreme Court refused to review Patterson's conviction. Alabama Governor Bibb Graves, asked to pardon the four convicted Scottsboro boys, agreed that "all were guilty or all should be freed." However, after setting a date for the pardon, he changed his mind.

Weems was freed in November 1943. Wright and Norris got out of jail in January 1944, but they were sent back to prison after they broke the terms of their parole by moving north. Wright was paroled again in 1950. Patterson escaped from prison in 1948. He was arrested in Detroit, but Michigan governor G. Mennen Williams refused a request to send him back to Alabama. Patterson was later convicted of manslaughter and died of cancer in prison in 1952. Norris, the last surviving "Scottsboro boy," was pardoned at age sixty-four by Alabama governor George C. Wallace in 1976.

Suggestions for Further Reading

Carter, Dan T. *Scottsboro: A Tragedy of the American South.* Baton Rouge: Louisiana State University Press, 1969.

Goodman, James. E. *Stories of Scottsboro.* New York: Vintage Books, 1995.

Haskins, James. *The Scottsboro Boys.* New York: Henry Holt, 1994.

Nash, Jay Robert. *Encyclopedia of World Crime.* Wilmette, IL: CrimeBooks, Inc., 1990.

Patterson, Haywood. *Scottsboro Boy.* Garden City, NY: Doubleday & Co., 1950.

Reynolds, Quentin. *Courtroom.* New York: Farrar, Straus and Cudahy, 1950.

The
Scottsboro
Trials:
1931–1937

Jomo Kenyatta Trial: 1952–1953

Defendants: Jomo Kenyatta, Fred Kubai, Richard Achieng Oneko, Bildad Kaggia, Paul Ngei, and Kungu Karumba—all executives of the Kenya African Union

Charges: Membership in the Mau Mau, a secret rebel group, and managing that "unlawful society" declared "dangerous to the good government of the Colony"

Chief Defense Lawyers: D. N. Pritt, A. R. Kapila, Chaman Lall, D. W. Thompson, H. O. Davis, Peter Evans, Fitzwell de Souza, and Jaswart Singh

Chief Prosecutor: Anthony Somerhough

Judge: Ransley S. Thacker

Place: Kapenguria, Kenya

Dates: November 24, 1952–April 8, 1953

Verdict: Guilty

Sentence: All defendants: seven years' hard labor for managing the Mau Mau, three years' hard labor for membership in the Mau Mau, the sentences to run at the same time; Kenyatta was also given "indefinite restriction" in a remote village

SIGNIFICANCE: Kenya convicted African nationalist leaders, including Kenyatta, by means of an unfair trial. This tactic backfired. Just over a decade later Kenya became independent, with Kenyatta as its first African president. Many historians believe the trial may well have helped Kenya reach independence sooner than it would have otherwise.

Although the British courts had a reputation for fairness, those in African and other colonies were not. This was especially true when they were part of an effort to crush movements for freedom from British rule.

In 1952, terrorists called the Mau Mau began killing British colonists and Africans alike. The Mau Mau, a secret society, wanted to push all whites, who numbered around 35,000, out of Kenya. On October 20, the Kenyan government declared a state of emergency, imposing military law. During the night of October 20, police and army units rounded up hundreds of suspects. Included was Jomo Kenyatta, an important nationalist and the leader of the Kenya African Union (KAU), which had more than 100,000 members.

Kenyatta's Background

Kenyatta was born Johnstone Kamau Ngengi on October 20, 1891. His parents belonged to the Kikuyu tribe. Scottish missionaries educated the young boy. In 1929, he went to London to study. He changed his name to Jomo ("Burning Spear") Kenyatta. His classic study of Kikuyu society, *Facing Mount Kenya,* earned him an advanced degree from the Lon-

Police round up suspects at Thompson Falls during the Mau Mau revolt in Kenya (1953).

HUMAN RIGHTS

don School of Economics. During the time, he helped organize the Pan-African Federation.

In 1946, Kenyatta returned to Kenya. There he turned the Kikuyu cultural association into a national political party, KAU. At the same time, he worked as the principal of a teachers' college that prepared teachers to work in independent African schools. Because of these activities, Kenyatta fell under the suspicion of Kenya's government. Officials suspected him of aiding the Mau Mau.

Whites Deport Kenyatta

Police arrested Kenyatta along with Fred Kubai, Richard Achieng Oneko, Bildad Kaggia, Paul Ngei, and Kungu Karumba. None were allowed to have lawyers. On November 18, the government sent them to the remote settlement of Kapenguria. The government hoped the location of the trial would enable it to avoid publicity. They also expected it would prevent Kenyatta's supporters from attending.

Kenyatta got out a message requesting the help of lawyers. Friends and supporters raised money and assembled an impressive international defense team. The team feared that government agents might seize and read their letters and telegrams or eavesdrop on telephone calls. So members drove long distances over hazardous roads to attend secret meetings or hand deliver documents.

Kenyatta obtained the services of one of the most gifted lawyers expert in English law, D. N. Pritt, a former member of the British Parliament. Pritt had defended anti-colonial leaders from Africa to India and the far East. Perhaps even more valuable than Pritt's legal skill was his ability to attract publicity for his clients.

The government appointed Ransley Thacker, a retired judge of the Kenya Supreme Court. A strong supporter of the colonialists, he would try the case without a jury. Taking charge of the case on November 24, Thacker refused a defense request to order Deputy Public Prosecutor Anthony Somerhough to release the details of the charges, which were so vague that it was nearly impossible to develop a defense to counter them. Thacker postponed the trial until December 3, when Pritt would be ready to lead the defense.

The defense requested a transfer of the trial to another court and to another judge. On December 1, the Kenya Supreme Court denied it. Pritt repeated this request in a telegram to British members of Parliament. English and African newspapers printed some of the telegram, causing the trial to be postponed. However, the prosecution served Pritt with a notice that he was in contempt of court (disrespect for authority of the court). On December 31, the Kenya Supreme Court dismissed the charge against Pritt.

A Weak Case

Finally the trial opened on January 2, 1953. The prosecution's case was weak. On the night of Kenyatta's arrest, the police had taken a ton and a half of papers, documents, and books from his house. They examined these, but they were unable to find anything connecting Kenyatta to the Mau Mau. The prosecution called African witnesses. It promised them money to help them protect themselves against Mau Mau revenge. However, the testimony of these witnesses was inconsistent and confused. Finally, in a harassing, seven-day cross-examination of Kenyatta, the government made Kenyatta appear to lie. Despite defense protests, the judge allowed the prosecution to ask numerous questions that should not have been allowed under Kenyan and English law. The judge also accepted the prosecution's view that Kenyatta had failed to denounce the Mau Mau at public KAU meetings. The defense countered with newspaper evidence. When the defense tried to bring in government tape recordings to prove their point, the judge ruled they could not.

Pritt stated that this was "the most childishly weak case ever brought against any man in the history of the British Empire." The judge, however, found the defendants guilty. He imposed maximum sentences and left Kenya immediately.

The defendants' attempts for an appeal (legal method for a new trial) lasted for over a year. The Kenya Supreme Court finally ruled in favor of the defense because of a technicality and ordered a retrial. When the East African Court of Appeal reversed this decision, the defense moved on to the highest court, the English Privy Council sitting in London. It refused to hear the case.

The Aftermath

The defendants served the first part of their sentences doing hard labor. They had to break rocks and dig holes and refill them. Because of his age, Kenyatta performed cooking duties.

In late 1958, chief prosecution witness Rawson Macharia admitted that he had lied in the Kenyatta trial. He said government agents had

KENYATTA'S COUNTRY

Anthropologists believe that Jomo Kenyatta's country, Kenya, was home to the first humans on earth some two million years ago. Farmers and herders inhabited the Kenya highlands as long ago as 1000 B.C. In the eighth century A.D., Arab traders first settled on the Kenya coast, establishing independent city-states. The first Europeans who came to Kenya were the Portuguese, who began to take over the Kenya coast in 1498. In 1729, however, the Arabs expelled the Portuguese. Then, in 1886, the British made an agreement with the Germans, which enabled them to take possession of much of modern Kenya. European settlers first came to Kenya in large numbers after 1903, when the first railroad made it easier to travel deep into the country. For half a century, the residents of Kenya protested the British occupation, resulting in the violent Mau Mau movement as well as Kenyatta's Kenya Africa Union.

bribed and coached him and other witnesses. In this, often called the second Kenyatta trial, Pritt defended Macharia. Although Macharia was found guilty, according to Pritt, the case had "done infinite political good, both directly and indirectly."

Kenyatta served out his sentence, extended by two years, in a remote village. Later, as president of an independent Kenya, he would demonstrate the statesmanlike qualities that he had displayed at his trial. When questioned about the aims of the KAU, replied:

> We do not believe in violence at all: we believe in negotiation, that is, we ask for our rights through constitutional means—through discussion and representation. We feel that the racial barrier is one of the most diabolical things that we have in this Colony, because we see no reason why all races in this country cannot work harmoniously together without any discrimination. . . . We believe that if people of goodwill can work together they can eliminate that evil.

Suggestions for Further Reading

Acacia Productions. *No Easy Walk.* (Videocassette.) Great Britain: Cinema Guild, 1987.

Howarth, Anthony. *Kenyatta, A Photographic Biography.* Nairobi, Kenya: East African Publishing House, 1967.

Kenyatta, Jomo. *Suffering without Bitterness, the Founding of the Kenya Nation.* Nairobi: East African Publishing House, 1968.

Macharia, Rawson. *The Truth about the Trial of Jomo Kenyatta.* Nairobi: Longman Kenya, 1991.

Murray-Brown, Jeremy. *Kenyatta.* London, Boston: Allen & Unwin, 1979.

Slater, Montagu. *The Trial of Jomo Kenyatta.* London: Mercury Books, 1965.

Jomo Kenyatta Trial: 1952–1953

Clarence Earl Gideon Trials: 1961 and 1963

Defendant: Clarence Earl Gideon

Crime Charged: Robbery

Chief Defense Lawyer: First trial: none; second trial: W. Fred Turner

Chief Prosecutors: First trial: William E. Harris; second trial: J. Frank Adams, J. Paul Griffith, and William E. Harris

Judge: Robert L. McCrary Jr.

Place: Panama City, Florida

Dates of Trials: First trial: August 4, 1961; second trial: August 5, 1963

Verdicts: First trial: guilty; second trial: not guilty

Sentence: First trial: five years imprisonment

SIGNIFICANCE: One man, without wealth, privilege, or education, went up against the entire legal establishment, arguing that his constitutional rights had been violated. In doing so, he brought about an historic change in the way American criminal trials are conducted. All defendants accused of felonies (serious crimes) are now entitled to legal representation, regardless of the crimes with which they have been charged. Also, courts will appoint attorneys to represent defendants who are too poor to hire their own.

At eight o'clock on the morning of June 3, 1961, a police officer in Panama City, Florida, noticed that the door of the Bay Harbor Poolroom was open.

Clarence Earl Gideon argued that his constitutional rights were denied because he could not afford an attorney.

Stepping inside, he saw that someone had burglarized a cigarette machine and jukebox. The evidence gathered by police led to the arrest of Clarence Gideon, a fifty-one-year-old drifter who sometimes helped at the poolroom. Gideon declared that he was innocent. Nonetheless, two months later he faced trial in the Panama City courthouse. No one present at the trial had any idea that they were about to witness history in the making.

Gideon's First Trial

Gideon, although poverty-stricken, was not entitled to the services of a court-appointed defense lawyer. A 1942 Supreme Court decision, *Betts v. Brady,* extended this right only to those defendants facing a charge punishable with the death sentence. Many states provided all defendants accused of a felony, or serious crime, with a lawyer. Florida did not. Judge Robert L. McCrary Jr. did his best to protect Gideon's interests when the trial opened August 4, 1961. Still he clearly could not assume the role of the defendant's lawyer. That task fell to Gideon himself. Gideon, a man of limited education, performed as well as he could, but he was not the equal of the Assistant State Attorney William E. Harris, who presented Henry Cook as one of the primary witnesses against Gideon.

Cook claimed to have seen Gideon inside the poolroom at 5:30 on the morning of the robbery. Cook said that he had watched Gideon for a few minutes through a window. Then Gideon came out. He was clutching a pint of wine in his hand. He then made a telephone call from a

nearby booth. Soon afterward a cab arrived and Gideon left.

During cross-examination Gideon questioned Cook's reasons for being outside the bar at that time of the morning. Cook replied that he had "just come from a dance, [and had] stayed out all night." Someone more experienced might have explored Cook's alibi further, but Gideon let it pass. Eight witnesses testified on Gideon's behalf. None proved helpful, and Gideon was found guilty. The whole trial had lasted less than one day. Three weeks later Judge McCrary sentenced Gideon to the maximum possible sentence: five years' imprisonment.

Clarence Earl Gideon's petition to the United States Supreme Court.

Gideon Fights Back

Gideon was outraged at the verdict, particularly because he had had no court-appointed lawyer. He applied to the Florida Supreme Court for an order freeing him on grounds that he was illegally imprisoned (a writ of *habeas corpus*). When this application was denied, Gideon wrote a five-page document petitioning the Supreme Court to review his case.

Each year the Supreme Court receives thousands of such petitions. Most are rejected. Against all odds, the Supreme Court decided to hear Gideon's petition. The case was heard as *Gideon v. H. G. Cochran, Jr.* (the director of Florida's Division of Corrections). Cochran's lawyers were Bruce R. Jacob and George Mentz. Abe Fortas, who would later become a Supreme Court justice, argued Gideon's suit. The date for oral argument was January 14, 1963. Before that date Cochran resigned his position and was replaced by Louie L. Wainwright. He thus earned an enduring if unwanted place in judicial history when the case was renamed *Gideon v. Wainwright.*

Fortas argued that the restrictions imposed after the ruling in *Betts v. Brady* resulted in unfairness to Gideon. This drew a pointed comparison between Gideon's situation and that of one of the nation's foremost legal personalities. "I was reminded the other night, as I was pondering this case, of Clarence Darrow when he was prosecuted for trying to fix a jury. The first thing he realized was that he needed a lawyer—he, one of the country's greatest criminal lawyers." It was time, said Fortas, for the law to change.

Jacob and Mentz disagreed, but the ruling went against them. On March 18, 1963, the Supreme Court unanimously overruled *Betts v. Brady,* saying that all felony defendants are entitled to legal representation, regardless of which crime they are charged with having committed. Justice Hugo L. Black wrote the opinion that set aside Gideon's conviction:

> **Reason and reflection requires us to recognize that in our adversary system of criminal justice, any person haled [hauled] into court, who is too poor to hire a lawyer, cannot be assured a fair trial unless counsel is provided for him. This seems to us to be an obvious truth.**

On August 5, 1963, Clarence Gideon again appeared before Judge Robert L. McCrary in the Panama City courthouse, but at his new trial he had an experienced trial lawyer, W. Fred Turner, to defend him. All of the publicity surrounding his Supreme Court victory also resulted in a stronger prosecution team at Gideon's second trial. State Attorney J. Frank Adams and J. Paul Griffith joined Harris to argue for Gideon's conviction a second time. Cook was again the main prosecution witness, but he did not stand up well under Turner's expert questioning. Particularly damaging to the prosecution was Cook's admission that he had withheld details of his criminal record at the previous trial. Due in large part to Cook's poor showing, the jury acquitted (found not guilty) Gideon of all charges.

Clarence Earl Gideon died in 1973 at age sixty-one.

Because one man took the time to write a letter, no felony defendant need ever face a court alone. *Gideon v. Wainwright* extended the law's protection to all. More than that, it gave American justice a better name.

HUMAN RIGHTS

HABEAS CORPUS: A CONSTITUTIONAL RIGHT

Clarence Gideon claimed that since he had not had his Constitutional right to a fair trial, he was being held illegally, and so he sought a "writ of *habeas corpus*." The "privilege of the writ of *habeas corpus*" is guaranteed by Article I, Section 9 of the U.S. Constitution. *Habeas corpus* is a Latin term that literally means "you have the body." It refers to a prisoner's right not to be held except under circumstances outlined by law. In other words, the police cannot simply pick up someone and hold him or her in prison. To hold a person in jail, the person must either be legally arrested and awaiting trial or convicted of a crime and serving a sentence. Moreover, the Fifth Amendment guarantees that citizens cannot be "deprived of life, liberty, or property, without due process of law." So Gideon claimed that since he had not had an attorney for his trial, he had not received due process of law.

Suggestions for Further Reading

Lewis, Anthony. *Gideon's Trumpet.* New York: Vintage Books, 1989.

Schwartz, Bernard. *History of the Law in America.* New York: American Heritage, 1974.

West Publishing Company Staff. *The Guide to American Law.* St. Paul, MN: West Publishing Co., 1985.

Ernesto Miranda Trials: 1963 and 1967

Defendant: Ernesto Miranda

Crimes Charged: Kidnapping and rape

Chief Defense Lawyers: First trial: Alvin Moore; second trial: John Flynn

Chief Prosecutors: First trial: Laurence Turoff; second trial: Robert Corbin

Judges: First trial: Yale McFate; second trial: Lawrence K. Wren

Place: Phoenix, Arizona

Dates of Trials: June 20–27, 1963; February 15–March 1, 1967

Verdicts: Guilty, both trials

Sentences: Twenty to thirty years, both trials

SIGNIFICANCE: Few events have altered the course of American justice more than the 1963 rape conviction of Ernesto Miranda. The primary evidence against him was a confession he made while in police custody. How that confession was obtained captured the nation's attention and prompted a landmark United States Supreme Court decision.

In Phoenix, Arizona, during the early hours of March 3, 1963, an eighteen-year-old movie theater attendant suddenly faced a stranger while on her way home from work. The stranger dragged her into his car and drove out to the desert, where he raped her. Later, he dropped the young woman off near her home. She told police her attacker was a Mexican in his late

HUMAN RIGHTS

twenties. She said he wore glasses and was driving an early 1950s car, either a Ford or Chevrolet.

By chance, one week later, the woman and her brother-in-law saw what looked like the car in which she had been held. It was a 1953 Packard, license plate DFL-312. However, records showed that this plate was actually registered to a late model Oldsmobile. The woman's identification of the license plate was close. DFL-317 was a Packard, registered to a Twila N. Hoffman. Hoffman's companion, Ernesto Miranda, twenty-three, fit the attacker's description almost exactly.

Police Jail Miranda

Under the Miranda decision, police must inform defendants of certain rights when an arrest takes place.

Miranda had a long history of criminal behavior. He had already served a one-year jail term for attempted rape. Police put him into a line-up with three other Mexicans of similar height and build, though none wore glasses. The victim did not positively identify Miranda. However, she said that he was the one who looked most like her attacker. Detectives Carroll Cooley and Wilfred Young then took Miranda into a room for question-

WARNING

The constitution requires that I inform you of your rights:

You have a right to remain silent. If you talk to any police officer, anything you say can and will be used against you in court.

You have a right to consult with a lawyer before you are questioned, and may have him with you during questioning.

If you cannot afford a lawyer, one will be appointed for you, if you wish, before any questioning.

If you wish to answer questions, you have the right to stop answering at any time.

You may stop answering questions at any time if you wish to talk to a lawyer, and may have him with you during any further questioning.

Rev. 9-79

ing. They told him, incorrectly, that the victim had picked him out of the line-up. Then they asked if he wanted to make a statement. Two hours later Miranda signed a written confession. He had not been physically or verbally abused or forced to sign the statement. Included in the confession was a section stating that he understood his rights. The detectives were pleased, although they did not realize the legal consequences that would result from their work.

E r n e s t o
M i r a n d a
T r i a l s : 1 9 6 3
a n d 1 9 6 7

Tainted Evidence

Miranda was financially unable to hire an attorney, so the state appointed him a lawyer, Alvin Moore. Moore studied the evidence. The state, which in criminal trials brings the charges, appeared to have a solid case. It was even stronger because of Miranda's confession. Still there was something about the confession that Moore found troubling. Convinced it had been obtained improperly, he intended to ask the court to rule that it could not be accepted in court as evidence of Miranda's guilt.

Only four witnesses appeared for the prosecution. They were the victim, her sister, and Detectives Cooley and Young. Moore cross-examined Cooley, making his most important point:

Question: Officer Cooley, in the taking of this statement, what did you say to the defendant to get him to make this statement?

Answer: I asked the defendant if he would . . . write the same story that he just told me, and he said that he would.

Question: Did you warn him of his rights?

Answer: Yes, sir, at the heading of the statement is a paragraph typed out, and I read this paragraph to him out loud.

Question: I don't see in the statement that it says where he is entitled to the advice of an attorney before he made it.

Answer: No, sir.

Question: Is it not your practice to advise people you arrest that they are entitled to the services of an attorney before they make a statement?

Answer: No, sir.

This admission prompted Moore to object to Miranda's confession being accepted as evidence. Judge Yale McFate overruled him. He then gave the jury a well-balanced and fair account of the law as it stood at the time. In 1963, the constitutional right to remain silent did not apply

to suspects detained by police. Consequently, on June 27, 1963, the court convicted Ernesto Miranda and sentenced him to two terms of twenty-to-thirty years' imprisonment, both running at the same time.

However, Moore's arguments about the confession had touched off a legal debate. Miranda's conviction was appealed all the way to the U.S. Supreme Court. On June 13, 1966, Chief Justice Earl Warren, speaking for a 5–4 majority, for the first time established guidelines for determining what is and what is not allowed in a police interrogation room:

> Prior to any questioning, the person must be warned that he has a right to remain silent, that any statement he does make may be used as evidence against him, and that he has a right to the presence of an attorney, either retained or appointed.

Court Overturns Conviction

With Miranda's conviction overturned, Arizona faced the prospect of having to free its most well-known prison inmate. Since the state could no longer use Miranda's confession as evidence in court, it had little chance of winning a retrial. It was Miranda himself who brought about his own downfall. He had expected to be released after retrial. So he had begun a battle for custody of his daughter with Twila Hoffman, his long-time companion. Hoffman, angry and fearful, told authorities about a conversation she had had with Miranda after his arrest, during which he had admitted the rape. This new evidence was all Arizona needed.

Miranda Retried

Miranda's second trial began February 15, 1967. Most of the arguments took place in the judge's private chambers. There was some question as to whether a common-law (not legal) wife could testify against her common-law husband. Finally the judge ruled that Hoffman's testimony could be allowed as evidence. Her story helped to convince the jury of Miranda's guilt. The court convicted him for a second time and sentenced him to a twenty-to-thirty-year jail term.

Miranda's Legacy

On January 31, 1976, four years after he was released on parole, someone stabbed Ernesto Miranda to death in a Phoenix bar fight. The killer

INFLUENTIAL CHIEF JUSTICE

Earl Warren was Chief Justice of the U.S. Supreme Court from 1953 to 1969. During this time, the "Warren Court" made some of the most influential decisions in modern U.S. history, establishing many civil rights and individual liberties issues. No one expected such landmark decisions from Warren whose previous history was as a rather unremarkable Republican politician. Warren was California's attorney general from 1939 to 1943 and its governor from 1943 to 1953, involving himself in a shameful chapter in the state's history. As attorney general during World War II, he pressed for the internment of Japanese Americans in detention camps, based on the fear that they might be enemy agents and spies. As governor, he presided over the internment process. In 1948, he was an unsuccessful vice-presidential candidate, running with Republican Thomas Dewey against President Harry S Truman. Yet as Chief Justice, Warren led the court to establish new precedents that outlawed school segregation, established the right to court-appointed attorneys, and asserted the right of arrested men and women to know their rights. While serving as Chief Justice, Warren also headed the "Warren Commission," established by President Lyndon Johnson on November 29, 1963, to investigate the assassination of President John F. Kennedy.

fled but his accomplice (helper) was caught. Before taking him to police headquarters, the arresting officers read the suspect his rights. This procedure was now referred to as "Mirandizing."

The importance of this case cannot be overstated. Although presidents from Richard Nixon to Ronald Reagan have publicly disagreed with it, the *Miranda* decision has not been overturned. Created originally to protect the poor and the ignorant, the practice of "reading the defendant his rights" has become standard in every police department in the country. The practice is seen so frequently in television police shows that today the words of the so-called "Miranda Warning" are as familiar to most Americans as those of the Pledge of Allegiance.

HUMAN RIGHTS

Suggestions for Further Reading

Baker, Liva. *Miranda: Crime, Law and Politics.* New York: Atheneum, 1983.

Graham, Fred P. *The Self-Inflicted Wound.* New York: Macmillan Co., 1970.

Skene, Neil. "The Miranda Ruling." *Congressional Quarterly* (June 6, 1991): 164.

Tucker, William. "The Long Road Back." *National Review* (October 18, 1985): 28–35.

U.S. v. Berrigan:
1968

Defendants: Philip Berrigan, Daniel Berrigan, and others

Crimes Charged: Willfully injuring government property, destroying public records, and hindering the operation of the Selective Service System

Chief Defense Lawyers: Harrop Freeman and William Kunstler

Chief Prosecutors: Stephen H. Sachs and Barnet D. Skolnik

Judge: Roszel C. Thomsen

Place: Baltimore, Maryland

Dates of Trial: October 7–10, 1968

Verdict: Guilty

Sentence: Three and a half years in prison for Philip Berrigan and three years in prison for Daniel Berrigan

SIGNIFICANCE: The courts refused to recognize moral opposition to the Vietnam War as a legal defense for prosecution of criminal acts of defiance. One example was the Berrigans' raid on a Selective Service office that housed young men's draft records.

Most people see the Roman Catholic Church as a conservative body, one that does not involve itself in American politics. During the late 1960s, however, Catholic priests began to take an active role in the movement to protest the increasingly unpopular Vietnam War. Two priests in particular—the Berrigan brothers, Philip and Daniel—got into serious trouble with the government.

HUMAN RIGHTS

Anti-War Activities

On October 26, 1967, Philip, Daniel, and three other people entered the Customs House in Baltimore, Maryland. The federal Selective Service Administration stored some draft records here. Philip, Daniel, and the others then broke into the file area, getting past a small staff of clerks. They emptied vials of blood into the file cabinets. This act symbolically demonstrated their belief that the Vietnam War was a "pitiful waste of American blood and Vietnamese blood." Afterward, they waited peacefully for the police to arrive.

Roman Catholic priest Philip Berrigan pours blood onto draft records at Selective Service Headquarters to protest the Vietnam War.

The federal authorities charged the Berrigans with destroying United States property, destroying public records, and hindering the administration of the Selective Service Act. A court found the Berrigans guilty of these charges. While awaiting sentencing, the Berrigans again demonstrated against the war. On May 17, 1968, they led seven people into the Selective Service office in Catonsville, Maryland, and seized nearly 400 files. They took these records to the parking lot and burned them with homemade napalm (jellied gasoline used in fire bombs). Once again, their actions were symbolic: napalm was the chemical weapon American troops used most often in Vietnam.

Philip and Daniel Berrigan Stand Trial

Police arrested the Berrigans. The government again charged them with violations of federal law. The Catonsville incident, however, inspired a nationwide wave of sympathetic anti-Vietnam protests unlike anything that followed the Baltimore Customs House affair. For example, in Milwaukee, Wisconsin, a group of Catholic activists stormed a Selective Service office and burned over 10,000 files.

The trial began on October 7, 1968. Philip Berrigan testified that his moral opposition to the Vietnam War led him to participate in the Catonsville incident:

> We have been accused of arrogance, but what of the fantastic arrogance of our leaders? What of their crimes against the people, the poor and the powerless? Still, no court will try them, no jail will receive them. They live in righteousness. They will die in honor. For them we have one message, for those in whose manicured hands the power of the land lies. We say to them: lead us. Lead us in justice and there will be no need to break the law.

The testimony of the rest of the "Catonsville Nine" was similar. They believed that America's fight in Vietnam was wrong. All of the defendants understood that they were breaking the law. However, they felt that their higher purpose in attempting to save human lives excused their actions. The prosecutors scornfully replied to this claim in their closing argument. "Our problems are not going to be solved by people who deliberately violate our laws, the foundation and support for an ordered and just and civilized society."

Before the jury retired to consider their verdict, Daniel Berrigan asked Judge Roszel C. Thomsen to interpret the law not according to its technical requirements, but according to human morality. Berrigan argued that the judge and the jury were responsible to a higher authority than the law. He said that if they believed as he did that the Vietnam War was wrong, they should acquit him and the others.

Thomsen was clearly sympathetic to these anti-war attitudes, but he knew that his responsibility as a judge was to uphold the law. Thomsen replied to Daniel Berrigan:

> You speak to me as a man and as a judge. I would be a funny sort if I were not moved by your sincerity on the stand, and by your views. I agree with you completely, as a person. We can never accomplish, or give a better life to people, if we are going to keep on giving so much money to war. It is very unfortunate but the issue of war cannot be presented as clearly as you would like. The basic principle of the law is that we do things in an orderly fashion. People cannot take the law into their own hands.

On October 10, 1968, after fewer than two hours of deliberation, the jury returned a verdict of guilty against the nine defendants. Philip Berrigan and another defendant were sentenced to three and a half years in prison. Daniel Berrigan and two other defendants were sentenced to three years in prison. The remaining four defendants received two-year sentences.

Convictions Appealed

The Berrigans' lawyers appealed their clients' convictions to the United States Court of Appeals for the Fourth Circuit. On June 10, 1969, both sides made their cases before the court, which issued its decision on October 15, 1969. There was one very interesting issue that the court had to consider. This was the defense's argument that the jury should have been free to clear the defendants if they chose to do so, regardless of the defendants' obvious guilt.

However, the Court of Appeals still upheld the Berrigans' convictions. It noted that the jury's freedom to do as it pleased had been greatly cut back in modern times. Even though the Berrigans' cause was noble,

THE BERRIGANS CONTINUE THEIR PROTESTS

Daniel and Philip Berrigan went on to lead many more actions for peace, including additional actions of civil disobedience (breaking one law to protest another law or issue). On March 12, 1997, for example, six members of the Prince of Peace Plowshares, a group founded by Philip Berrigan, broke into the Navy destroyer USS *The Sullivans*. The protestors, including Berrigan, disabled the ship by pouring their own blood onto its computer circuits and using hammers to beat on the hatches that covered the tubes used to fire nuclear missiles. Over the ship they hung a banner quoting from the biblical prophet Isaiah: "They shall beat their swords into plowshares and their spears into pruning hooks." The six members of the group were arrested and charged with two felonies in federal court. "We've alerted people once again to this killing machine that Clinton is refurbishing," said Philip Berrigan in a phone interview from the Cumberland County (Maryland) Jail with *The Progressive,* a monthly news magazine. "And we've alerted the peace movement that things aren't over yet. Disarmament is not a fact. The Clinton Administration wants the American people to believe that it is, but that is far from the truth."

the law could not approve their criminal acts, because the alternative was to allow every group with a particular political viewpoint to do as it pleased.

The Berrigans and the rest of the Catonsville Nine went to prison. The courts did not accept their defense that moral opposition to a war was a legal defense to criminal conduct. In essence, Judge Thomsen and the judges of the Fourth Circuit had held that there was no place in the law for the belief that "extremism in the defense of liberty is no vice." That phrase, however, originated with Senator Barry Goldwater, a major supporter of the Vietnam War.

Suggestions for Further Reading

Berrigan, Daniel. *No Bars to Manhood.* Garden City, NY: Doubleday & Co., 1970.

HUMAN RIGHTS

Berrigan, Daniel. *To Dwell in Peace: An Autobiography.* New York: Harper & Row, 1987.

Casey, William Van Etten. *The Berrigans.* New York: Avon, 1971.

Curtis, Richard. *The Berrigan Brothers: the Story of Daniel and Philip Berrigan.* New York: Hawthorn Books, 1974.

Halpert, Stephen. *Witness of the Berrigans.* Garden City, NY: Doubleday & Co., 1972.

Lockwood, Lee. *Daniel Berrigan: Absurd Convictions, Modest Hopes.* New York: Random House, 1972.

Polner, Mary. *Disarmed and Dangerous: The Radical Lives and Times of Daniel and Philip Berrigan.* New York: Basic Books, 1997.

In the Matter of
Karen Ann Quinlan:
1975

Plaintiff: Joseph T. Quinlan

Defendant: St. Clare's Hospital

Plaintiff Claim: That doctors at St. Clare's Hospital should obey Joseph Quinlan's instructions to disconnect his comatose daughter from her respirator and allow her to die

Chief Defense Lawyers: Ralph Porzio (for Karen Quinlan's physicians), Theodore Einhorn (for the hospital), New Jersey State Attorney General William F. Hyland, and Morris County Prosecutor Donald G. Collester Jr.

Chief Lawyers for Plaintiff: Paul W. Armstrong and James Crowley

Judge: Robert Muir Jr.

Place: Morristown, New Jersey

Date of Decision: November 10, 1975

Decision: Denied Joseph Quinlan the right to authorize termination of "life-assisting apparatus" (machines that kept patients alive) and granted Karen Quinlan's physicians the right to continue to treat her over the objections of the Quinlan family. Overturned by the New Jersey Supreme Court, which, on March 31, 1976, ruled that Karen's "right of privacy" included a right to refuse medical treatment and that her father, under the circumstances, could assume this right for her

SIGNIFICANCE: This case brought about the adoption in some states of "brain death" (no brain activity) as the legal definition of death. It also caused the adoption in other states of laws recognizing "living wills" (documents directing that life support assistance be ended if person cannot recover) and the "right to die" (the right to end one's life).

HUMAN RIGHTS

The parents of Karen Ann Quinlan (center)—with their attorney, Paul Armstrong, and their family pastor, Thomas Trapasso— speak to the press on March 31, 1976, after the New Jersey Supreme Court decided the fate of their daughter.

On April 15, 1975, twenty-one-year-old Karen Ann Quinlan fell into a coma. Doctors found she had taken tranquilizers along with alcohol. Unable to breathe on her own, she was put on a mechanical respirator.

By the fall of 1975, Quinlan's family and doctors had given up hope for her recovery. Her parents, Julia and Joseph Quinlan, were devout Roman Catholics. The Quinlans consulted their parish priest, Father Thomas Trapasso. He told them that they could, without guilt, request that Karen be removed from the respirator. They made the request. However, Karen's primary doctor, Dr. Robert Morse, refused to end the artificial life support. Joseph Quinlan went to court.

Parents Ask the Court to Allow Karen to Die

The trial began on October 20, 1975. The court appointed attorney Daniel R. Coburn as Karen Quinlan's guardian. Morris County prosecutor Donald Collester and New Jersey State Attorney general William Hyland represented the state. State law prohibited taking the young woman off her respirator. They defined this as murder. Hyland claimed that the suit challenged New Jersey's very definition of death, that is, when all "vital signs,"

such as breathing, stop. He felt it could result in a new definition of death, one based on the end of all brain-wave activity (brain death).

The week before the trial, however, doctors revealed that Karen Quinlan still had brain-wave activity. She could also breathe on her own for short periods and had occasionally shown muscle activity. Some doctors described these as her will to live. Clearly the trial would not focus on New Jersey's definition of death. Instead it would answer the even more complicated question of whether Karen Quinlan had a "right to die."

Medical Values and the Right to Die

One of Karen Quinlan's doctors, Robert Morse, was the first person to testify. He said that Karen would never resume a normal life. However, he said he saw no medical grounds for disconnecting her breathing machine. He would not obey a court order to do so. Arshad Jarved, another of Quinlan's doctors, had also refused Joseph Quinlan's request. He said that the standards of medical practice did not permit the removal of the respirator.

The Quinlans' attorney argued that the rights of privacy and religious freedom included a right to die. He said that the Quinlans felt that the machine that breathed for her was keeping their daughter from God and heaven.

Karen Quinlan's court-appointed guardian saw the matter differently: "This isn't a terminal cancer case where someone is going to die. Where there is hope, you cannot just extinguish a life because it becomes an eyesore."

The following day, Armstrong called an expert witness. He was Dr. Julius Korein, a specialist on the nervous system. The doctor worked at Bellevue Hospital and New York University Medical School. Korein described the seventy-five-pound Karen Quinlan as having serious brain damage. He testified that she had only unconscious reactions, such as blinking or rolling her eyes, to stimulation. He also said doctors often withheld aggressive treatment from patients who were near death and in pain. He added, "[t]hat is the unwritten law and one of the purposes of this trial is to make it the written law."

Family Pleads for Removal of Life Support

Then an emotional Joseph Quinlan took the witness stand. He asked the court to "take her from the machine and the tubes and let her pass into the hands of the Lord."

HUMAN RIGHTS

THE "SLIPPERY SLOPE"

The question of a person's "right to die" is what lawyers call a "slippery slope." What they mean is that once you make one exception to a rule, it is hard to know where the exceptions will stop, as if you were sliding down a slippery slope. The case of Karen Ann Quinlan, for example, centered on her parents' wish to speed her death by turning off her respirator. Later, similar cases centered on whether people in comas should be allowed to die by starvation. Other cases have concerned whether physicians should actively induce death, such as by giving a comatose or even a conscious patient a higher dose of medication. Formerly, the "right to die" was considered only in cases where the patient was comatose or suffering from a painful illness that would soon bring death anyway. Now doctors and bioethicists are debating other forms of physician-assisted suicide, in which conscious patients might choose death because they are suffering from pain or disability—but might otherwise still live for months or even years. People who favor physician-assisted suicide say that the quality of life is more important than its length. People who are concerned about the "slippery slope," however, worry that sick or elderly people might be pressured into choosing death out of guilt, depression, or financial concerns.

On the third day, Karen's mother, Julia Ann Quinlan, testified that Karen had made her wishes known three times in the past. Karen had told her, "Mommy, please don't ever let them keep me alive by extraordinary means." She stated this after two friends and an aunt finally died after long battles with cancer. "Karen loved life," her mother said. "If there was any way that she could not live life to the fullest she wanted to be able to die in her own surroundings, instead of being kept alive for months or years." Mrs. Quinlan continued: "I visit her every day and as I see her in her present condition I know in my heart as a mother she would not want to be there. We discussed this many times."

AFTERMATH

The Quinlan case prompted the formation of "bioethics" committees (groups that study ethical problems stemming from medical practices) in many hospitals. In 1985, the New Jersey Supreme Court ruled that all life-sustaining medical treatment, including artificial feeding, could be withheld from terminally ill patients incapable of expressing their desires, provided such action reflected the ailing person's past wishes.

The defense lawyers objected to admitting such reported conversations as evidence in court. However, Judge Robert Muir Jr. permitted Karen's sister and one of her friends to give similar testimony.

On October 23, three doctors testified. They were Dr. Fred Plum of the American Association of Neurologists, Dr. Sidney Diamond of Mount Sinai Hospital, and Dr. Stuart Cook of the New Jersey College of Medicine and Dentistry. The three agreed that Karen Quinlan's loss of "higher" brain function (anything beyond minor, unconscious reactions) could not be reversed or repaired. Yet they agreed that Karen was alive according to both legal and medical definitions, and that it would be improper to remove the respirator.

Judge Says Let Karen Live

On November 10, 1975, Judge Muir handed down his decision. He refused permission for the removal of the respirator. Then he appointed Coburn to continue acting as Karen's guardian. Muir rejected the Quinlans' plea that their daughter be allowed to pass into life after death. "This Court will not authorize that life to be taken away from her."

On November 17, 1975, the Quinlans filed an appeal (legal method for a new trial). The New Jersey Supreme Court agreed to hear it immediately. On January 26, 1976, the case was argued before the seven justices of New Jersey's highest court. Their unanimous decision came on March 31 and was a major upset. They named Joseph Quinlan Karen's

guardian and authorized him to order the removal of the breathing machine.

However, the court stated that the ruling was not based on the freedom of religion argument favored by the Quinlans. Instead, Chief Justice Hughes wrote, the court's decision was based on "Karen's right to privacy." It was a right, he continued, that could "be asserted on her behalf by her guardian under the peculiar circumstances here present."

Lastly, Justice Hughes dismissed the attorney general's and the Morris County prosecutor's assertion that the person removing Karen's respirator should be charged with homicide when she died.

None of the interested parties appealed this decision to the U.S. Supreme Court. Karen's respirator was removed in May 1976. She managed to breathe on her own and remained in a coma for another ten years. She died on June 11, 1985.

Suggestions for Further Reading

Colen, B. D. *Karen Ann Quinlan.* New York: Nash, 1976.

Kubler-Ross, Elizabeth. *On Death and Dying.* New York: Touchstone Books, 1997.

Quinlan, Joseph. *Karen Ann: The Quinlans Tell Their Story.* Garden City, NY: Doubleday & Co., 1977.

Los Angeles Police Officers' Trials: 1992 and 1993

Defendants: Theodore J. Briseno, Stacey C. Koon, Laurence M. Powell, and Timothy E. Wind

Crimes Charged: First trial: assault, excessive force by a police officer, and filing a false report; second trial: violating civil rights

Chief Defense Lawyers: First trial: Paul DePasquale, Darryl Mounger, and Michael P. Stone; second trial: Harland W. Braun, Paul DePasquale, Ira M. Salzman, and Michael P. Stone

Chief Prosecutors: First trial: Terry L. White; second trial: Steven D. Clymer, Barry Kowalski, Lawrence Middleton, and Alan Tieger

Judges: First trial: Stanley M. Weisberg; second trial: John G. Davies

Places: First trial: Simi Valley, California; second trial: Los Angeles, California

Dates of Trials: First trial: March 4–April 29, 1992; second trial: February 3–April 17, 1993

Verdict: First trial: not guilty; jury deadlocked on one charge against Powell; second trial: Koon and Powell, guilty; Briseno and Wind, not guilty

Sentence: Koon and Powell sentenced to thirty months imprisonment each

SIGNIFICANCE: What was already one of the most well-known cases in American legal history became even more important when a second jury had to wrestle not only with questions of guilt or innocence, but how best to deal with public anger over the verdict in the first trial.

HUMAN RIGHTS

In the early hours of March 3, 1991, Los Angeles police officers stopped a car after chasing it at high speed for three miles. It belonged to Rodney King. Police later reported that King refused orders to get out of his car. They said he put up such a struggle that officers had to use night sticks and stun-guns (guns that deliver an electric shock) to control him.

However, a person who lived nearby secretly filmed the incident. The eighty-one-second videotape of King's arrest told a surprising story. On the tape King seemed not to resist as several officers kicked and beat him to the ground, as a dozen other officers looked on. Public anger over the much-televised tape led to a grand jury investigation. The District Attorney charged the officers involved with state criminal offenses.

The First Trial

Because of the huge amount of publicity the case received, the trial took place outside Los Angeles. On March 4, 1992, the trial began in Simi Valley, well outside the city. California Highway Patrol Officer Melanie Singer testified for the state. She said that she saw Officer Laurence Powell strike King six times with his metal night stick for no reason. "He had it in a power swing and he struck the driver right across the top of the cheekbone, splitting his face from the top of his ear to his chin," she said. "Blood spurted out." Singer added that defendants Stacey Koon and Theodore Briseno tried to stop Powell from beating King more.

Prosecutors never called King, a tall, heavyset African American, to the witness stand. Perhaps they feared the ex-convict would not make a good impression on the jury.

Under questioning, Briseno admitted that he did not consider King's actions to be threatening. He repeatedly described Officers Powell and Timothy Wind as having been "out of control." He also blamed Sergeant Koon, the highest ranking officer present, for not stopping the beating.

The officers' defense lawyers said that the police had believed King was under the influence of PCP, a powerful drug that can make people dangerous. (King admitted that he *had* been drinking alcohol on the night he was arrested.) In his closing statement, defense lawyer Michael P. Stone said of the videotape, "We do not see an example of unprovoked police brutality. We see, rather, a controlled application of baton strikes, for the very obvious reason of getting this man into custody."

*Lawrence Powell
(left) answers
questions from
reporters on the
steps of the federal
courthouse in Los
Angeles during his
trial. Standing next
to Powell is his
attorney, Michael
Stone. In the
background Stacey
Koon also talks to
reporters. Powell
and Koon were
charged with
violating the civil
rights of Rodney
King.*

The jury clearly agreed. On April 29, 1992, they declared all of the defendants to be innocent of the charges against them, only deadlocking on one charge against Powell.

A City In Flames

The verdict rocked Los Angeles. Within hours rioters initially protesting the Simi Valley jury's decision had left fifty-eight people dead and caused

$1 billion in damage. In the aftermath of this tragedy the U.S. government filed charges of criminal civil rights violations against the four officers.

Lead federal prosecutors Barry Kowalski and Steven D. Clymer faced a difficult task when the second trial began in Los Angeles on February 3, 1993. They had to convince a jury that the officers had deliberately deprived Rodney King of his constitutional rights. First, though, they had to select that jury.

Many had criticized the fact that no African American jurors took part in the first trial. However, this time the jury consisted of people of many ethnic backgrounds. In his opening statement Clymer declared, "Rodney King is not on trial.

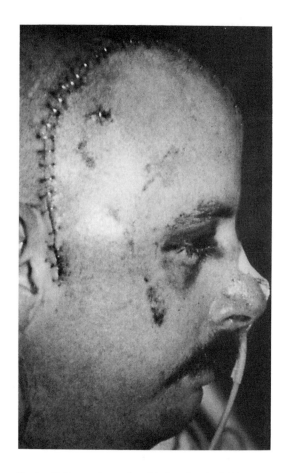

Reginald Denny just after his beating in 1992 during the riots that erupted after the acquittal of Los Angeles police officers following the Rodney King trial.

The issue of whether he was guilty or innocent that night is not the issue in this trial." He went on: "While he was being beaten, while he was on the ground, he didn't kick a police officer, he didn't punch a police officer, he didn't grab a police officer, he didn't injure a police officer."

Dorothy Gibson, an eyewitness, agreed. "He was lying on the ground, face down with his hands stretched out like a cross shape." Another eyewitness, Robert Hill, described hearing King scream in pain as officers beat him.

Sergeant Mark Conta, an expert on police procedure with the Los Angeles Police Department, condemned the tactics used by the officers.

He criticized Koon in particular for not stopping the other officers from beating King.

Throughout a grueling day of cross-examination King managed to undo an earlier impression—conveyed by lawyers for the accused officers—that he was a menacing brute. Attorney Stone got King to admit that he had lied to investigators when he denied driving drunk on the night of the beating. King responded that, being on parole (release from prison for good behavior), he had been afraid of being returned to prison if he had admitted to drunk driving.

Another defense team member, Harland W. Braun, addressed King's varied and conflicting versions of the events that occurred on the night of the beating. Implying that charges that the arresting officers used racial epithets (words or phrases that insult a person's race) had been brought out only lately to increase King's chances of winning his second suit. "You can become a rich man," said Braun, suggesting that King stood to gain $50 million in this suit.

King did admit to having a bad memory. "Sometimes I forget things that happened and sometimes I remember things," he said, confessing that he was uncertain about whether the officers' taunts had actually included

Los Angeles Police Officers' Trials: 1992 and 1993

The prosecution team in the LAPD Police Officers' Trial (left to right): Barry Kowalski, Steve Clymer, Alan Tieger, and Lawrence Middleton.

the word "nigger." "I'm not sure. I believe I did hear that." In earlier testimony before the investigating grand jury, King had not mentioned the racial insults.

Braun was astounded. "As an Afro-American who admittedly was beaten, you would forget that police officers called you nigger?. . . The fact is that you were trying to improve your case or lawsuit and really didn't care about the impact it would have on anyone else!"

The assault was continued by Paul DePasquale, attorney for Timothy Wind. He also highlighted King's hazy memory by referring to an interview in which King had mistakenly claimed that he was handcuffed all through the beating. Despite such errors, however, King stepped down from the stand having left the majority of people in the courtroom with a positive impression.

In a strange turn of events, Officer Singer was this time called to the witness stand by the defense. However, the content and manner of her testimony under cross-examination by Tieger only helped the prosecution. Defense attorneys could do little as she tearfully condemned their clients' conduct. It was a devastating setback.

Textbook Tactics

Now only the defendants could help themselves. Stacey Koon was the first to take the stand, insisting that his actions were a textbook example of how to subdue an aggressive suspect. Judge John G. Davies then refused to allow Steven Clymer to question Koon about some allegedly racist passages included in a book the sergeant had written about the Rodney King incident.

To the astonishment of many, the defense team announced that none of the other accused officers would testify. Following the closing arguments, Judge Davies gave the jurors a careful reading of the complex law involved after which they went away to discuss their verdict.

The media, many public officials, and ordinary citizens predicted more riots if the four officers went free. Tension in Los Angeles continued to grow as the jury deliberated. Police officers' saw their workdays increased to twelve hours. California Governor Pete Wilson called up National Guard units. Gun stores experienced a rush of customers as shopkeepers and residents prepared to protect themselves.

On April 17, 1993, one week after jurors began to deliberate, they had reached a decision. Koon and Powell sat emotionless as the guilty verdicts were read. The jury found Briseno and Wind not guilty. On August 4, 1993, it sentenced Koon and Powell to thirty months in jail.

RIOTS IN LOS ANGELES

The Los Angeles riots that erupted in response to the first Rodney King verdict recalled to many another Los Angeles riot, which had taken place in 1965, in the African American neighborhood known as Watts. The Watts riots were also sparked by an encounter between an African American man and the Los Angeles Police Department. In the mid-1960s, a number of other riots took place in American cities, mostly as a result of what African American residents perceived as police brutality. In response, President Lyndon Johnson charged the Kerner Commission with investigating the causes of America's urban unrest in 1968. In 1992, California Congresswoman Maxine Waters recalled the Kerner Commission report as she reflected on the connection between Watts and the more recent riots: "There was an insurrection in this city before, and, if I remember correctly, it was sparked by police brutality. We had a Kerner Commission report. It talked about what was wrong with our society. It talked about institutionalized racism. It talked about a lack of services, a lack of government responsiveness to the people. Today, as we stand here in 1992, if you go back and read the report, it seems as though we are talking about what that report cited some twenty years ago, still exists today."

Few jury decisions have so affected everyday life as the verdicts handed down in these two trials. The first prompted violence on a huge scale, while an entire city held its breath awaiting the second. Almost unnoticed in all of the turmoil was the question of "double jeopardy" (being charged twice for the same crime). Some felt the officers were tried a second time for essentially the same crimes they had been acquitted for in the first trial. Many felt that the second trial in federal court had more to do with public outrage than with civil rights protected by the Constitution.

Suggestions for Further Reading

Boyer, Peter J. "The Selling of Rodney King." *Vanity Fair* (July 1992): 78–83.

HUMAN RIGHTS

Duffy, Brian and Ted Gest. "Days of Rage." *U.S. News & World Report* (May 11, 1992): 20–26.

Koon, Stacey and Robert Dietz. *Presumed Guilty.* Chicago, Regnery Gateway, 1992.

Newton, Jim. "How the Case Was Won." *Los Angeles Times Magazine* (June 27, 1993): 20–26.

Prudhomme, Alex. "Police Brutality." *Time* (March 25, 1991): 16–19.

Right to Die: 1997

Plaintiffs: New York: Timothy E. Quill, Samuel C. Klagsbrun, and Howard A. Grossman; Washington: Harold Glucksberg, Thomas A. Preston, Abigail Halperin, and Peter Shalit

Defendants: Dennis C. Vacco (New York State and Washington State)

Chief Defense Lawyers: Walter Dellinger, Dennis C. Vacco, and William L. Williams

Chief Plaintiff Lawyers: New York: Laurence H. Tribe; Washington: Kathryn L. Tucker

Judges: Chief Justice William H. Rehnquist, Antonin Scalia, Sandra Day O'Connor, David H. Souter, Ruth Bader Ginsburg, Stephn G. Breyer, Anthony M. Kennedy, Clarence Thomas, and John Stevens

Place: Washington, D.C.

Date of Decision: June 26, 1997

Ruling: The Supreme Court unanimously upheld state laws prohibiting assisted suicide

SIGNIFICANCE: Does anyone have a constitutional right to die? In these cases the Supreme Court addressed one of the most controversial issues of the day.

Fom the beginning of time people have tried to kill themselves. Poor health is high on their list of reasons. Few people want to suffer with a lingering, painful illness with no hope of recovery. However, in almost

every Western democracy and nearly every U.S. state, it is illegal for doctors to help patients die. Therefore, these people privately kill themselves. Some doctors ignore the law altogether and assist in suicides, even though they may be charged with manslaughter or even murder.

To address this unsatisfactory situation the Supreme Court agreed, on October 1, 1996, to review rulings by two lower courts in New York and Washington states. In the New York case of *Vacco v. Quill,* three physicians had filed suit against Dennis C. Vacco, the Attorney General of New York State, on behalf of three patients. Each patient was terminally ill. Each wished their doctor to prescribe lethal medications that he or she could take privately.

The three patients were Jane Doe (who chose to conceal her actual identity), George A. Kingsley, and William A. Barth. Jane Doe was a seventy-six-year-old retired physical education instructor who was dying of thyroid cancer. Kingsley was a forty-eight-year-old publishing executive stricken with AIDS (Acquired Immunodeficiency Syndrome). Barth was a twenty-eight-year-old former fashion editor, also suffering from AIDS. Each of them understood that they had a deadly illness with no hope of recovery.

In their medical practices, said the doctors, they encountered competent, terminally ill patients who requested help in dying. The three doctors—Timothy Quill, Samuel C. Klagsbrun, and Howard A. Grossman—each said that medical values permitted doctors to help some patients die by prescribing sedatives. Current law, the doctors claimed, barred them from recommending the drugs.

In the State of Washington

At the same time, a similar case, *Washington v. Glucksberg,* was being decided in the Washington State courts. Finally, the courts in both states ruled that the laws against physician-assisted suicide were unconstitutional. Specifically, they violated the equal protection clause of the Fourteenth Amendment. This set the stage for a confrontation in the Supreme Court.

Even before arguments began, Justice Antonin Scalia—the conservative "conscience" of the current Supreme Court— took the highly unusual step of broadcasting his views in public. Speaking to a university audience on October 18, 1996, he said, "It's absolutely plain there is no right to die." He meant it was not a "right" protected by the Constitution. Scalia believed early Americans had accepted the laws against suicide at the time they drafted the Constitution. "There was clearly understood not to be any federal right to die."

Justice Scalia brought this mood of skepticism with him when the Supreme Court heard arguments on January 8, 1997. He was not alone. The entire court seemed reluctant to regard "the right to die" as a constitutional matter. However, Kathryn L. Tucker, counsel for Glucksberg, said that Washington's law against assisted suicide violated the due process rights of terminally ill patients who want a doctor's help in dying. Justice David H. Souter abruptly responded: "Why shouldn't we conclude that as an institution, we are not in a position to make the judgment you want us to make?"

Even Justice Ruth Bader Ginsburg, one of the more liberal justices, expressed doubts that the Supreme Court was the right place to decide such a dispute. She said, "Everything you have said, it seems to me, could go on in a legislative chamber."

Still Tucker urged the court to find that the Constitution protected the right to die. She spoke of "the underground practice, available to mainly the educated and the affluent."

Washington State's response was led by its assistant attorney general, William L. Williams. He asserted that "the state has an important interest in maintaining a clear line between physicians as healers and curers and physicians as instruments of death of their patients."

Justice Ginsburg injected a dose of practicality. She commented, "The reality is that in practice it happens," referring to situations where doctors give large doses of opiates or barbiturates to relieve pain, in the knowledge that the patient will slip into a coma and die.

Walter Dellinger, the acting solicitor general, had no problem with this. Speaking for the federal government, he said that such action was not unlawful "so long as the physician's intent was to relieve pain and not cause death."

Constitutional Doubts

For Laurence H. Tribe, chief lawyer for the New York plaintiffs, outlawing doctors from helping patients to die was a violation of their constitutional right to liberty. Justice John Stevens asked Tribe to define that right. Tribe replied that it was "the liberty when facing imminent death not to be forced by the government to experience pain and suffering that you can bear only by being unconscious, and to have a voice in deciding how much pain you will take."

HUMAN RIGHTS

EUTHANASIA: A MERCIFUL DEATH?

The right-to-die cases have centered on the notion of *euthanasia* (yoo-than-AY-zha). This can mean a painless putting to death (positive euthanasia), or it can mean the withdrawal of life-support systems such as respirators, intravenous feeding, or artificial kidney machines (negative euthanasia). A painless putting to death—particularly when assisted by physicians—remains illegal in the United States. However, negative euthanasia—a doctor's refusal to artificially prolong life—is legal. Naturally, this distinction is not always a clear one. Supporters of the "right to die" argue that patients have both the right to refuse so-called extraordinary measures to prolong life, and to actively seek their own deaths. Opponents of physician-assisted suicide argue that both positive and negative euthanasia raise the spectre of a society that refuses to save or prolong the lives of those it considers "undesirable."

"This is lovely philosophy, but is it in the Constitution?" observed Scalia. He repeatedly derided Tribe's efforts to read the constitutional guarantee of liberty as a protection of dignity in dying. Scalia also had searching questions for Tucker, wondering why she had limited her constitutional claim to people with terminal illnesses. Why, he mused, would someone faced with ten years of "terrible suffering" not have a similar right?

Because, said Tucker, the dying patient "does not have a choice between living and dying. The dying process has begun." At which point Scalia delivered a crushing answer: "I have to tell you, the dying process of all of us has begun!"

The court reached its pair of 9–0 decisions on June 26, 1997. It rejected the constitutional challenges to the laws that made doctor-assisted suicide a crime. The court answered the question presented by both the New York and Washington cases—do laws against doctor-assisted suicide violate the Fourteenth Amendment—by ruling they do not. However, this ruling had no direct bearing on the six patients mentioned in the two briefs. All had died before their suits had reached the Supreme Court.

The court's decision did not close the door to the debate over whether doctors could sedate a patient to the point of unconsciousness, then allow that person to die. Some of the justices had suggested that in the future some terminally ill people might be able to claim they had a constitutional right to a doctor's help in committing suicide. "Our opinion does not absolutely foreclose such a claim," said Chief Justice William H. Rehnquist.

The "right to die" is an argument being fought around the globe. On March 24, 1997, the Australian parliament overturned, by a narrow margin, the world's only right-to-die law, which had been introduced in that country's Northern Territory the year before. Elsewhere, although euthanasia is tolerated in some countries, most notably the Netherlands, it remains technically illegal.

—*Colin Evans*

Right to Die: 1997

Suggestions for Further Reading

Greenhouse, Linda. "High Court Hears 2 Cases Involving Assisted Suicide." *The New York Times* (January 9, 1997): 1.

Jones, Constance. *The Complete Book of Death and Dying.* New York: HarperCollins, 1997.

Kubler-Ross, Elizabeth. *On Death and Dying.* New York: Touchstone Books, 1997.

NEGLIGENCE

The Triangle Shirtwaist Fire Trial: 1911

Defendants: Max Blanck and Isaac Harris
Crime Charged: Manslaughter
Chief Defense Lawyer: Max D. Steuer
Chief Prosecutors: Charles S. Bostwick and J. Robert Rubin
Judge: Thomas C. T. Crain
Place: New York, New York
Dates of Trial: December 4–27, 1911
Verdict: Not guilty

SIGNIFICANCE: The Triangle Shirtwaist fire spurred the efforts of the International Ladies' Garment Workers' Union (ILGWU) to organize garment workers, and increased support for the vote among wage-earning women. Politicians passed legislation to improve sweatshop conditions in the garment industry.

At the turn of the twentieth century, poor working conditions and long hours were common for most factory employees—especially for female workers. Male unions and employers kept women out of better-paying jobs, forcing them into industries such as garment-making (making clothes), where sweatshop (a place where employees work long hours for low pay) conditions prevailed, pay was low, and employees had to pay for their cutting and sewing supplies. Factories had few fire-prevention regulations—no sprinklers, poor ventilation, and almost no usable emergency exits.

NEGLIGENCE

The Uprising of the 20,000

The first major strike (refusal to work) by working women took place among the shirtwaist (type of women's shirt) makers of New York and Philadelphia on November 22, 1909, and continued until February 15, 1910. Called the "Uprising of the 20,000," the strike was an important demonstration of the beginning of the women's labor movement.

New York's Triangle Shirtwaist Factory, a maker of women's clothing, became a strike target. That winter, women and girls in their teens left their cramped and filthy work rooms, and marched to Union Square to protest their poor working conditions at a meeting called by the IL-GWU. Although the intent of the meeting was not to call a strike, remarks made by teenager Clara Lemlich stirred up members of the group and motivated them to walk out. She interrupted the speeches of Samuel Gompers, president of the American Federation of Labor (AFL), and Margaret Dreier Robins of the New York Women's Trade Union League (WTUL)—an organization that joined women factory workers with women from the upper and middle classes—to yell: "I am tired of listening to speakers who talk in general terms. What we are here for is to decide whether or not we shall strike. I offer a resolution that a general strike be declared now!" The following day, the women walked out.

One of the strikers, Pauline Newman, remembering the day, recalled:

> Thousands upon thousands left the factories from every side, all of them walking down toward Union Square. It was November, the cold winter was just around the corner, we had no fur coats to keep warm, and yet there was the spirit that led us out of the cold at least for the time being.

Striker Esther Lobetkin was arrested during the strike:

> The officer wouldn't let us girls sit down on the [police] benches because we were strikers. . . . One of our girls got so tired she went to crouch down to rest herself, when one of the officers came over and poked her with his club and says, 'Here, stand up. Where do you think you are? In Russia?'

The WTUL aided the strikers. Well-known society leaders Anne Morgan, Alva Belmont, Mrs. Henry Morgenthau, and Helen Taft (President William Howard Taft's daughter) were active members. They joined the picket lines, faced arrest, raised bail money for the factory workers, monitored the courts, and brought charges against police—despite resentment and harassment from policemen.

One policeman yelled at the WTUL's Helen Marot, "You uptown scum, keep out of this or you'll find yourself in jail." A judge told the arrested women, "You are striking against God and Nature, whose prime law is that man shall earn his bread with the sweat of his brow." Thirteen weeks after it began, the protest against the Triangle Shirtwaist Company ended but that year also saw 404,000 women petition Congress for the right to vote. Of 339 shops involved, over 300 settled with the workers. These women won a fifty-two-hour work week, a promise that employers would provide supplies, no punishment for striking, and an equal division of work in during slow seasons. (The latter discouraged bosses from firing workers during slow times.)

The Triangle
Shirtwaist
Fire Trial:
1911

The Triangle Fire

Located on the ninth floor of a building that overlooked Washington Place on one side and Greene Street on the other, Triangle's workrooms had to few fire escapes and no sprinklers—conditions the workers had been protesting. Worse, supervisors locked the doors to the workplace from the outside to prevent the women and girls, crowded next to each other on benches, from taking breaks during working hours or removing materials. Only one stairway led to the roof.

On March 25, 1911, a fire broke out on the eighth floor, rising to the ninth through the Greene Street stairwell. As smoke and flames filled the air, the women rushed to the Washington Place exit. It was locked. About 500 women were trapped; many clung to the breaking fire escapes. Firefighters tried to reach them, but their ladders stopped at the sixth floor. Women jumped hand-in-hand from the windows, falling through the nets, and crashing on the sidewalk. Other women, caught inside, died of burns or suffocation (death from lack of oxygen). That night, the Twenty-Sixth Street Pier held 146 corpses. Two thousand people searched for their loved ones' bodies.

It took one week to identify the dead; seven were unknown. The angry members of the ILGWU and WTUL planned a funeral for the unnamed women. New York's grieving population turned out in full on the rainy, cold April day. Throughout the steady downpour, they marched to Washington Square Arch, from which they formed a parade. There were so many people at the square that the last one waited until 6:00 P.M. to pass below the arch.

NEGLIGENCE

Police dispose of bodies from the Triangle Shirtwaist fire which killed 146 employees on March 25, 1911.

On December 4, Max Blanck and Isaac Harris, the owners of the company, went on trial for manslaughter. Max D. Steuer was their attorney. Assistant District Attorneys Charles S. Bostwick and J. Robert Rubin prosecuted the defendants in the three-week trial.

There were more than 150 witnesses. Kate Alderman told how both she and Margaret Schwartz tried and failed to open the door. Alderman ultimately escaped by covering herself with dresses and a coat and leaping through the flames to where firemen rescued her. Despite the dramatic testimony, Judge Thomas C. T. Crain instructed the jury that the key to the case was whether the defendants knew the door was locked. If so, and Margaret Schwartz died because she was unable to pass through, would she have lived if the door had not been locked?

On December 27, 1911, the jury acquitted both defendants of manslaughter. One jury member said, "I believed that the door was locked at the time of the fire. But we couldn't find them guilty unless we believed they knew the door was locked." Another member of the all-male jury remarked that the women—who they did not believe were as intelligent as those in other occupations—probably panicked, causing their deaths. The court denied a prosecution demand for a retrial, so Blanck and Harris went free.

Out of the Ashes

The tragedy of the fire galvanized working women. Despite arrests and beatings, strikes across the nation increased, and the membership of the ILGWU grew. In 1912, women were among 20,000 textile workers to strike in Lawrence, Massachusetts. One of them explained her continued support: "It is not only bread we give our children. . . . We live by freedom, and I will fight till I die to give it to my children."

Female labor leaders such as Leonora O'Reilly demanded the vote for women so they could protect themselves by electing politicians who would pass laws to change the sweatshop conditions under which they worked. In 1912, when the next New York City suffrage parade (demonstration in support of the right for women to vote) took place, 20,000 people marched and another half million lined the sidewalks.

Out of public outrage, officials imposed new laws that required strict building codes and inspections on sweatshops, for example. New York City created a Bureau of Fire Prevention that established and enforced stricter safety regulations. Other cities and states did the same during the following years. Finally, the federal government, under the administration

The Triangle Shirtwaist Fire Trial: 1911

On April 5, 1911, the International Ladies' Garment Workers' Union and the New York Women's Trade Union League organized a memorial parade for the employees who died in the Triangle Shirwaist fire.

NEGLIGENCE

THE GROWTH OF THE ILGWU

Both women and men came in large numbers to join the International Ladies' Garment Workers' Union (ILGWU) as the union movement spread. From 1910 to 1920, the union expanded from its base in New York to include workers in Chicago, Boston, Cleveland, and other cities. By 1920, it had a membership of over 100,000. During the same ten-year period, women greatly increased their role in the labor movement in general: from 76,784 women in all U.S. trade unions in 1910 to 379,000 in 1920.

of Franklin D. Roosevelt, developed workplace safety measures, which eventually led to the creation of the Occupational Safety and Health Administration (OSHA).

Suggestions for Further Reading

Frost, Elizabeth and Kathryn Cullen-DuPont. *Women's Suffrage in America: An Eyewitness History.* New York: Facts on File, 1992.

Frost-Knappman, Elizabeth. *The ABC-Clio Companion to Women's Progress in America.* Santa Barbara, CA: ABC-CLIO, 1994.

Wertheimer, Barbara Mayer. *We Were There: The Story of Working Women in America.* New York: Pantheon Books, 1977.

Titanic Inquiry: 1912

Chief Lawyers: Sir Rufus Isaacs and Sir John Simon
Judge: Lord John Mersey
Place: London, England
Dates of Inquiry: May 2–July 3, 1912

SIGNIFICANCE: Cover-up or thorough investigation? Doubts about the British *Titanic* investigation have never been resolved.

The *Titanic* was 46,328 tons and 882 feet in length, with eight decks that together reached the height of an eleven-story building. The ship was not only the largest afloat in 1912, but also the grandest. It was considered safe, too. Beneath the splendor of public rooms and cabins, the engineers who designed the ship had created an arrangement of watertight compartments above a double hull. One English journalist had described the *Titanic* as "practically unsinkable." Yet on her first voyage across the Atlantic on the night of April 14, she sank in calm seas off the coast of Newfoundland.

The Iceberg

The iceberg that sank the *Titanic* was spotted at 11:40 P.M. The collision with the iceberg came seconds later. The huge wall of ice ripped a 300-foot gash through the ship. Freezing water poured in, and two and a half hours later the ship sank quietly beneath the surface of the North Atlantic.

The loss of life was enormous: 1,522 passengers and crew died, and only 705 survived by boarding lifeboats and rafts that were left half empty. Why there were so few lifeboats and how they came to be occupied by so few passengers outside of first-class were just two of the questions that gave rise to official investigation on both sides of the Atlantic.

How could It have Happened?

To decide the matter, the British Board of Trade took the unusual step of appointing a wreck commissioner, Lord John Mersey, to head the investigation. The British inquiry began sooner than expected because an American investigation was already underway. The British commission met in a hall in London, England, starting on May 2, 1912.

Facing Lord Mersey was a long line of lawyers. Besides the two primary barristers (British lawyers), the White Star Line, owner of the *Titanic,* had its own lawyer. Another lawyer represented the interests of third-class passengers. Still another represented the national Sailors' and Firemen's Union. Among the half dozen other lawyers was Henry Duke. He represented Sir Cosmo and Lady Duff Gordon, wealthy passengers who were accused of having attempted to bribe those rowing their lifeboat so they would not go back to pick up more passengers.

Survival of the Richest?

One of those oarsmen, Charles Henrickson, testified that "there was plenty of room for another dozen in the boat," but that the lifeboat had been prevented from going back to the ship.

One of the lawyers representing the third-class passengers asked, "You say that . . . this was due to the protests of the Duff Gordons?"

"Yes," said Henrickson.

"You say you heard cries?"

"Yes."

"Agonizing cries?"

"Yes, terrible cries."

"At what distance?"

"About two hundred yards."

In response, Duff Gordon explained that he had offered the seamen "a fiver [5 pounds] each" after learning that they would not be receiving

NEGLIGENCE

any wages. His wife, too, angrily rejected any suggestion that she had prevented efforts to return.

Tragically, the person who could have done most to clear up the matter was not present. Edward Smith, captain of the *Titanic,* had gone down with his ship. This meant that the spotlight fell on J. Bruce Ismay, president of the White Star Line. It was charged that he had ordered Captain Smith to proceed at maximum speed even after icebergs had been sighted in the area. He had survived in one of the last lifeboats.

Under questioning, Ismay admitted having received a telegraphed warning. He was asked: "If you were approaching ice in the night, it would be desirable, would it not, to slow down?"

"I am not a navigator," replied Ismay.

"Answer the question," insisted Lord Mersey.

"I say no. I am not a navigator."

The questioning continued, and finally Ismay said, "I say he [Smith] was justified in going fast to get out of it if the conditions were suitable and right and the weather clear."

Asked about the lack of lifeboats, Ismay again answered in a misleading fashion. The *Titanic* had carried the minimum number of lifeboats required by the Board of Trade, he said, because the ship was thought to be unsinkable. This explained why it was decided to reduce the number of lifeboats to one per davit (the device for lowering lifeboats into the water from the deck), even though the davits were designed to carry four lifeboats each. This change was made so that there might be more deck space for passengers.

Next, the inquiry looked into one of the more mysterious aspects of the tragedy. Officers from the *Titanic* told of seeing another ship five or six miles away. This ship failed to respond either to the eight distress rockets (flares shot into the sky to attract attention) fired from the *Titanic*'s decks or to repeated distress signals sent by Morse code (method of wireless communication). Most believed the other ship to have been the *Californian,* a 6,000-ton ship under the command of Captain Walter Lord and heading for Boston. Called to testify, Lord failed to impress his questioners favorably. From the start, his answers were full of contradictions. He admitted that he had seen a ship at around 11 P.M., and that a number of his officers had seen the distress rockets. Still, he insisted that the ship he saw was *not* the *Titanic.* "You never can mistake those ships," he said, "by the blaze of light."

SCANDALS OF THE TITANIC

The tragedy of the *Titanic* had a great impact on the shipping industry. Stronger safety rules for ships were ordered to prevent another such disaster. An iceberg patrol was also established. Still, the *Titanic*'s story continued to fascinate and horrify the public. Newspaper accounts told of how the lifeboats were supposed to take "women and children first," and how some men dressed as women so as to be allowed onto the lifeboats. Later historians told of how women in steerage—the lower, cheaper decks—were not allowed into the lifeboats. In fact, ship's personnel were actually stationed at the tops of the stairways leading out of steerage, to prevent the less wealthy passengers from climbing onto the upper deck to the lifeboats.

Radio Officer Asleep

When asked why he had not asked his radio officer for help, Lord exploded, "At one o'clock in the morning?" The questioning continued: "You have already told us that you were not satisfied that [the flares were] a company's signal." (At the time, ships identified themselves to other vessels at night by using rockets much smaller then distress flares.)

Lord responded: "I asked the officer, 'Was it a company signal?'"

"And he did not know?"

"He did not know," agreed Lord.

"That did not satisfy you?"

"It did not satisfy me."

Next came what was perhaps the most telling question of the entire inquiry. "Then, if it was not that, it might have been a distress signal?"

"It might have been," Lord squirmed. With those four words, his guilt was exposed for all the world to see.

Lord Mersey certainly thought Lord was guilty. In his report, delivered on July 30, 1912, he wrote: "These circumstances convince me that the ship seen by the *Californian* was the *Titanic* and if so, according to Captain Lord, the two vessels were about five miles apart at the time of the disaster. . . . When she first saw the rockets, the *Californian* could have pushed through the ice . . . and . . . come to the assistance of the *Titanic*. Had she done so she might have saved many if not all of the lives that were lost."

A Cover-Up?

Other than the testimony of Lord, Mersey found little to criticize. Captain Smith had been merely following orders. The White Star Line met every requirement of the Board of Trade guidelines. There was no truth to the charges that those manning the lifeboats favored first-class passengers. Charges of bribery against the Duff Gordons were "unfounded," although Mersey added: "I think that if he had encouraged the men to re-

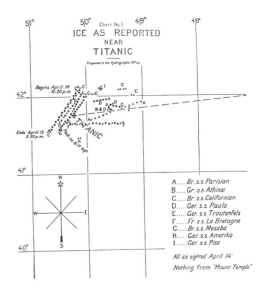

A map drawn after the sinking of the Titanic. This sketch, drawn by the U.S. Navy Hydrographic Office, clearly shows a huge field of ice in the direct path of the Titanic.

turn . . . they would probably have made an effort to do so and could have saved some lives." Ismay, too, was declared free of blame. In conclusion, Mersey recommended "more watertight compartments in ocean-going ships, the provision of lifeboats for all on board, and a better lookout."

Such conclusions brought charges that the inquiry was a coverup intended to dismiss blame rather than discover who was responsible for the tragedy of the *Titanic*. Certainly the American inquiry dealt more harshly with all concerned. The American report, issued May 30, 1912, also prompted U.S.-backed support for the International Ice Patrol, a fleet of ships that has since watched over traffic in the dangerous North Atlantic.

On September 1, 1985, the world got its first photographic view of the *Titanic* in more than seven decades. An expedition led by Dr. Robert Ballard managed to locate the sunken ship on the ocean floor, 13,000 feet beneath the surface.

Suggestions for Further Reading

Davie, Michael. *Titanic: The Death and Life of a Legend.* New York: Alfred A. Knopf, 1986.

Lord, Walter. *A Night to Remember.* New York: Holt, Rinehart & Winston, 1955.

Marcus, Geoffrey. *The Maiden Voyage.* New York: Viking Press, 1969.

Reade, Leslie. *The Ship That Stood Still.* New York: W. W. Norton, 1993.

Titanic Inquiry: 1912

Silkwood v. Kerr-McGee: 1979

Plaintiff: Estate of Karen Silkwood

Defendant: Kerr-McGee Nuclear Company

Plaintiff Claim: Damages for negligence leading to the plutonium contamination of Karen Silkwood

Chief Defense Lawyers: Elliott Fenton, John Griffin Jr., Larry D. Ottoway, William Paul, L. E. Stringer, and Bill J. Zimmerman

Chief Lawyers for Plaintiff: Gerald Spence, Arthur Angel, and James Ikard

Judge: Frank G. Theis

Place: Oklahoma City, Oklahoma

Dates of Trial: March 6–May 18, 1979

Verdict: Defendant was found negligent and was ordered to pay $505,000 in actual damages and $10 million in punitive damages

SIGNIFICANCE: This precedent-setting action between the estate of a dead woman and a giant industrial conglomerate sparked a public uproar about the issue of safety at nuclear facilities and held a company responsible for negligence (failure to uphold required standards).

In 1974, Karen Silkwood was a laboratory worker and union activist at the Kerr-McGee Nuclear Company in Cimarron, Oklahoma. The plant produced plutonium. That year Silkwood found evidence that made her believe that the management had been careless in the way it ran the plant. So she gave the federal Atomic Energy Commission (AEC) a list of the management's violations of safety standards. On November 13, three months later, she died in a mysterious car crash. She had been on her way to meet with a *New York Times* reporter. She was supposed to give him documents that proved her suspicions.

An autopsy revealed that Silkwood's body was contaminated with plutonium, just as tests had shown when she was still alive. At the time these tests were taken, some said Silkwood had deliberately contaminated herself in an effort to make the Kerr-McGee Company look guilty. Silkwood had denied these rumors. Kerr-McGee just as strongly denied that its plant violated any federal guidelines. The company said that any nuclear contamination Silkwood had suffered must have come from somewhere else.

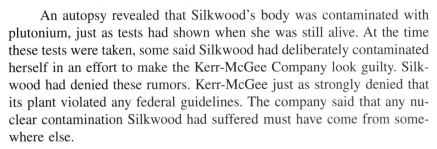

Silkwood's Family Goes to Court

After four years of delay, Silkwood's family's suit (legal action to obtain justice) against Kerr-McGee finally went to trial on March 6, 1979. The trial lasted three months and was the longest civil trial in Oklahoma history. Gerry Spence opened the case for Silkwood's estate by calling to the witness stand John Gofman. He was a doctor and outspoken critic of careless nuclear regulation. Gofman stated, "The license to give out doses of plutonium is a legalized permit to murder."

"Was Karen in danger of dying from the plutonium inside her?" asked Spence.

"Yes, she was."

Asked about Kerr-McGee's employee training program, Gofman responded: "My opinion is that it is clearly and unequivocally negligen[t]."

The only member of the Kerr-McGee management team to testify against his former employers was ex-supervisor James Smith. Although he did not care for Silkwood personally—he found her hard to deal with as a union organizer—he believed her findings about safety violations were correct. Most alarming was his claim that there were forty pounds of Material Unaccounted For (MUF). This meant that a deadly amount of plutonium was missing. He brushed aside Kerr-McGee's claims that the MUF was in fact still at the plant. Part of Smith's job at Cimarron had been to supervise the process of cleaning the plant's pipes: "Let me put it this way, if there's forty pounds still at Cimarron, I don't know where it is."

Another former employee at the plant, Ron Hammock, told of defective fuel rods, packed full of plutonium pellets, being shipped to other

NEGLIGENCE

plants. "Who told you to ship them?" Spence asked. "My supervisor," Hammock replied.

New Disaster

Three weeks into the trial something happened that raised questions about nuclear safety throughout the United States. The Three Mile Island nuclear reactor in Pennsylvania had a near meltdown. For most Americans, the accident at that nuclear plant was a hint of nuclear disaster. The incident cast a shadow over the Silkwood trial. Even Kerr-McGee's chief attorney, Bill Paul, asked the judge to declare a mistrial. Paul feared that all the negative publicity about Three Mile Island would unfairly effect the outcome of the case. Judge Frank Theis denied the request. The Silkwood legal team was relieved. They did not have the unlimited sources of money available to Kerr-McGee and a delay delay would have favored the giant company.

Paul called Kerr-McGee's star witness, Dr. George Voelz, who was the health director at the important Los Alamos Scientific Laboratory. Voelz testified that, in his opinion, the level of contamination carried by Silkwood fell within AEC standards. Spence thought this was untrue. In a cross-examination that lasted two days, he forced the scientist to take back one statement after another. Central to Voelz's testimony was the model he had used to arrive at the AEC standards. Spence showed that Silkwood was in no way the average person that had been used as this model. She weighed less than 100 pounds and had been a heavy smoker. Both of these factors increase the chances of becoming contaminated. Also, Spence got Voelz to grudgingly admit that he did not really know what level of plutonium exposure would produce cancer.

In his final instructions to the jury, Judge Theis spelled out the law: "If you find that the damage to the person or property of Karen Silkwood resulted from the operation of this plant . . . Kerr-McGee . . . is liable."

Nuclear Martyr?

On May 18, 1979, after four days of deliberation, the jurors decided that Kerr-McGee had indeed been negligent. They awarded Karen Silkwood's estate $505,000 in damages. A gasp swept the courtroom when the jury added an amount for punitive damages, meant not so much to pay back Silkwood's family as to punish Kerr-McGee: $10 million.

PLUTONIUM

Plutonium, a silver-gray mineral, is used as fuel in both nuclear reactors and nuclear weapons. It is a very dangerous poison that collects in the bones, where it changes the production of white blood cells. Plutonium was first produced artificially (made by man, not by nature) in 1940 by chemist Glenn Seaborg and his colleagues. Although plutonium exists in nature as the result of the decay of uranium, only small amounts can be found that way.

It was a huge award. Kerr-McGee filed an appeal (legal method to request a new trial or reversal of decision). The suit dragged on until August 1986 when, in an out-of-court settlement, Kerr-McGee agreed to pay the Silkwood estate $1.38 million. This amount was less than the interest the original award would have earned in a year.

Many regarded Karen Silkwood as a nuclear martyr. To this day, the circumstances of her death remain a mystery. Was she killed so that she would be silenced? That may never be known. What is known is that the Silkwood victory—even in its final, reduced form—sent the nuclear industry a clear message: dangerous sources of energy demand careful regulation.

Suggestions for Further Reading

Kohn, Howard. *Who Killed Karen Silkwood?* New York: Summit, 1981.

Rashke, Richard. *The Killing of Karen Silkwood.* New York: Houghton Mifflin, 1981.

"Silkwood Case Laid to Rest." *Science News* (August 30, 1986): 134.

Spence, Gerry. *With Justice For None.* New York: Times Books, 1989.

Stein, J. "The Deepening Mystery." *Progressive* (January 1981): 14–19.

Index

Italic type indicates volume numbers; **boldface** indicates main entries and their page numbers; (ill.) indicates illustration

Note: Trial names have been treated as titles, so that *In the Matter of Baby M* falls under "I" and "John Brown Trial" is listed under "J," while John Brown himself is listed under "B"—Brown, John.

A

Index

Bizos, George *3:*773
Black, Hugo L. *1:*33, 37, 136, 213
Black, William P. *2:*404
Black Consciousness Movement *2:*468, 470
Black Hand *2:*303, 307
Black Local Authorities Act *2:*486
Blackard, Pamela *1:*53
Blacklist *1:*132, 134
Blackmun, Harry A. *1:*39, 41, 47, 89, 93-94
Blair, Montgomery *1:*15, 19
Blake, Timothy *2:*454
Blakeney, Ben Bruce *3:*814
Blanck, Max *1:*249, 252
Blasphemy *3:*608, 610
Blatman, Yonah *3:*829
Bleeding Kansas *3:*706
Blewett, George Francis *3:*814
Bligh, William *3:*588-592, 588 (ill.)
Bliss, Theodore *2:*386
Bloch, Alexander *2:*364, 366-367
Bloch, Emanuel H. *2:*364, 366
Bloom, Molly *1:*126-127
Blow, Peter *1:*16
Blow, Taylor *1:*19
Blowers, Sampson Salter *2:*381, 386
Blunt, Anthony *1:*150
Blythin, Edward C. *2:*439, 442-444
Boda, Chen. *See* Chen Boda
Boda, Mike *2:*423, 426
Bodart, Philippe *2:*354
Bodkin, Archibald *3:*718
Boer War *2:*471
Bogart, Humphrey *1:*131
Bokassa, Jean-Bédel *2:*491-495, 492 (ill.)
Boleyn, Anne *3:*660, 665, 670
Bollingen Prize for Poetry *3:*752
Bolsheviks *2:*309, 313; *3:*730-733, 745
Bolt, Robert *3:*663
Bonaparte, Napoleon. *See* Napoleon Bonaparte
Bonfield, John *2:*406
Book of Daniel *2:*370
Booth, John Wilkes *2:*517
Borah, William E. *2:*297, 300
Borgerhoff-Mulder, W. G. Frederick *3:*814
Bormann, Martin *3:*807, 811, 823
Boston massacre *2:*381-391, 382 (ill.)
Boston Massacre Trials *2:***381-391,** 382 (ill.)
Bostwick, Charles S. *1:*249, 252
Bothwell, earl of. *See* Hepburn, James (earl of Bothwell)
Botts, Lawson *3:*704, 707
Bounty *3:*587-592
Bounty* Mutineers Court-Martial** *3:587-592,** 588 (ill.), 590 (ill.)
Bradford, William *1:*105, 107
Bradley, Daina *2:*508
Bradley, Richard *1:*105, 109, 168, 170
Bradshaw, John *3:*684-685, 687, 689
Brain death *1:*227, 229
Branch Davidians *2:*505
Brandeis, Louis D. *1:*81, 118
Brando, Marlon *3:*591
Brandt, Willy *2:*373, 375, 463
Brannon, John *3:*814
Branton, Leo Jr. *2:*446, 449-451
Braun, Harland W. *1:*233, 237-238
Breach of confidence *1:*148, 151
Breach of office *2:*516
Brennan, William J. Jr. *1:*39, 41, 47, 89, 95, 101, 136-137, 137 (ill.), 139
Brewer, David J. *1:*29
Brewer, James *2:*388-389
Brewer, Roy *1:*130
Bribery *1:*260; *2:*374, 528, 549-550
Bridges, R. R. *1:*199, 201
Briseno, Theodore J. *1:*233-234, 238

Brisset, André *3:*710, 713
Britano, Jacob *3:*631
British Board of Trade *1:*256
British Broadcasting Corporation (BBC) *2:*321
British Commonwealth *3:*814
British North America *1:*168
British Parliament *1:*75, 110, 206; *2:*383
British rule *1:*80, 205; *2:*328, 333, 457
British Security Service *1:*148-150
Brodsky, Joseph *1:*196
Bromley, Thomas *3:*664, 668
Brooks, Alfred W. *3:*814
Broun, Heywood *2:*428
Brown, Henry B. *1:*29
Brown, J. W. *1:*70-71
Brown, Jim *2:*496-497
Brown, John *3:*704-709, 707 (ill.)
Brown, Linda *1:*34
Brown, Oliver *1:*34, 38
Brown, William *2:*390
Brown v. Board of Education *1:*5, **33-38,** 37 (ill.)
Brownell, Herbert *1:*136
Broz, Josip ("Tito") *3:*764-767
Bruno, Giordano *3:*628-633, 629 (ill.), 630 (ill.)
Bruno Richard Hauptmann Trial *2:***431-438,** 432 (ill.)
H.M.S. *Brunswick* *3:*591
Bryan, William Jennings *3:*648-649, 651, 651 (ill.), 655
Buback, Siegfried *2:*459, 462, 464
Buchanan, James *1:*20
Buchenwald concentration camp *3:*809
Buck, Carrie *1:*81-88, 86 (ill.)
Buck, Emma *1:*82-83
Buck v. Bell *1:***81-88,** 85 (ill.), 86 (ill.)
Buck v. Priddy *1:*83
Buenger, Wilhelm *3:*724, 727
Bukharin, Nikolai *3:*733-734
Burdick, Benjamin *2:*386
Burger, Warren E. *1:*39, 41, 43, 47, 89
Burgess, Guy *1:*150
Burkett, Thomas *3:*587, 590-591
Burkinshaw, Neil *2:*523
Burmeister, Steven *2:*508
Burnett, McKinley *1:*34
Burnham, Margaret *2:*446, 450
Burns, Lucy *1:*191, 194
Burns, Sherman *2:*523
Burns, William J. *2:*523, 527
Burr, Aaron *2:*513, 515; *3:*699-703, 700 (ill.), 701 (ill.)
Burr, Richard H. III *2:*503,
Burr *3:*702
Burroughs, George *3:*644
Burton, Harold H. *1:*33, 37
Burton, Mary *1:*169-170
"Butcher of Lyons" *3:*837
Butler, Benjamin *2:*520-521
Butler, Eddie *2:*456
Butler, John Washington *3:*649
Butler, Pierce *1:*81, 85
Butler Act *3:*652, 654
Butt, Charles *1:*75, 77
Butterfield, Alexander *1:*42
Byrn, Michael *3:*587, 589, 591

C

Čabrinovič, Nedeljko *2:*302-303, 305
Caesar *1:*168-170
Caiaphas *3:*608, 610
Cain and Abel *3:*653
Cajetan, Thomas de Vio *3:*623
Caldwell, James *2:*385
Calef, Daniel *2:*386

Index

Index

Index

H

Index

Index

Index

Index

Montané, Jacques *2:*392, 396
Monteith, Robert *3:*719
Montes, Pedro *1:*173-175
Montgomery, Hugh *2:*381, 384
Montgomery, Olin *1:*196-197
Montgomery, Robert *1:*131
Montluc Prison *3:*837
Moody, Milo *1:*196
Moon Young-ho *2:*548, 550
Moore, Alfred *1:*3
Moore, Alvin *1:*215, 217-218
Moore, Fred H. *2:*422
Moore, Howard Jr. *2:*446
Moore, Stephen *1:*69
Morín, Sorí *3:*768-769
More, Thomas *3:*659-663, 660 (ill.)
Morejon, Pedro *3:*768
Moretti, Mario *2:*473, 475-477
Morgan, Anne *1:*250
Morgan, John H. *3:*718
Morgenthau, Mrs. Henry *1:*250
Mormons *1:*22-23, 26-28
Mornard, Jacques *2:*314-315, 317-318
Mornet, André *3:*736
Moro, Aldo *2:*473-478
Morrill Anti-Bigamy Act *1:*23
Morrison, James *3:*587, 590-591
Morrow, Anne *2:*431
Morse, Robert *1:*228-229
Moscow Purge *3:*730-734
Moscow Purge Trials *3:***730-735**
Moses *2:*404, 417; *3:*613
Motion Picture Alliance for the Preservation of
    American Ideals *1:*131
Motsoaledi, Elias *3:*773, 776
Moulin, Jean *3:*837
Mount Sinai Hospital *1:*231
Moyer, Charles H. *2:*299
Muir, Robert Jr. *1:*227, 231
Muller, Arndt *2:*459
Mullowney, Alexander *1:*190, 192-193
Multiple sclerosis *1:*99
Murphy, Frank *1:*133
Murphy, Thomas F. *2:*357, 360-361
Murray, Joseph *1:*168
Murray, Robert *1:*143
Murrow, Edward R. *1:*134
Musmanno, Michael A. *2:*422; *3:*825
Muspratt, William *3:*587, 591
Mussolini, Benito *3:*737, 746
Mutiny *1:*173, 176; *2:*548-549; *3:*587-592, 750
Mutiny on the Bounty *3:*591
Muto, Akira *3:*814-815
My Lai massacre *3:*593-599
Myers, Eric *2:*452-453

N

Nachman, M. Roland Jr. *1:*136
Nagano, Osami *3:*814-815
Nagy, Imre *3:*757
Napalm *1:*223
Napoleon Bonaparte *2:*491
Narvaiz, Pedro Carlos *2:*530
Nasjonal Samling (National Unity Party) *3:*743,
    745-746
National Assembly *3:*692-693
National Association for the Advancement of Col-
    ored People (NAACP) *1:*34, 36-37, 139, 200
National Commission on Disappeared Persons
    (CONADEP) *2:*481-482
National Convention *1:*141; *3:*691, 693
National Guard *1:*201, 238

National Pencil Company *2:*417
National Security Council (NSC) *2:*537-538, 537
    (ill.), 540
National Socialist Party *3:*724, 746
National Unity Party *3:*743, 746
National Woman's Party *1:*190-191, 195
Nationalist Party *2:*467, 471; *3:*777
Native Americans *1:*161
Nau, Claude *3:*667-669
Naud, Albert *3:*736
Naumowicz, Bogdan *2:*302
Naval Petroleum Reserves *2:*524-525, 528
Nazis *1:*82; *2:*309, 320-321, 322 (ill.), 323, 324
    (ill.), 373; *3:*724-729, 736, 738, 743, 745-746,
    753, 764, 805-808, 808 (ill.), 810-811, 816, 823,
    826, 834, 836-837, 840
Nebelung, Günther *2:*320
Neebe, Oscar *2:*404, 407-409
Nehru, Jawaharlal *2:*341, 347
Nelson, Henry John *1:*118
Nelson, Samuel *1:*15, 19-20
Nelson, Thomas *1:*112; *2:*521
Nelson Mandela Trial *3:***773-778,** 775 (ill.)
Nesbit, Evelyn *2:*410-411, 413-415
Neubert, Dr. *2:*320
Neurath, Konstantin von *3:*812
New China News Agency *3:*800
The New Class *3:*765
New Jersey College of Medicine and Dentistry
    *1:*231
New Jersey Supreme Court *1:*97, 101, 227-228, 231
New York City suffrage parade *1:*253
New York Gazette *1:*107
New York state constitution *1:*111
New York Supreme Court *1:*111
The New York Times *1:*102, 136, 137, 138, 245;
    *2:*313, 347, 363, 413, 438, 442, 472, 478, 484,
    535; *3:*764, 767
New York Times Company v. Sullivan *1:***136-140,**
    137 (ill.), 138 (ill.)
New York University Medical School *1:*229
New York Weekly Journal *1:*105
New York Women's Trade Union League (WTUL)
    *1:*250-251, 253
Newman, Pauline *1:*250
Ngei, Paul *1:*204, 206
Nicaraguan Contras *2:*536-538, 540, 545
Nicholas, Philip *1:*112
Nichols, Terry *2:*504, 506, 508-509
Nicolls, Richard *1:*168
Nietzsche, Friedrich *3:*653
Niewoudt, Gideon *2:*470
Nigh, Robert Jr. *2:*503
Nikolayev, Leonid *3:*731-732
1916 Easter Rebellion *2:*457
1964 Civil Rights Act *1:*54
1975 Helsinki Accords *3:*780
Nineteenth Amendment *1:*177, 192, 195
Ninety-five Theses *3:*621-624
Ninth Amendment *1:*5, 92-93
Nixon, Richard M. *1:*39-45, 44 (ill.), 49, 56, 219;
    *2:*357, 359-360, 463; *3:*597, 802
Nixon v. Fitzgerald *1:*56
Nolan, Henry *3:*815
Noriega, Manuel Antonio *2:*542-547, 543 (ill.)
Norman, Charles *3:*587, 589, 591
Norris, Clarence *1:*196-197, 199, 201, 203
Norris, Lyman D. *1:*15
North, Oliver Laurence *2:*536-541, 537 (ill.)
North Atlantic Treaty Organization (NATO) *2:*465
Northcroft, Harvey *3:*815
Noske, Gustav *2:*313
Notelet, Pierre *2:*396
Noyes, Nicholas *3:*645
Nuclear policy *2:*465

Index

S

Index

Index

Index

Index